Diversity, Autism, and
Developmental Disabilities:

GUIDANCE FOR THE
CULTURALLY SUSTAINING
EDUCATOR

Council for Exceptional Children

DADD
Division on Autism and
Developmental Disabilities

Elizabeth A. Harkins Monaco
Marcus C. Fuller
L. Lynn Stansberry Brusnahan

© 2021 by Council for Exceptional Children
All rights reserved.

No part of this publication may be reproduced, stored in a retrieval system, or transmitted, in any form or by any means, electronic, mechanical, photocopying, recording, or otherwise, without prior written permission of the copyright owner.

Council for Exceptional Children
3100 Clarendon Blvd, Suite 600
Arlington, VA 22201-5332
www.exceptionalchildren.org

Library of Congress Cataloging-in-Publication data

Diversity, Autism, and Developmental Disabilities: Guidance for the Culturally Sustaining Educator

Editors: Elizabeth A. Harkins Monaco, Marcus C. Fuller, L. Lynn Stansberry Brusnahan

Authors: Christine Ashby, Diana Baker, Kathlene Holmes Campbell, Kelly M. Carrero, Beth A. Ferri, Megan-Brette Hamilton, JoDell R. Heroux, Djanna Hill, William Hunter, Deeqaifrah Hussein, Tian (Jessie) Jiang, Talya D. Kemper, Hyejung Kim, Endia J. Lindo, Helen McCabe, Meaghan M. McCollow, Tracy McKinney, Kelly McNeal, Nanette Missaghi, Shelley Neilsen Gatti, Martin Odima Jr., Jamie Pearson, Nigel P. Pierce, Phillandra Smith, Calvin Stanley, Peggy Schaefer Whitby

p. cm.
Includes biographical references.

ISBN 978-0-86586-547-1 (soft cover edition)
ISBN 978-0-86586-548-8 (eBook edition)
CEC Product No. P6333 (soft cover edition)

Cover design by Tom Karabatakis, Tompromo Marketing
Layout by Tom Karabatakis, Tompromo Marketing

Printed in the United States of America by Gasch Printing

First edition

10 9 8 7 6 5 4 3 2 1

DADD PRISM Series

The Board of Directors of the Division on Autism and Developmental Disabilities of the Council for Exceptional Children is pleased to offer its 13th publication in the PRISM series. Each issue in the series is intended to provide practical and timely information related to serving children and youth with developmental disabilities, including cognitive disabilities, intellectual disability, autism, and related disabilities.

We thank Drs. Harkins Monaco, Fuller, and Stansberry Brusnahan for editing this volume in the series, and thank all the volume contributing authors as well. We are confident that readers will find the information offered in this work to be of significant value.

James R. Thompson, Prism Series Executive Editor and Chair, DADD Publications

DADD 2021 Board of Directors

Executive Director: Emily Bouck

President: Robert Pennington

President-Elect: Peggy Schaefer-Whitby

Vice President: Leah Woods

Past-President: Ginevra Courtade

Treasurer: L. Lynn Stansberry Brusnahan

Secretary: Angi K. Stone-McDonald

At Large Representative and Membership Chair: Jenny Root

At Large Representative and Diversity Chair: Elizabeth A. Harkins Monaco

Communication Chair and Web Coordinator: Bree Jimenez

Canadian Member: Jordan Shurr

ETADD Journal Editor: Stanley H. Zucker

Conference Coordinator: Cindy Perras

Contents

Editors and Contributors vii

Foreword *Christopher J. Cormier* xv

Introduction xvii

Chapter 1   Introducing cultural competence in the context of disability and additional social identities
Marcus C. Fuller, Elizabeth A. Harkins Monaco, L. Lynn Stansberry Brusnahan, and Endia J. Lindo 1

Chapter 2   Interrogating assumptions about culture and disability: Becoming a critical and reflexive educator
Christine Ashby, Beth A. Ferri, and Phillandra Smith 23

Chapter 3   Acknowledging other cultural identities and their beliefs around culture and disability
Tracy McKinney, Nigel P. Pierce, and Nanette Missaghi 47

Chapter 4   Working with diverse languages and disability
Diana Baker, Tian (Jessie) Jiang, Hyejung Kim, Helen McCabe, and Calvin Stanley 67

Chapter 5   Supporting the right to gender and sexuality diversity and disability
Meaghan M. McCollow, JoDell R. Heroux, and Talya Kemper 83

Chapter 6   Creating positive relationships with diverse students with disabilities and ensuring academic success through culturally sustaining pedagogies
Shelley Neilsen Gatti, Martin Odima, and Kathlene Holmes Campbell 103

Chapter 7   Empowering families by utilizing culturally sustaining strategies in the education of children with multi-layered identities
Jamie Pearson, Megan-Brette Hamilton, L. Lynn Stansberry Brusnahan, and Deeqaifrah Hussein 131

Chapter 8   Teaching diverse students with disabilities socio-political consciousness and self-advocacy
Peggy J. Schaefer Whitby, Elizabeth A. Harkins Monaco, Djanna Hill, and Kelly McNeal 157

Chapter 9   Preparing practitioners and coaching cultural competence and disability awareness
Marcus C. Fuller, Kelly M. Carrero, and William Hunter 175

Editors and Contributors

Editors

Elizabeth A. Harkins (Monaco), Ed.D., is an Assistant Professor in the Department of Special Education, Professional Counseling, and Disability Studies at William Paterson University. She is currently the program director of the autism and developmental disabilities advanced master's program. She is a former special education administrator, classroom teacher, and family advocate who has served students with disabilities, in a variety of settings. Dr. Harkins' scholarly interests focus on the critical importance of social justice pedagogy alongside educational excellence for all students, specifically the coexisting experiences of multiple, overlapping social identities for students with disabilities and the teaching strategies and learning opportunities that incorporate these social constructs. Publications include manuscripts that examine the impacts of social and emotional health; comprehensive sexuality education; gender, race, and sexuality injustices for individuals with disabilities; and intersectional pedagogy.

Marcus C. Fuller, Ph.D., is a Visiting Lecturer in the Department of Education at The University of Vermont. He earned his doctorate in special education at Texas A&M University. He has served teachers and parents from various ethnic backgrounds, socio-economic status, and age groups within urban and rural areas. Dr. Fuller's scholarly interests focus on empowering families, educators, and researchers by helping them increase their implementation skills during interventions with children with behavior disorders, autism, and/or complex communication needs through the use of educational coaching and performance feedback. Dr. Fuller has served as a reviewer for multiple journals and conference proposals as an active member of the Council for Exceptional Children (CEC) Division on Autism and Developmental Disabilities (DADD), and the Council for Children with Behavioral Disorders (CCBD). He completed a summer internship with the Office of Special Education Programs (OSEP) in Washington, D.C.

L. Lynn Stansberry Brusnahan, Ph.D., is a Professor in and Chair of the Department of Special Education at the University of St. Thomas in Minnesota. She coordinates the autism and developmental disabilities master's programs. She is a private educational consultant and parent of an adult son with autism. She earned her doctorate at the University of Wisconsin-Milwaukee, where she studied contemporary educational issues within urban settings. She has served on the board of directors for the Autism Society of America and CEC's Division on Autism and

Developmental Disabilities (DADD). She co-authored *Do-Watch-Listen-Say: Social and communication skills for autism spectrum disorder.* Dr. Stansberry Brusnahan's scholarly interests focus on autism and teacher preparation. In 2012, she was the Autism Society Professional of the Year.

Authors

Christine Ashby, Ph.D., is an Associate Professor of Inclusive Special Education and Disability Studies at Syracuse University. She coordinates both undergraduate and graduate special education programs along with directing the Center on Disability and Inclusion. She is a former special education teacher. Dr. Ashby's scholarly interests focus on inclusive education broadly, with emphasis on support for students with autism and developmental disabilities, disability studies, and inclusive teacher preparation. She has published in numerous journals including *Equity and Excellence in Education, International Journal of Inclusive Education, Teacher Education and Special Education, and Intellectual and Developmental Disability.* Her co-edited book, *Enacting change from within: Disability studies meets teaching and teacher education* explores how disability studies can inform the practical work of teachers.

Diana Baker, Ph.D. and BCBA, is an Associate Professor of Education at Hobart and William Smith Colleges. She has worked as a preschool teacher for students with autism, where she developed a special interest in culturally and linguistically diverse children and their families. Dr. Baker's scholarly interests focus on multilingual students with autism and the inclusion of students with disabilities in dual immersion settings.

Kathlene Holmes Campbell, Ph.D., is the Dean of the School of Education at the University of St. Thomas in Minnesota. She has experience as a classroom teacher, college professor, interim dean, university instructor and supervisor, and non-profit consultant. She worked with the National Urban Alliance for Effective Education (NUA), helping teachers improve their practice and infuse culturally relevant teaching practices into classrooms. She holds a B.A. in elementary education and M.Ed. in early childhood intervention and family studies from the University of North Carolina at Chapel Hill, and a Ph.D. in curriculum and instruction from The University of Texas at Austin. She has taught numerous courses focused on social justice and equity.

Kelly M. Carrero, Ph.D. and BCBA, is an Associate Professor in the Department of Psychology and Special Education at Texas A&M University - Commerce. She earned her doctorate in special education with an emphasis on behavioral disorders at the University of North Texas. She has served children from culturally and linguistically diverse backgrounds identified with exceptionalities and behavioral health concerns (including autism) in a variety of settings. Dr. Carrero's scholarly interests focus on investigating interventions that increase access to social capital for children and families from diverse backgrounds who are affected by communicative and behavioral health disorders; and disseminating socially valid and culturally responsive practices in research and service delivery. Dr. Carrero serves as a reviewer for several journals and as an active member and leader within CEC and its respective divisions.

Beth A. Ferri, Ph.D., is a Professor of Inclusive Education and Disability Studies at Syracuse University, where she also coordinates the doctoral program in special education. She has published widely on the intersection of race, gender, and disability, including recent articles in *Teachers College Record, Race Ethnicity and Education, Educational Studies, Review of Research in Education, International Journal of Inclusive Education, Remedial & Special Education, Multiple Voices for Ethnically Diverse Exceptional Learners, History of Education Quarterly,* and the *Journal of African American History.* Dr. Ferri has published several books, including *Righting Educational Wrongs: Disability Studies Law and Education* (Syracuse University Press, 2013, with Kanter); and *DisCrit: Critical Conversations Across Race, Class, & Dis/ability* (Teachers College Press, 2016, with Connor & Annamma).

Megan-Brette Hamilton, Ph.D. and CCC-SLP, is an Assistant Professor in the Department of Speech, Language, and Hearing Sciences at Auburn University. She is an ASHA certified speech-language pathologist (SLP) and has worked as an SLP for 10 years in New York city where the majority of her caseload included African American and Hispanic students. Dr. Hamilton's scholarly interests include the educational and clinical experiences (e.g., literacy, communication interactions) of speakers of non-mainstream dialects of English, with a particular focus on African American English-speakers. Megan-Brette's work also explores cultural-linguistic competence/perspectives of professionals and students working with culturally-linguistically diverse populations.

JoDell R. Heroux, Ph.D., is an Associate Professor of Special Education at Central Michigan University. She has worked with students with disabilities in various public school contexts. Dr. Heroux's scholarly interests focus on disability studies and how social and rights-based models of disability can be used to challenge narrow conceptions of disability as a deficit. She co-authored a book chapter on the tensions between special education and inclusion and how the rights-based model of disability can be used to inform the way we think about inclusion. She is collaborating with faculty to develop a minor in Disability Studies at her university.

Djanna Hill, Ed.D., is a Professor of Teacher Education PreK-12 at William Paterson University. She serves as Chair of the Department of Community and Social Justice Studies. She is a former middle and high school science teacher with extensive experience preparing teachers for K-12 classrooms. Her academic degrees from Howard University and Columbia University lead her to teach courses in educational foundations, multicultural education, and science methods at the undergraduate and graduate levels. Dr. Hill's most recent co-authored book entitled, *Star teachers of children in poverty* (Routledge, 2018), brings the ideas of community teachers, teacher disposition, and efficacy to the forefront when analyzing our current involvement in K-12 classrooms.

William Hunter, Ed.D., is an Associate Professor of Special Education at the University of Memphis. He earned his doctorate degree in Special Education from the University of Cincinnati. He has worked as a special education teacher and administrator in urban schools in addition to working as a residential mental health intervention specialist at youth residential facilities. He has numerous publications and presentations including those with a focus on culturally relevant pedagogy. He serves on the CEC Board of Directors as a Member-at-Large and on the CEC Division for Culturally and Linguistically Diverse Exceptional Learners (DDEL) Finance Committee.

Deeqaifrah Hussein, M.A., is a Director of Special Education at Minneapolis Public Schools. She is a licensed teacher in autism and emotional behavior disorders. She is pursuing her doctorate in educational leadership with a focus on autism at the University of St. Thomas in Minnesota. Ms. Hussein is a parent of two children with autism, a community advocate, and the vice president of Somali Parents Autism Network. She serves on the board of Autism Society of Minnesota, is a former Leadership Education in Neurodevelopmental Disabilities (LEND) Fellow from University of Minnesota, and is a member of her state senate autism council.

Tian (Jessie) Jiang, M.S. and BCBA, is a Doctoral Student at the Warner School of Education and Human Development at the University of Rochester. Her work involves translating techniques from applied behavior analysis (ABA) into Chinese, training teachers and parents to effectively implement interventions, and advising policymakers on creating initiatives that suit China's cultural context. Her scholarly focus includes providing training to special education teachers in inclusive settings in China.

Talya D. Kemper, Ph.D., (she/her/hers) is an Assistant Professor in the Teacher Education Department at California State University East Bay. She has worked as a paraprofessional, inclusive support teacher and as a home support provider for individuals with disabilities across the life span. She received her teaching credential at San Francisco State. She has a master's degree in special education and a doctorate from the University of Washington. Dr. Kemper's scholarly interests focus on issues of diversity in the design and research of educational interventions for students with autism.

Hyejung Kim, Ph.D., is an Assistant Professor in the Department of Teaching, Learning and Educational Leadership at Binghamton University, State University of New York. Informed by her own experiences as a transnational scholar who is bilingual and, within the American context, a minority, Dr. Kim's scholarly interests focus on individuals with autism from diverse backgrounds including the intersectionality of autism, race, and language during individuals' transition from high school to adulthood.

Endia J. Lindo, Ph.D., is an Associate Professor of Special Education at Texas Christian University, core faculty in the Alice Neeley Special Education Research and Service (ANSERS) Institute, and President of Council for Exceptional Children (CEC) Division for Culturally and Linguistically Diverse Exceptional Learners (DDEL). Dr. Lindo worked as a resource teacher prior to earning her Ph.D. in Special Education from Vanderbilt University and completing an Institute of Education Science (IES) Postdoctoral Fellowship at Georgia State University. In addition to serving on the DDEL executive board, she is a member of the Professional Development, Standards, and Ethics Committee for the Division of Learning Disabilities (DLD). Dr. Lindo's scholarship focuses on improving the reading comprehension of students with learning difficulties and disabilities by examining approaches for implementing and enhancing school and community-based interventions and increasing the teaching and cultural competence of our teaching force.

Helen McCabe, Ph.D. and BCBA, is an Associate Professor in the Education Department at Daemen College. She has collaborated with China-based educational organizations for children with autism for many years, as a volunteer and as a provider of parent and teacher training. Fluent in Mandarin Chinese, she serves as an interpreter for Chinese-speaking families of children with disabilities in the United States. Dr. McCabe's scholarly interests focus on intervention and support for children with autism, along with their families and teachers in China.

Meaghan M. McCollow, Ph.D. and BCBA-D, (she/her/hers) is an Assistant Professor in the Department of Educational Psychology at California State University East Bay. She has supported individuals with disabilities in a variety of capacities and across age groups from preschool through young adulthood. Her training includes sexuality education for individuals with intellectual and developmental disabilities. Dr. McCollow's scholarly interests focus on examining the contexts in which research and evidence-based practices are implemented and on developing independence and rights of individuals with disabilities. Her publications include practitioner-focused articles on gender and sexuality issues for individuals with intellectual and developmental disabilities.

Tracy McKinney, Ph.D. and BCBA-D, is a Special Education Assessor with the Department of Defense Dependent Schools. She previously worked at Georgia State University as a Clinical Assistant Professor of Special Education in the Department of Learning Sciences and as an affiliated faculty member while at Georgia State University. She received her doctorate from the University of Central Florida and was a postdoctoral research associate at the University Illinois-Chicago. Dr. McKinney's scholarly interests include a focus on teacher preparation infusing culturally relevant pedagogy in teacher preparation. She has published in numerous journals and presented her work at numerous international and national conferences.

Kelly McNeal, Ph.D., is a Professor in the Department of Special Education, Professional Counseling, and Disability Studies at William Paterson University in New Jersey. She is the Chair of the Department and has previously served as Graduate Director of the Teacher of Students with Disabilities program. She has worked as a classroom teacher and a special education diagnostician as well as a parent advocate. Dr. McNeal's scholarly interests focus on literacy, assessment, urban education, and accreditation. She has served in numerous positions on the American Educational Research Association Urban Learning, Teaching and Research special interest group, including program chair, editor of their journal, and session chair of its annual program.

Nanette Missaghi, M.A., is the Director of Equity and Inclusion at Minneapolis Community and Technical College. Ms. Missaghi is a licensed Intercultural Development Inventory (IDI) coach. She was the Director of the Collaborative Urban Educator (CUE) program and an adjunct faculty at the University of St. Thomas. She has a master's degree from the University of Minnesota. Ms. Missaghi's scholarly interests focus on racial equity, culturally responsive pedagogy, and the intersection of culture and race in educational settings and she has contributed to numerous publications on these topics.

Shelley Neilsen Gatti, Ph.D., is an Associate Professor in the Department of Special Education at the University of St. Thomas in Minnesota. She coordinates the license program in emotional and behavioral disorders and residency programs. She was a special education teacher in Montana and worked in the special education department in Minneapolis schools. She completed her doctorate in educational psychology at the University of Minnesota studying multi-tiered systems of support for young children at risk in urban settings. She is the president of the Minnesota Council for Children with Behavioral Disorders chapter. Dr. Neilsen Gatti's scholarly interests focus on embedding culturally sustaining pedagogy across all sectors of education and teacher preparation and evaluation.

Martin Odima Jr., M.A., is a Special Education Teacher in the Saint Paul Public School District in Minnesota. He is Adjunct Faculty at the University of St. Thomas in Minnesota. He studied psychology at the University of Minnesota and completed his master's degree in special education at the University of St. Thomas. His scholarly interests focus on educational equity, inclusive practices for students with disabilities, and retention of teachers of color. His publications include a chapter that focuses on teaching strategies for special education teachers to thrive and persist in the field.

Jamie Pearson, Ph.D., is an Assistant Professor of Special Education in the Department of Teacher Education and Learning Sciences at North Carolina State University. She is a former behavioral interventionist and autism program consultant. She earned her doctorate in Special Education from the University of Illinois at Urbana-Champaign where she developed Families of Children with Autism (FACES), a parent advocacy program designed to support African American families of children with autism. Dr. Pearson's scholarly interests focus on equity in special education for historically marginalized populations, disparities in autism diagnoses, service access, and service utilization among minority families, and strategies for building effective partnerships between educators and parents of children with disabilities. She has presented at national and international conferences and published in journals such as the Journal of Special Education, Journal of Autism and Developmental Disorders, and Teaching Exceptional Children.

Nigel P. Pierce, Ph.D., is an Assistant Professor in the School of Education at North Carolina Central University. Dr. Pierce received his Bachelor's degree in Early Childhood/Special Education from Bowie State University, his Master's degree from Johns Hopkins University, and his doctorate from the University of Texas at Austin. He was a Postdoctoral Research Associate with the Frank Porter Graham Child Development Institute at the University of North Carolina at Chapel Hill. Dr. Pierce's scholarly interests include the effects of ethnicity, socioeconomic status, and linguistic differences on treatment and accessibility of services for individuals with autism.

Phillandra Smith, M.S., is a Doctoral Candidate in Special Education and pursuing a Certificate of Advanced Studies in Disability Studies at Syracuse University. Originally from the Bahamas, the driving force for her interest in special education is an increasing awareness that some students, particularly those with disabilities, exist on the fringe of the school community and the realization that her classroom was no different. Her scholarly interests focus on cultural reciprocity and the integration of student culture in the transition planning of culturally and linguistically diverse students with disabilities, retention and recruitment of racially and ethnically diverse students to inclusive education teacher programs and the experiences of Caribbean migrant students with disabilities in U.S. schools.

Calvin Stanley, M.Ed. and BCBA, is an in-home Applied Behavior Analyst (ABA) supervising clinician in Boston, Massachusetts, working with culturally and linguistically diverse students ranging in age from early childhood to adolescence. He has served as a teacher and school administrator in Guangzhou, China. He returned to the United States when his daughter was diagnosed with autism. His scholarly interests focus on promoting autism awareness, exploring multilingual and multicultural issues in the field, and serving local immigrant communities as a resource on autism-related issues.

Peggy Schaefer Whitby, Ph.D. and BCBA-D, is an Associate Professor at the University of Arkansas. Dr. Schaefer Whitby's scholarly interests focus on providing behavior support to children with autism in school settings including sexuality education, skill acquisition in academics, and reduction of problem behaviors. She is researching access to services for children living in rural areas of poverty and the sociopolitical constructs that may impact advocacy and service issues. She has numerous publications in peer-reviewed journals, book chapters, and books on educating children with autism.

Foreword
Christopher J. Cormier, Ph.D., is a Postdoctoral Fellow at Stanford University in the Stanford Graduate School of Education. He is a former special education teacher. His scholarly interests focus on how marginalization is indexed across the globe. More specifically he studies the functions of marginalization for students who are overrepresented in special education programs in addition to exploring how this issue is exacerbated by the underrepresentation of minoritized teachers who are historically marginalized both domestically and internationally. He also explores the mental health of teachers and students domestically.

Foreword

Christopher J. Cormier, Ph.D., Stanford University

When I taught special education, always in "Title 1" schools in areas considered by many to be challenging and distressed, I was always the department's only Black man, though minoritized students dominated my caseload and classes. I was constantly called upon to be the disciplinarian for a wide array of students. This gave me a view of my colleagues' failures of cultural responsiveness, as students frequently arrived with accounts of behavior I could easily recognize as appropriate within the cultural norms that we shared. My singularity as a Black man in Individualized Education Program meetings also required me to compensate for colleagues who would speak in such a way that was often difficult to understand by parents of different cultural backgrounds. As one of the few teachers who grew up in similar environments as my students and their parents, I often became the social justice advocate and cultural broker for all minority students. This was a heavy burden and I hope this book will help others handle similar situations.

I was honored to be asked to write this Foreword. The title of the book indicates that *all* educators have the responsibility to implement culturally sustaining practices. The editors could have chosen a title such as, *Guidance for Those Who Want to Be Culturally Responsive or Guiding Principles in How to Be Culturally Responsive*. But it is clear that *all* students, especially the most vulnerable, such as the minoritized students receiving special education services I once taught, deserve cultural responsiveness from *all* their teachers. The few teachers of color in schools deserve to work with colleagues with these skills as well; we never received any recognition or extra pay for the extra responsibilities we assumed. Taking on the role of lead disciplinarian often interfered with my own teaching.

For too long school practices that are touted as culturally neutral (Positive Behavior Intervention Supports, Response to Intervention, or Universal Design for Learning) have produced unequal results; minoritized students of color are still suspended at higher rates than their White counterparts and are disproportionately identified and qualified for special education services. These practices are not working, and it is vital to respect the culture of the students.

Researchers have long known of the need for cultural awareness and responsiveness, particularly in special education, and the work of scholars documents the dire impact of our ongoing failure to do so. The contributors to this book continue this discussion while providing relevant contemporary examples to help open the minds of the teaching population. They explore the complexities of intersectional identities of those with disabilities, identify practices to not only advocate for families but to allow parents to feel empowered as they advocate for the success of their children, and challenge assumptions about culturally diverse students' abilities.

In a time of greater awareness of racialized experiences, especially those of Black Americans, I hope this book will soon be part of the standard curriculum in every preservice general and special education program and used in professional development at all the districts in the country – or even around the globe. There is reason to hope that this book will help more teachers, administrators, students, and parents recognize the benefits of culturally responsive teaching for all students regardless of background, as an increasingly diverse nation moves beyond White-dominated expectations and practices and learns to value all the backgrounds of all its students while positioning every student for success.

Introduction

The PRISM series, developed by the Council for Exceptional Children (CEC) – Division on Autism and Developmental Disabilities (DADD), is a collection of volumes that highlight evidence-based, research-to-practice teaching strategies and interventions geared toward supporting students with developmental disabilities (DD) including autism and intellectual disability (ID). The volumes in the PRISM collection address interventions in the classroom, home, and community and focus on how to help students build needed skills.

The chapters in this PRISM volume help practitioners become more culturally competent by identifying and examining beliefs about their own and their students' cultures, including disability, race, ethnicity, language, gender, and sexuality diversity. The book offers practical strategies and prepares practitioners to create positive integral connections with students and their families from diverse communities while infusing culturally sustaining practices. This volume discusses teaching socio-political consciousness and self-advocacy and explains why it is important to coach cultural competency.

This book consists of nine chapters written by 29 authors. We sought to include authors who represent a variety of diversity amongst social identities such as race, ethnicity, sexuality, and gender. In addition to their social identities, we sought authors with expertise related to the subject of each chapter. While we strived for a diverse representation of voices, we recognize that some chapters do not represent a full intersectional spectrum. We also recognize that there are greater risks for people who may identify as part of some social groups and therefore this may inhibit their participation in these projects.

In this publication, the word diversity is used very broadly. Throughout the text, we have adopted the term "diverse" to describe groups of individuals who share similar identities. Diversity doesn't mean one thing (e.g., race, culture, ethnicity, gender). Just because we possess a social identity doesn't mean we think or act exactly the same as others who share our backgrounds. Our individual differences influence the way we think about social and cultural norms within the inclusive groups we are members of. People who ascribe to a particular identity can have very different experiences and, therefore, outlooks.

The target population highlighted in this book is individuals with DD and ID. We use the terms individuals, people, youth, and students interchangeably. We also use person-first language. Rather than defining people primarily by their disability or racial or cultural backgrounds, we use people-first language in this book to convey respect by emphasizing the fact that people are—first and foremost—people. We respect that some individuals and communities may prefer other terminology such as identity-first language. For example, people with autism see their disability as an intrinsic part of their identity and view being autistic as a different way of perceiving and interacting with the world with benefits. Although autism spectrum disorder (ASD) is a common diagnostic term (e.g., American Psychiatric Association [APA], 2013), the word "disorder" is increasingly viewed negatively, thus we use the term "autism" to describe individuals across the spectrum. In this publication, we will also use respectful gender terminology involving individuals who self-identify with a non-binary gender (something other than "male" or "female").

The target audience for this volume include practitioners (e.g., special education teachers, general education teachers, educational administrators, related service providers, school psychologists, Department of Education personnel, and other school professionals) and special education stakeholders (e.g., school personnel plus the community, mental health providers, medical professionals, individuals with disabilities along with their families). Throughout this book, you will see references to practitioners which includes the aforementioned professionals. At the end of each chapter, we provide guiding questions for practitioners that are linked to chapter objectives and meant to guide reflexive practice.

The following descriptions highlight the contents of the chapters in this volume.

Chapter 1 *Introducing cultural competence in the context of disability and additional social identities* introduces the topic of cultural competence as it relates to youth with DD, including those with autism and ID. This chapter presents the importance of culturally sustaining practices used by practitioners and describes cultural competence through the lens of disability and another social identity. Readers will learn key terminology related to culturally relevant pedagogy and special education.

Chapter 2 *Interrogating assumptions about culture and disability: Becoming a critical and reflexive educator* introduces the topic of the cultural mismatch between teachers and students and the adoption of a "culturally minded and reflexive stance," (Artilles, 2011)--one that promotes cultural relevance, reciprocity, and competence. This chapter presents a process of how to interrogate one's own assumptions about disability and difference and what it means to develop habits of cultural reflexivity and critical consciousness in our work with students with developmental disabilities, including those with autism and intellectual disability.

Chapter 3 *Acknowledging other cultural identities and their beliefs around culture and disability* introduces knowledge and skills related to acknowledging one's own cultural identity, the identities of the students and families we work with, and how to learn to accept the differing beliefs related to disability that are different than one's own. This chapter presents practical skills to learn how to acknowledge the cultural beliefs of others different from one's own around culture and disability and discusses the impact of these beliefs on their interactions with individuals of other cultures including individuals with disabilities. Readers will examine the ways an individual with a disability is viewed by various cultures.

Chapter 4 *Working with diverse languages and disability* introduces the benefits of multilingualism for students with developmental disabilities such as autism and ID. This chapter presents strategies for working effectively with multilingual students with disabilities and their families. Readers will learn about the challenges associated with educating multilingual students with autism and ID.

Chapter 5 *Supporting the right to gender and sexuality diversity and disability* introduces how a rights-based model of disability can be used to understand issues related to sexual identity and disability and rationalizes the importance of sexuality education as a right for individuals with DD, including autism and ID. This chapter presents issues related to the intersection of sexual identity and disability, explains and dispels common myths related to sexuality education and DD, and defines key terms in regard to sexuality and gender identity.

Chapter 6 *Creating positive relationships with diverse students with disabilities and ensuring academic success through culturally sustaining pedagogies* introduces relationships and why they matter for students with disabilities. The chapter presents how relationships are pivotal to student success and barriers to developing student relationships. Readers will learn ways practitioners can develop relationships in culturally sustaining ways to influence academic success and social emotional well-being.

Chapter 7 *Empowering families by utilizing culturally sustaining strategies in the education of children with multi-layered identities* introduces culturally sustaining strategies, rooted in empowerment, to address identified needs of families who have children with disabilities. This chapter presents how to support empowerment among all families, including those who identify with historically marginalized racial and ethnic groups in the United States.

Chapter 8 *Teaching diverse students with disabilities socio-political consciousness and self-advocacy* introduces the sociopolitical constructs that impact people from oppressed populations ability to advocate for themselves and others. This chapter presents how the intersection of multiple sociopolitical constructs further impacts students with DD, including autism and ID. The chapter identifies teachers' biases that may impact how they teach students with developmental disabilities to self-advocate. Readers will learn ways in which to teach self-advocacy while addressing the sociopolitical constructs using a cultural competency approach.

Chapter 9 *Preparing practitioners and coaching cultural competence and disability awareness* introduces practices and strategies to use during coaching sessions on culture, diversity, and disability awareness. This chapter describes how the Cultural Proficiency Continuum (CPC; Lindsey, Robins, & Terrell, 2009) can be used as a coaching component in assessing where classroom practices and behavior fall on the continuum, as well as how to move along the CPC. Readers will learn how to provide clear expectations between the coach and coachee and create and maintain a culturally proficient relationship during the coaching experience.

Chapter 1

Introducing cultural competence in the context of disability and additional social identities

Marcus Fuller, Elizabeth A. Harkins Monaco, L. Lynn Stansberry Brusnahan, and Endia J. Lindo

> **Objectives**
> - Develop an understanding of cultural competence in the context of disability and a second social identity.
> - Rationalize the importance of culturally sustaining practices utilized by culturally responsive special educators.
> - Explain key terms related to culturally relevant pedagogy and special education.

This book is relevant to practitioners who wish to better understand cultural competence and intersectionality and how issues of race, culture, and other differences shape lived experiences with disability in American society. Throughout this book, we discuss membership in dual social identities and the consequences of double marginalization. Chapter 1 introduces the topic of intersectionality, which is the multidimensionality of disability and at least one other social identity, such as a child with a disability who also identifies as Black or gay or Somali. Cultural competence is the ability to be firmly grounded in one's own culture of origin and fluent in at least one other culture. We include disability and other identities in this lens, as constructions with social meaning rather than biological phenomena (Hartlep, 2009; Hosking, 2008). We also introduce terminology, frameworks, and concepts that will lay the foundation for understanding the important topics raised throughout this text. Each chapter focuses on youth with developmental disabilities (DD), including those with autism and intellectual disability (ID), who experience the intersection of race, ethnicity, class, disability, language, sexual identity, and gender. The key terminology introduced in this chapter will be utilized throughout the other chapters in this text.

Table 1.1 Key Terminology

Ableism	An uncritical assertion that particular ways of being and performing are preferable, often privileging the experience of individuals who do not experience disabilities.
Autism	A developmental disability that impacts social, communication, and behavioral skills (IDEA, 2004).
Bias	A preference for or against something or someone (Harry et al., 1999). Implicit or hidden biases are stereotypes held by all individuals without their awareness (Staats et al., 2015).
Culture	Refers to socio-demographic markers like race and ethnicity that are often taken as proxies for culture; yet culture is dynamic, multidimensional, and imbued with power and complexity (Artiles, 2015). Culture is a combination of thoughts, feelings, attitudes, beliefs, values, behavior patterns, and practices that are shared by racial, ethnic, religious, or social groups. Student identities reflect strategic sampling of multiple identity and cultural resources, yet because of reductionist and problematic views of culture, culturally diverse students are often seen through a deficit lens (Artiles, 2014).
Cultural competence	The ability to build understanding, communicate, and interact with people across cultures in a way that demonstrates respect and openness to different cultural perspectives and strengthens cultural security. A first step toward cultural competence is understanding the ways in which our own perspectives are rooted in cultural, racial, and ethnic identity and history. Competence is about being comfortable with at least one culture outside of your own and 1) Being culturally self-aware 2) Valuing diversity 3) Understanding the social and historical dynamics of cultural interactions and 4) Institutionalizing cultural knowledge and adapting to diversity (The Continuum, 2020).
Cultural reciprocity	A self-reflective and dialogic process used to identify our own cultural norms and the cultural norms of others with the goal of identifying a reference point or frame to understand different cultural perspectives.

Table 1.1 Key Terminology (continued)	
Cultural relevance	A pedagogical strategy that "uses the cultural knowledge, prior experiences, frames of reference, and performance styles of ethnically diverse students to make learning more relevant and effective" (Gay, 2010).
Cultural informant	A person who is highly self-aware of his/her own cultural values, norms, and appropriate behaviors and who understands the nuances well enough to express this knowledge to others who are less familiar with the culture.
Culturally sustaining practice	Practices that extend on culturally responsive practices in moving beyond respecting or valuing diverse languages, cultures, ways of being. An explicitly anti-colonialist and anti-deficit stance, culturally sustaining practice seeks to center and sustain the diverse linguistic, literate, and cultural practices of our students (Paris & Alim, 2017).
Developmental disability	"A group of conditions due to an impairment in physical, learning, language, or behavior areas. These conditions begin during the developmental period, may impact day-to-day functioning, and usually last throughout a person's lifetime" (Facts about Developmental Disabilities, 2019).
Disability	Any condition of the body or mind (impairment) that makes it more difficult for the person with the condition to do certain activities (activity limitation) and interact with the world around them (participation restrictions).
Dis/Ability	Dis/Ability is an identity marker that includes ways notions of ability are relied on and constructed in tandem with other identity markers (e.g., gender, race, language) (Gillborn, 2015). Students with dis/abilities have experienced oppression with great consequence for who accesses learning, whose abilities are recognized and valued, and who participates in decision making in schools. Thus, pedagogies that value ethnic, racial, and language differences simultaneously and intentionally must be committed to disrupting those that have historically pathologized students' abilities (Waitoller & King-Thorius, 2016).

Table 1.1 Key Terminology (continued)	
Disability Critical Race Theory / Studies **DisCrit**	A framework that theorizes about the ways in which race, racism, disability and ableism are built into the interactions, procedures, discourses, and institutions of education, which affect students of color with disabilities qualitatively differently than White students with disabilities (Annamma, Connor, & Ferri, 2013; Crenshaw, 1993; Solorzano & Yosso 2001).
Disproportionality	Occurs when a group of students is overrepresented in special education classification, placement, or disciplinary sanctions, such as suspension relative to their percentage of the school or district population (Voulgarides & Zwerger, 2013). Disproportionality is sometimes described as a student's risk factor for being labeled or suspended compared to their peers.
Impairment	Any loss of or challenges in psychological, physiological, or anatomical structure or function.
Intellectual disability	A disability characterized by significant limitations in both intellectual functioning and in adaptive behavior, which covers many everyday social and practical skills. This disability originates before the age of 18.
Intersectionality	A framework used to understand how multiple overlapping social identities (e.g. race, gender, socioeconomic status, sexual orientation, or disability) impact and oppress certain populations (Crenshaw, 1989). The problems certain people face stem from the multiplied oppressions that accompany a particular combination of identities (Bell, 2016).
Intersectional blind spots	A lack of recognition and acceptance of cultural difference, which can serve to perpetuate barriers to equity and inclusion in our schools (Bazerman & Tenbrunsel, 2011; Chugh, Bazerman, & Banaji, 2005).
Instructional pedagogy	Teaching strategies and learning opportunities that incorporate the coexisting experiences of multiple, overlapping social identities (e.g. race, gender, socioeconomic status, sexual orientation, or disability) in a classroom environment.

Table 1.1 Key Terminology (continued)	
Minoritized	An extension of the term "minority" that notions while groups may not be subordinate to the dominant group (as defined in minority), they are pushed aside or seen as second citizens by means out of their own control (Paniagua, 2015).
Multiple minoritized identities	Varied social categories such as race, gender, socioeconomic status, sexual orientation, or disability – explains how multiple identities intersect to create systems of oppression, power, and discrimination (Proctor, Williams, Scherr, & Li, 2017).
Neurodiversity	The recognition of autism, and other diverse neurological conditions and ways of being, as a variation of human experience, rather than a deficiency in need or remediation or cure.
Oppression	The unjust or cruel exercise of authority or power.
Othering/Otherness	When one is mentally classified in somebody's mind as "not one of us." This practice communicates instances of perpetuating prejudice, discrimination, and injustice.
Privilege	A right or immunity granted as a peculiar benefit, advantage, or favor (Merriam Webster, 2020). It is "a set of unearned benefits given to people who fit into a specific social group" (Ferguson, 2014).
White Privilege	Often used in the phrase "White privilege" to describe the advantages White Americans have over minoritized populations. For example, American history written through the lesson of White men, and other American cultures only taught as electives.
Race	Refers to socially constructed grouping of people based on the physical characteristics they share (e.g., skin color, facial features, hair texture).
Racism	An attitude or action that can be deliberate or unintended and is based on the belief of White superiority and oppression of non-Whites (Gay, 1973).

Table 1.1 Key Terminology (continued)	
Representation	Trends of overrepresentation or underrepresentation of individuals based on demographics, in comparison to their presences in the overall population or unit.
Overrepresentation	"Overrepresentation" refers to circumstances in which a racial or ethnic group has greater representation than in the general population. For example, more students from one racial group are represented in a special education disability category based on their overall presence in the school population.
Underrepresentation	"Underrepresentation" refers to circumstances in which a racial or ethnic group has lesser representation in aspects of education than in the general population. For example, less students from one racial group are represented in gifted educational programs based on their overall presence in the school population.
Self-determination	The ability to autonomously engage in self-directed skills, strategies, and actions that are consistent with one's values, preferences, strengths, and needs (Turnbull & Turnbull, 2001; Cartledge et al., 2009). This includes the ability to engage in actions to set and attain goals, and use skills like choice-making, problem-solving, and self-regulation (Burke, Shogren, & Wehmeyer, 2018).
Self-advocacy	An individual's ability to effectively communicate, convey, negotiate, or assert his or her own interests, desires, needs, and rights (VanReusen et al., 1994)
Special education	The practice of educating students in a way that addresses their individual differences and special needs. Ideally, this process involves the individually planned and systematically monitored arrangement of teaching procedures, adapted equipment and materials, and accessible settings.

To right systemic racial inequities and to cultivate culturally sustaining practices, it is critical to understand the multiple overlapping experiences of youth with DD and how these experiences differ because of intersecting identities. Here we discuss Critical Disability Theory, examine social identity constructs, and introduce the adoption of intersectionality as a framework for special education practice.

Chapter 1

Critical Disability Theory

To understand the intersectionality between diversity and disability requires an examination of theories from a broad perspective. One theory that is used frequently when discussing the issue of diversity and disability is Critical Disability Theory (CDT). CDT postulates that the social disadvantages experienced by individuals with disabilities are caused by attitudes and environments that do not meet their needs and not by the disability itself (Pearson, Hamilton, & Meadan, 2018). CDT promotes the understanding of the impact of preconceived societal notions, norms, and values on the daily lives of people with disabilities (Hosking, 2008).

CDT is based on two concepts. First is the principle that disability is a social construct. There is a difference between an actual condition and the notion of disability, that is constructed by society of how a person can or cannot function. The second concept is that disability is best characterized as a complex interrelationship. This interrelationship involves the individual's challenges, the individual's response to the challenges, and the social environments that the individual is a part of and has access to. All these factors help define how the individual with disability sees themselves, how society sees them, and how these two components interact to form societal norms. This can create a disadvantage for people with disabilities that is then supported by the social environment which fails to meet the needs of people who do not match the typical expectation. These concepts will be discussed further in Chapter 5 and revisited throughout this text.

The framework of CDT derives from combining medical understanding of disabilities and societal understanding of disabilities. From the medical perspective, CDT acknowledges the effects a disability has on an individual. This includes the biological, neurological, and hereditary impacts on an individual. From the social perspective, CDT acknowledges the experience an individual has with their environment. This includes how society views people with disabilities, how they function in society, and how abilities across people differ. The World Health Organization defines this framework that combines the medical and social perspective as a "biopsychosocial model" (Dogar, 2007). The effects of the biopsychosocial model are discussed throughout this book.

When using CDT, researchers question deep-valued concepts that society has around disabilities. Some of these concepts include the personal independence and interdependence that is both assumed and needed for a person with a disability. Independence refers to the way in which individuals think, function, or act as their own isolated entities without help or advice from others. Conversely, interdependence refers to the relationship in which an individual relies on or desires assistance from others. Another concept that is questioned is the social construction of disability as well as "non-disability." CDT seeks to challenge the concept of what society views as typical, how it is defined, and who decides what is considered typical. This theory also challenges the value of dignity and respect shown by society to persons with disabilities. Finally, CDT seeks to bring to light the intersectional issues of disability with concepts of class, gender, race, sexual orientation, and ethnicity, as noted in the chapters in this text.

CDT supports that within the category of people with disability, just like any broad-overarching category, there is great diversity amongst the population. Furthermore, each member of this category are members of many other categories such as countries of origin, ethnic groups, religions, professions, and socio-economic status. CDT combats the notion that disability is a monolithic category and showcases how the term disability should be redefined broadly as one would consider the term "American" or "man," expressing that while individuals may share one commonality of disability, each person is unique and a part of many other groups. By focusing on the intersectionality of the different groups people with disabilities are a part of, CDT challenges society to look at how expectations and norms impact people with disabilities.

Advocates of CDT provide a voice to support people with disabilities that society attempts to silence. These advocates embrace legal rights as an indispensable means to promote the equality of people with disability and support the full integration of people with disabilities into all aspects of society, without forcing people with disability to conform to societal norms. While self-advocates with disabilities have spoken up for themselves in terms of their rights, expectations, and ability to function in society, many have been silenced due to the assumptions society has imposed on them. For example, some assume that an inability to communicate by an individual with a disability translates to an inability to comprehend. Chapter 8 further discusses how to support advocacy, but the first step in fully understanding Critical Disability Theory is to fully examine identity and why social identity constructs matter in special education.

Evolution of Identity

Civil rights activist Kimberlé Crenshaw explored the complexities of social identity in 1989, when she studied how Black women face a double layer of oppression due to issues with both their race and their gender. She connected this double oppression to systems of oppression, power, and discrimination (Proctor, Williams, Scherr, & Li, 2017). Crenshaw's work provides the structure for how we frame the relationship between intersectional social identities and systems of power today. We are using the coexisting experiences of "multiple minoritized identities," or people who identify among various social categories such as race, gender, socioeconomic status, sexual orientation, or disability and how these social categories intersect to create or support unfair systems of oppression (Proctor, Williams, Scherr, & Li, 2017). For example, a female with Down syndrome who also identifies as Black and gay will have different experiences than her White, straight, male peers without disabilities. The intersection of this individual's race, gender, sexuality, and disability means she faces higher risks of oppression in contexts such as schools (National Association of School Psychologists, 2017; Proctor, et al., 2017). Crenshaw warned that ignoring the importance of multiple layered identities erases the experiences of people who are significantly oppressed (Cooper, 2016; Crenshaw, 1989). "For example, people without disabilities may not notice or recognize certain challenges people with disabilities face, which ultimately erases their experiences – and in turn, their opportunities – in society" (Harkins Monaco, 2020).

Racial Identity

The United States has a complicated history in defining race and its definitions very much reflect political and scientific trends and societal pressures. The United States most often recognizes five categories when it comes to race: White, Black or African American, American Indian or Alaska Native, Asian, and Native Hawaiian or Other Pacific Islander. The U.S. census' categorical definitions reflect a social definition of race recognized in this country that represents antiquated trends; see Chapter 5 for a similar issue with the census and gender. The first formal acknowledgement of multiracial ethnicities did not occur until 2000, and it took until 2020 for the term "Negro" to be dropped and for people who chose White or Black to expound upon their ethnic or racial origins.

The reality is that race can be defined biologically, anthropologically, genetically, or be derived from racial and national origin or sociocultural groups. Race becomes more complex when we examine elements of culture within these stereotypes. It is challenging to define race in its true context, especially when many people may choose to report more than one race to indicate their racial mixture. Furthermore, those who identify their origin as Hispanic, Latinx, or Spanish may see this as their ethnicity and still identify with other races. The concept of race, a social notion that does not have a scientific base in biology or genetics, was created by early European colonizers to identify those with different phenotypical traits (i.e. skin color) from their "superior" selves (James & Burgos, 2020). Historically, these classifications have significance as they were used in the United States to enslave people. Currently, racial biases of people have created institutionalized oppression that perpetuates stereotypes based on skin color (Race & Ethnicity, 2020).

Culture is the way of life of a group of people (Griswold, 2012). It utilizes tools, artifacts, and other tangible elements, and it is grounded in the interpretations, perceptions, and values of those items (Banks, 2010). People with the same culture usually share these views. However, these groups are not monolithic and may differ based on additional factors such as (but not limited to) region, education, and socio-economic status. Traditionally in the educational setting, culture describes the backgrounds of students and how they learn. It should also take into consideration students' implicit and explicit funds of knowledge, ways of speaking, traditions, and backgrounds. Chapters 2 and 3 further explore these concepts.

Why Social Identity Constructs Matter in Special Education

Multidimensionality of social identity is the presence of multiple interconnected memberships in an individual's daily life (Hosking, 2008). "Intersectional concepts . . . are especially critical in academic environments because multiple minoritized identities in schools are on the rise while practitioners primarily identify as members of the dominant society" (Niles & Harkins Monaco, 2019, p. 116). When disability and other social identities are combined, it is the axis of one or more oppressions with another (Pearson, et al., 2019).

The majority of special education teachers are female and White and only a small portion of special educators are Black or African American (U.S. Census Bureau, 2016). Conversely, half of our U.S. public school students identify in multiple minoritized racial or ethnic groups. It has been posed that this cultural disconnect between teachers and the students they serve plays a role in the trends of students of color being systemically treated differently and given disparate opportunities than their White school-aged peers, resulting in overrepresentation in special education (Ford, 2012; National Center for Education Statistics [NCES], 2017). This is connected with a discussion of familial systems in Chapter 7.

Special education practitioners are typically unaware of the importance of intersectional differences for many reasons (Gay & Howard, 2000; Owen, 2010). Historically, practitioners have only been prepared to address cultural perspectives during awareness days and certain elements of school curricula, or discuss it diagnostically (Linton, 1998), such as part of an educational plan or a need to learn English as a second language. See Chapters 4 for the implications this has on issues of language and culture. Other issues stem from the value system of the special educator practitioners themselves; some are not willing to engage in these concepts (Darling-Hammond, 2002), while others still "define fairness and equity as treating all children the same; to some, being 'colorblind' [is] valuing diversity" (Owen, 2010, p. 18). Even when special educator practitioners attempt to address injustices on behalf of their students, they tend to center only on the student's disability which means they are ignoring or erasing other aspects of their students' identities. These issues highlight the importance of building the cultural competence of our teaching force. The rest of the book is dedicated to helping practitioners build this competence in their own spheres of influence.

This book will guide a process of enhancing cultural competence, so practitioners can respectfully 1) infuse students' culture and language into their learning environments which ultimately reinforces students' cultural identities and 2) embed instructional strategies that meet the cultural and linguistic needs of their students (Chu, 2011; Lindo & Lim, 2020; Siwatu, 2011). Building cultural competence is an ongoing process that requires teachers to intentionally work to develop what Bennett (2017) refers to as Intercultural Sensitivity or the ability to communicate across cultures adeptly. Bennett's Developmental Model of Intercultural Sensitivity notes six stages of intercultural relations with the least competent being denial, followed by defense, minimization, acceptance, adaptation, and those most proficient at intercultural engagement being in the integration stage (Bennett, 2017).

Table 1.2 Summary of Bennett's Stages of Intercultural Sensitivity
1. Denial: Cultural differences not recognized; one's culture is the only reality.
2. Defense: Cultural differences are recognized; differences perceived as inferior to one's own or the dominant culture.
3. Minimization: Lack of awareness of own cultural values; one's values seen as universal.
4. Acceptance: One's own culture is recognized and centered; other cultures are accepted and/or tolerated.
5. Adaptation: One holds a broader perspective of other cultures; can see the world from a different cultural perspective and adapt behavior accordingly.
6. Integration: One's expansive cultural experiences allows them to serve as a cultural mediator; can engage skillfully across cultures and shift cultural perspectives.

Research suggests that fewer than one percent of people actually reach the integration stage with the majority (65.5%) of surveyed individuals falling within the minimization stage where they see their own culture as universal and often trivialize key aspects of other cultures suggesting they do not see them; and nearly another 19% being in the defense (15.55%) and denial (3.05%) stages (Braxton, 2019). This lack of recognition and acceptance of cultural difference serves to perpetuate barriers to equity and inclusion in our schools.

These kinds of intersectional blind spots (Bazerman & Tenbrunsel, 2011; Chugh, Bazerman, & Banaji, 2005) place students with disabilities at higher risks for discrimination. The reality is that special education practitioners, despite the best of intentions, end up perpetuating systems of inequities.

> When practitioners do not recognize these nuances or counteract them in their daily interactions, they are inadvertently contributing to further oppressive acts. For example, a practitioner can interpret the world through a cultural frame of reference that is female, middle class, and be

influenced by personal religious beliefs, and while a student might share some of these perspectives like class or religion, s/he may identify more with other social identities and experiences that have been oppressed due to race and a [disability] .... (Niles & Harkins Monaco, 2019, p. 116).

Another example of an intersectional blind spot is when a practitioner teaches a student how to self-advocate to receive support to accomplish a task within a job site, but not teach them what to do if someone is discriminating against them. Chapter 8 will discuss this further.

Practitioners may not understand the long-term consequences of intersectional blind spots on students (Brown, 2007). This lack of knowledge or awareness "is problematic (a) when it skews our personal interactions and judgments and (b) when it contributes to or blinds us to systemic barriers for those who do not possess a certain privilege, thereby creating or perpetuating inequity" (National Association of School Psychologists [NASP], 2016, p. 24). This is especially critical for our most vulnerable students. Ultimately, this means that special education programs are not designed to incorporate the actions, feelings, and needs of their students with multiple minoritized identities or address how these intersectional oppressions contribute to systematic marginalization (Carroll, 2009; Proctor & Meyers, 2015). Practitioners must be equipped to acknowledge intersectional differences between practitioners and students and their families. When navigating this book, we recommend practitioners adopt an iterative process for building their cultural competence and apply the three steps of C.A.P. (Lindo & Lim, 2020) to the concepts presented in each chapter.

C - Cultural self-study

A - Acquisition of cultural knowledge

P - Putting the acquired knowledge to practice

This reflective and active practice is critical to raising practitioner awareness of the barriers they may present or perpetuate, but also to better recognize instructional and institutional barriers hindering the development of equitable and inclusive environments.

Infuse Intersectional Pedagogy

Adopting intersectionality as a framework in the classroom means that practitioners must be prepared to engage in introspective reflection that interrogates one's role when participating in systemic injustices (Niles & Harkins Monaco, 2019). Reflecting upon our own culture, personal perspectives, and biases (Lindo & Lim, 2020; Spring, 2000) will help practitioners better understand the impact of intersectional identities that are different from their own. Chapter 2 discusses how interrogating assumptions will help you become a critical and reflexive educator.

Assumptions are often directly connected to strongly held value systems for school stakeholders and are exacerbated when practitioners do not understand 1) the power of social influences and structures, 2) intergroup communications, or 3) how to constructively deal with conflict. In addition to practitioners building their own cultural competence through procedures like C.A.P. (Lindo & Lim, 2020), engaging in the following exercises can serve to aid in identifying assumptions and areas that need reshaping within the broader systems and settings. These models aim to help practitioners improve equity in the classroom and ensure they are meeting the intersectional needs of students.

Bell, et al.'s (2016) *Five Dimension of Diversity and Equity in the Classroom* serves to identify the connections between pedagogy and student learning, student relationships, and classroom climate. It emphasizes the importance of considering course design alongside facilitation and suggests evaluating the following five dimensions: 1) pedagogical methods; 2) curricula; 3) student learning; 4) classroom climate; and 5) group dynamics.

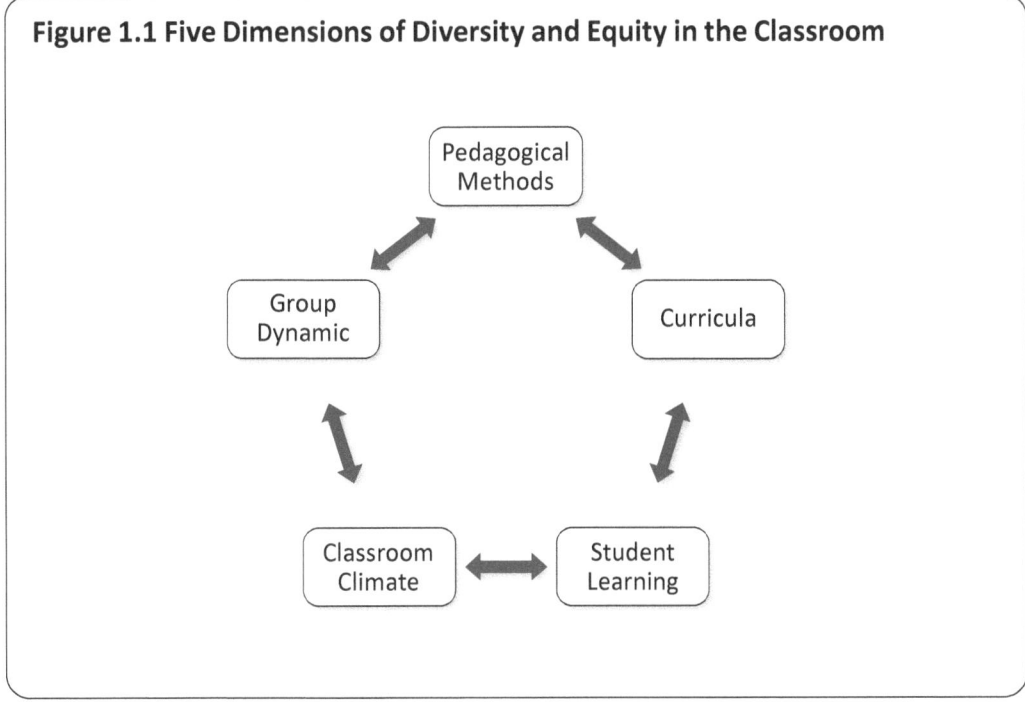

Figure 1.1 Five Dimensions of Diversity and Equity in the Classroom

Each dimension is interrelated and interconnected and offers a point of entry for considering how classrooms may be shaped and improved (Adams, et al., 2016). We suggest pairing classroom elements with interactive activities that emphasize student-centered learning (Harkins Monaco, 2020). To start, ask yourselves the following questions:

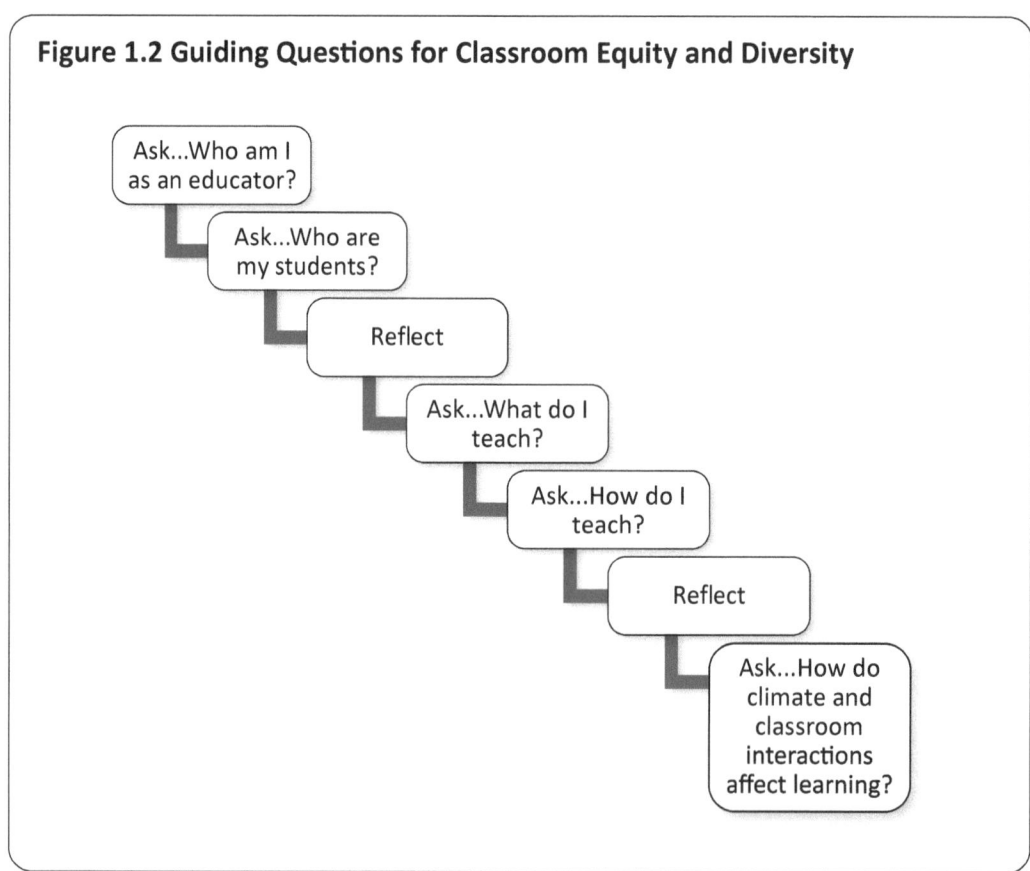

Figure 1.2 Guiding Questions for Classroom Equity and Diversity

After examining who we and our students are (see Chapters 2 and 3 for further guidance), practitioners should examine how they teach and assess the current classroom climate for peer interactions, social justice, and inclusive behaviors. The following questions nicely connect with these concepts. Additionally, keep them in mind when reading Chapter 9.

Table 1.3 Social Justice and Inclusive Behaviors in the Classroom: Questions for Practitioners

Do you balance the emotional and cognitive elements of your students' learning?
Do you highlight individual student's experiences alongside illuminating any systemic issues?
Do you support social relationships and communication within the classroom?
Do you have and utilize a wide variety of tools for student-centered learning?
Do you value awareness, personal growth, and change as outcomes of students' learning?
Do you use inclusive language such as "she," "he," as well as the singular "they?"
Do you avoid use of phrases that exclude some students such as "It's easy to see…" or "I'm sure you all know the answer…"?
Do you use terminology that is respectful and avoid outdated terms for social groups?
Do you try to learn student's names and pronounce them correctly?
Do you address diversity issues in class discussions?
Do you treat students equally?
Do you respond consistently to students? For example, when you notice that a student is unprepared for class, do you respond the same regardless of their backgrounds or gender?
Do you allow students to interrupt?
Do you give feedback that includes praise to all students?

Reflect on your answers. *What are you allowing to happen in your classroom? What can you control? What can you address?*

To start shaping these reflections directly into your daily practices, review Adams et al.'s (2010) *Pedagogical Framework for Social Justice Education*. They suggest prioritizing relationships and personal growth through emotional and cognitive learning, individual student experiences, and student-centered learning.

Table 1.4 Five Basic Teaching Approaches For Social Justice Education

1. *Balance the emotional and cognitive components of the learning process.* Pay attention to personal safety, classroom norms, and guidelines for group behavior when teaching.

2. *Acknowledge and support the personal (the individual student) while illuminating the systemic (the interactions among social groups) experiences.* Call attention to the here-and-now of the classroom setting and ground the systemic or abstract in an accumulation of concrete, real-life examples when teaching.

3. *Attend to social relations within the classroom.* Help students name behaviors that emerge in group dynamics, understand group processes and improve interpersonal communications, without blaming or judging each other when teaching.

4. *Utilize reflection and experience as tools for student-centered learning.* Begin from the student's world view and experience as the starting point for dialogue or problem-posing when teaching.

5. *Value awareness, personal growth, and change as outcomes of the learning process.* Balance different learning styles and is explicitly organized around goals of social awareness, knowledge, and social action, although proportions of these three goals change in relation to student interest and readiness when teaching.

(Adams, et al., 2016, p. 56-57)

These five norms will help you actively prepare for infusing intersectional concepts into your daily practices. Use these concepts to guide you through further exploration into culturally sustaining pedagogies in Chapter 6.

Summary

Throughout this book, we aim to provide you with context-specific background information around discipline-specific intersectional concepts. The reality is that we face critical disparities in special education and unfortunately many of us are unaware of the importance of intersectional differences. Ultimately teaching practices must be improved to refocus on social justice education and increase the cultural competence in the context of disability. The first step in dismantling any biased or unjust structures is to create awareness of intersectional identities, beliefs, and practices. Once practitioners can recognize their own cultural identities and the various intersected identities represented in today's classrooms, they can more proficiently engage cross-culturally and are better able to address the structures of inequality in classrooms and schools.

The second step in dismantling any biased or unjust structures is to identify opportunities to infuse intersectionality into one's daily professional practices. Practitioners can use the suggested models from Chapter 1 to reflect upon sustaining intersectional practices and ultimately combat systemic challenges within their purview. Each subsequent chapter provides strategies to infuse various contexts of intersectional pedagogy into daily practices (Gay & Howard, 2000; King & Butler, 2015). Once a practitioner has determined needs and which areas to focus on, they can align current practices to a framework, such as those presented in this text, and determine new practices to take on.

The chapters in this text will help readers become more culturally competent by identifying and examining beliefs about their own and their students' cultures including disability, race, ethnicity, language, gender, and sexuality diversity. This text offers practical solutions for improving respect and communication while prioritizing student engagement. The chapters prepare practitioners to create positive integral connections with students and their families from diverse communities while infusing culturally sustaining practices. Lastly, the text discusses how to teach diverse students socio-political consciousness and self-advocacy and the importance of coaching cultural competency.

References

Adams, M., Bell, L. A., Goodman, D. J., & Joshi, K. Y. (2016). *Teaching for diversity and social justice.* Routledge.

Adams, M., Blumenfeld, et. al. (Eds.) (2010). *Readings for Diversity and Social Justice*. Routledge.

ABazerman, (Eds.), *Conflict of interest: Challenges and solutions in business, law, medicine, and public policy.* Cambridge University Press.

Bazerman, M.H. & Tenbrunsel, A.E. (2011). *BlindSpots: Why we fail to do what's right and what to do about it.* Princeton, NJ: Princeton University Press.

Bell, M. (2016). Teaching at the intersections. *Teaching Tolerance.* https://www.tolerance.org/magazine/summer-2016/teaching-at- the-intersections

Bennett, M. (2017). Development model of intercultural sensitivity. In Y. Kim (Ed.), International encyclopedia of intercultural communication. New York, NY: Wiley. https://doi.org/10.1002/9781118783665

Braxton, P. (2019) *Creating a Culture of Inclusion on Campus*. College and University Professional Association for Human Resources.

Brown, M. (2007). Educating all students: Creating culturally responsive teachers, classrooms, and schools. *Intervention in School and Clinic. 43*(1), 57-62.

Carroll, D. W. (2009). Toward multicultural competence: A practice model for implementation in the schools. In J. M. Jones (Ed.), *The psychology of multiculturalism in schools: A primer for practice, training, and research* (pp. 1–16). National Association of School Psychologists.

Census Bureau. (2016). Data USA: Special education teachers. Retrieved from https://datausa.io/profile/soc/252050/

Chu, S. (2011). Teacher efficacy beliefs toward serving culturally and linguistically diverse students in special education: Implications of a pilot study. Education and Urban Society, 45(3), 385–410. https://doi.org/10.1177/0013124511409401

Chugh, D., Bazerman, M. H., Banaji, & M. R. (2005). Bounded ethically as a psychological barrier to recognizing conflicts of interest. In D. Moore, D. Cain, G. Loewenstein, & M.

Cooper, B. (2016). Intersectionality. In L. Disch & M. Hawkesworth (Eds.), *The Oxford handbook of feminist theory* (385–406). New York, NY: Oxford University Press.

Crenshaw, K. (1989). Demarginalizing the intersection of race and sex: A Black feminist critique of antidiscrimination doctrine, feminist theory, and antiracist politics. *University of Chicago Legal Forum, 8*(1), 139–167. https://chicagounbound.uchicago.edu/uclf/vol1989/iss1/8

Darling-Hammond, L. (2002). Educating a profession for equitable practice. In L. Darling-Hammond, J. French, & S. P. Garcia-Lopez (Eds.), *Learning to teach for social justice* (201–212). Teachers College Press.

Definition of Intellectual Disability. (n.d.). Retrieved October 26, 2020, from http://www.aaidd.org/intellectual-disability/definition

Diversity Issues for the Instructor: Identifying Your Own Attitudes, Center for Teaching and Learning, University of North Carolina, Chapel Hill, 1998;

Diversity Issues for the Instructor: Identifying Your Own Attitudes, http://www.crlt.umich. edu/gsis/p3_2.

Dogar, I. A. (2007). Biopsychosocial model. *Annals of Punjab Medical College*, *1*(1), 11-13.

Facts About Developmental Disabilities. (2019, September 26). Retrieved October 25, 2020, from https://www.cdc.gov/ncbddd/developmentaldisabilities/facts.html

Ferguson, S. (2014, September 29). What is privilege? Everyday Feminism. https://everydayfeminism.com/2014/09/what-is-privilege/

Ford, D.Y. (2012). Culturally different students in special education: Looking backward to move forward. *Exceptional Children, 78*(4), 391-405. https://doi.org/10.1177/001440291207800401

Garibay, J. *Creating a Positive Classroom Climate for Diversity*. UCLA. Contact UCLA's office of Diversity & Faculty Development for permission to reproduce this booklet for educational purposes. Email facdiversity@conet.ucla.edu or call (310) 206-7411.

Gay, G., & Howard, T. C. (2000). Multicultural teacher education for the 21st century. *The Teacher Educator, 36*(1), 1–16. http://dx.doi.org/10.1080/08878730009555246

Griswold, Wendy. 2012. *Cultures and Societies in a Changing World*. Thousand Oaks: Pine Forge Press.

Harry, B., Kalyanpur, M., & Day, M. (1999). Building cultural reciprocity with families. Paul H. Brookes.

Hosking, D.L. (2008). Critical disability theory: a paper presented at the 4th biennial disability studies conference at lancaster university, UK. 2008. http://www.lancaster.ac.uk/fass/events/disabilityconference_archive/2008/papers/hosking2008.pdf 2008. Accessed 18 Oct 2018.

Individuals with Disabilities Education Act, 20 U.S.C. § 1400 (2004).

Ilrish, C. & Scrubb, M. (2012). Five Competencies for Culturally Competent Teaching and Learning, Faculty Focus, Higher Ed Teaching Strategies, Magna Publications. http://www.facultyfocus.com/articles/teaching-and-learning/five-competencies-for-culturally-competent-teaching-and-learning/

James, M., & Burgos, A. (2020, May 25). Race. Retrieved October 29, 2020, from https://plato.stanford.edu/entries/race/

King, E. & Butler, B. R. (2015). Who cares about diversity? A preliminary investigation of diversity exposure in teacher preparation programs. *Multicultural Perspectives, 17*(1), 46–52. http://dx.doi.org/10.1080/15210960.2015.994436

Lindo, E. J., & Lim, O. J. (Spring, 2020). Becoming more culturally competent educators.

Perspectives on Language and Literacy, 46(2), 33–38. https://dyslexiaida.org/perspectives/

Linton, S. (1998). *Claiming disability: Knowledge and identity.* University Press.

National Association of School Psychologists (2016). *Understanding race and privilege*. [Handout]. Bethesda, MD: Author.

National Association of School Psychologists (2017). *Understanding intersectionality*. [Handout]. Bethesda, MD: Author.

National Center for Educational Statistics. (2017). Condition of education 2017. Washington, DC: Author.

National Center for Educational Statistics. (2018). Children and Youth with Disabilities. Retrieved from https://nces.ed.gov/programs/coe/indicator_cgg.asp

National Institute of Health. National Human Genome Research Institute. https://www.genome.gov/genetics-glossary/Race

Niles, G. & Harkins Monaco, E.A. (2019). Privilege, social identity and Autism: Preparing preservice practitioners for intersectional pedagogy. *DADD Online Journal (DOJ), 6*(1), 112-123.

Owen, P. M. (2010). Increasing preservice teachers' support of multicultural education. *Multicultural Perspectives, 12*(1), 18–25. http://dx.doi.org/10.1080/15210961003641310

Paniagua, A. (2015, September 20). Opinion: Minoritized, not a minority. Retrieved October 26, 2020, from http://www.kentwired.com/latest_updates/article_dc83f7e0-5fe9-11e5-b6c0-2b8c8a9b5266.html

Pearson, J. N., Meadan, H., Malone, K. M. & Martin, B. M. (2019) Parent and Professional Experiences Supporting African-American Children with Autism. Journal of Racial and Ethnic Health Disparities. https://doi.org/10.1007/s40615-019-00659-9

Pew Research Center (2020). *What census calls us.* https://www.pewresearch.org/interactives/what-census-calls-us/

Pew Research Center (2020). *The changing categories the U.S. census has used to measure race.* https://www.pewresearch.org/fact-tank/2020/02/25/the-changing-categories-the-u-s-has-used-to-measure-race/

Privilege. 2020. In Merriam-Webster.com. Retrieved April 22, 2020, from https://www.merriamwebster.com/dictionary/privilege

Proctor, S. L., & Meyers, J. (2015). Best practices in primary prevention in diverse schools and communities. In P. L. Harrison & A. Thomas (Eds.)., *Best practices in school psychology: Foundations.* (pp. 33–47). National Association of School Psychologists.

Proctor, S. L., Kyle, J., Fefer, K., & Lau, C. (2017). Examining racial microaggressions, race/ethnicity, gender, and bilingual status with school psychology students: The role of intersectionality. *Contemporary School Psychology.* Advance online publication. doi:10.1007/s40688-017-0156-8

Proctor, S. L., Williams, B., Scherr, T., & Li, K. (2017). Intersectionality and School Psychology: Implications for Practice. *National Association of School Psychologists (NASP).* Retrieved from https://www.nasponline.org/resources-and-publications/resources-and-podcasts/diversity/social-justice/intersectionality-and-school-psychology-implications-for-practice

Race & Ethnicity. (n.d.). Retrieved October 29, 2020, from https://genderedinnovations.stanford.edu/terms/race.html

Siwatu, K. O. (2011). Preservice teachers' culturally responsive teaching self-efficacy-forming experiences: A mixed methods study. *The Journal of Educational Research, 104*, 360–369. https://doi.org/10.1080/00220671.2010.487081

Staats, C., Capatosto, K., Wright, R. A., & Contractor, D. (2015). State of the science: Implicit bias review 2015. https://kirwaninstitute.osu.edu/wp-content/uploads/2015/05/2015-kirwan-implicit-bias.pdf

Spring, Joel (2000). *The intersection of cultures: Multicultural education in the United States and the global economy.* McGraw Hill Higher Education.

Teaching for Inclusion: Valuing the Diversity of Our Students, Southern Methodist University, http://www.smu.edu/Provost/CTE/Resources/TeachCourse/TeachingSituations/Inclusion;

Teaching in Racially Diverse College Classrooms, Derek Bok Center for Teaching and Learning, Harvard University, http://isites.harvard.edu/fs/html/icb.topic58474/TFTrace.html

The Continuum. (n.d.). Retrieved November 02, 2020, from https://ccpep.org/home/what-is-cultural-proficiency/the-continuum/

Chapter 2

Interrogating assumptions about culture and disability: Becoming a critical and reflexive educator

Phillandra Smith, Christine Ashby, and Beth A. Ferri

> **Objectives**
> - Consider how you are situated in terms of identity and culture and how those positionalities may align with or differ from those of individuals with developmental disabilities, including autism and intellectual disability.
> - Understand your own cultural assumptions about disability and culturally responsive and sustaining education for individuals with developmental disabilities, including autism and intellectual disability.
> - Examine how your cultural identity informs your "habitus" (internalized ways of knowing, being, and acting), which influence your views about disability and neurodiversity.
> - Examine your practice for the development of cultural reflexivity and critical consciousness using a list of considerations.

Chapter 2 provides an overview of culture and disability. Given the diversity present in our classrooms and the frequent cultural mismatch between teachers and students there remains an urgent need to support all teachers in adopting a "culturally minded and reflexive stance," (Artiles, 2011)—one that promotes cultural relevance, reciprocity, and competence. As defined in Chapter 1, culture is a combination of thoughts, feelings, attitudes, beliefs, values, behavior patterns, and practices that are shared by racial, ethnic, religious, or social groups. Culture is dynamic, multidimensional, and imbued with power and complexity (Artiles, 2015). This chapter presents a process of how to interrogate one's own assumptions about disability and difference and what it means to develop habits of cultural reflexivity, reflexive practice, and critical consciousness in our work with students with developmental disabilities, including those with autism and intellectual disability.

Table 2.1 Key Terminology	
Assumptions	An idea that is accepted as true or as certain without finite evidence.
Interrogate	The act of asking questions.
Reflexive practice	An action that involves "active, persistent, and careful consideration of any belief or supposed form of knowledge in light of the grounds that support it and the further consequences to which it leads" (Dewey, 1933).

Almost half of all students in U.S. public schools are culturally, linguistically, and economically diverse (CLED) (Thoma, Agran, & Scott, 2016). Yet, despite schools becoming more diverse (de Brey, Musu, McFarland, Wilkinson-Flicker, Diliberti, Zhang, & Wang, 2019) and despite findings that suggest that students from minoritized backgrounds who are instructed by teachers also from minoritized backgrounds have better outcomes (e.g., higher achievement and graduation rates) (Rocha & Hawes, 2009; Skiba & Williams, 2014), teachers of color make up a small percentage of the U.S. teaching force (Department of Education [DOE], 2016).

Special education (SE) identification and placement are deeply influenced by cultural, racial, and linguistic factors. Students from CLED backgrounds, particularly males, are identified for special education at much higher rates than their White peers (Fish, 2019; U.S. Department of Education (USDOE), 2018). American Indians and African Americans are more likely to receive special education services than all other racial/ethnic groups combined (USDOE, 2018). The category of intellectual disability is one of several disability classifications that are disproportionately assigned to students of color. In this chapter, we share their experiences and journeys in examining their assumptions about culture and disability and becoming critical and reflexive practitioners. We invite practitioners to examine their practices for cultural reflexivity and critical consciousness using a list of considerations.

Interrogation: *How am I situated in terms of identity and culture and how similar is my positionality to the students I will teach in terms of race, class, gender, disability, and culture?*

Case Study: Phillandra

I (Phillandra) did not recognize my culture or identity until I was confronted with differing cultural views and identities. Outside of a few specialty foods and cultural events in the form of street parades or festivals, I could not describe my identity and beliefs with any level of detail or nuance. When I left my home country to further my tertiary education at the age of 18—my first time living away from 'home' for a period longer than two weeks—I was forced to figure out who I was and what I believed. My identity up to that point was obscured by my affiliation with the majority culture, and each time I found myself on the margins of another culture I discovered more about what I believed. As Delpit (2006) put it, "...many of us don't even realize that our own worlds exist in our heads and in the cultural institutions we have built to support them" (xxiv). I had lived in my own world—or a world where I was a part of the dominant group—so, naturally, I took that world with me as I entered and negotiated different spaces. I had to learn alternate ways of viewing and interacting with another world where I was now the "other." This was neither easy nor comfortable.

At 18 years old I struggled to adapt to my new context, but this "struggle," mostly in the form of a series of faux pas, is what helped me to understand, recognize, and appreciate other realities. I would love to tell you that following those four years or the multiple countries I have lived in since that I became an expert in cultural understanding, but the only thing I would claim to know well is what it feels like to exist on the margins. I have learned to lean into these experiences in new ways to help me think about the experiences of diverse students in my classroom.

Although I experience living on the margins in terms of race and culture in the United States, my experience of marginalization does not adequately describe my entire existence, since I am a part of the "majority" in some ways as well. Identity is not a unitary construct and as a nondisabled, cis-gender, Afro-Caribbean woman, I have access to membership in the dominant groups for gender and ability. This membership comes with hegemonic, contextual assumptions about those outside these groups.

The K-12 teaching workforce in the United States is predominantly White (National Collaborative on Diversity of the Teaching Force, 2004) and there is little to suggest that it will become more diverse in the near future; the vast majority of all current teacher education students are White females (Cochran-Smith, 2004). Approximately half of all schools in the United States do not have a single teacher of color on staff, yet almost half of all students in public schools are considered culturally, linguistically, and economically diverse (CLED) (Thoma, Agran, & Scott, 2016). *Can you think of any possible ramifications of the disparity between the demographics of the teaching force compared to our student population?*

Many students will leave high school without ever having been taught by a person of color (Jordon-Irvine, 2003) and denied the opportunity to see themselves reflected in the teaching profession. Many students of color will not have the opportunity to connect with practitioners who share, value, honor, and affirm their cultural views, beliefs, ideals, and experiences, while exploring other cultural perspectives. Without intervention, diverse students will experience education from the borders of their classroom community because they lack membership in the dominant cultures. It is therefore crucial for teachers, especially those who identify as members of the dominant cultural group, to examine their positionality in relation to that of their students. C.A.P. (Lindo & Lim, 2020), as explained in Chapter 1, can help with this. Sometimes this begins with understanding that we are all part of one or more cultural groups, a racial identity, and that we are all sometimes insider and outsider. As Ladson-Billings (2001, p. 81) contends:

> Typically, White, middle-class prospective teachers have little to no understanding of their own culture. Notions of Whiteness are taken for granted. They rarely are interrogated. But being White is not merely about biology. It is about choosing a system of privilege and power.

Researchers in the field of culturally relevant teacher education stress the importance of White teachers developing awareness, or critical consciousness, around issues of race, privilege, power, and oppression in order to be successful with students from diverse settings (Cochran-Smith, 2004; Jordan-Irvine, 2003). However, as a teacher who is also a member of a dominant cultural group, understanding the relevance of teaching from the culturally relevant, sensitive, and sustainable perspective may present a challenge (Cochran-Smith, 2004; Jordan-Irvine, 2003). Life experiences and positionality may hinder one's ability to interrogate personal ideals (Picower, 2009), taken for granted beliefs, and ability to engage in cultural reflexivity—all practices that are essential to successfully teaching students of color. Using C.A.P. (Lindo & Lim, 2020) to approach this challenge may assist starting your personal interrogation.

Special education and students with disabilities are not immune to the implications of this cultural mismatch and hegemonic (i.e., dominant in a social context) framing that positions difference as deficit. Racially, ethnically, and culturally diverse students with disabilities face a "double jeopardy" as multiple minoritized individuals. As students and families are invited to participate in special education meetings, they often bring with them different expectations and understandings of disability, race, and gender, for example. Research points to the significance of parents' culture in the way they interpret their child's disability (Ticani et al., 2009). One study found that African American mothers perceived a less negative impact associated with having a child with autism than did Caucasian mothers (Bishop, Richler, Cain, & Lord, 2007). An implication of their findings is that some African American parents may interpret their children's impairments differently (and perhaps less negatively) based on their cultural beliefs. Similarly, another study found that parents from cultures that have strong religious beliefs, such as Columbian, Puerto Rican, Mexican cultures, were more accepting of their children's limitations (Rogers-Adkinson et al., 2003). Thus, differences in cultural understandings of disability might lead teachers to misinterpret parents' behavior and response to their child's impairment. More information about caregivers of children with disabilities who have multiple social identities is presented in Chapter 7.

Generally, non-Western cultures possess varying definitions of conditions such as autism and these definitions often do not adhere to the strict clinical definitions used within the dominant cultures of the United States (Welterlin & LaRue, 2007). Autism and intellectual disability labels may be fully absent in some cultures. For example, in immigrant cultures in which education is seen as the primary path toward economic advancement and as a result is highly valued and sought after, the effect of a disability might be interpreted solely as a student failing to meet family aspirations (Huer, Saenz, & Doan, 2001). Unfortunately, practitioners who lack cultural reflexivity may be inclined to dismiss differing views toward disability and perceive families as being in denial about the students' impairments (Rogers-Adkinson et al., 2003), or as disinterested in their child's education (see Chapter 7). Given the vastly different cultural and linguistic contexts from which students and families originate, as practitioners we must refrain from generalizing about students on the basis of our own preconceptions. To do this, we begin by identifying our preconceptions, something addressed throughout this chapter.

If you are a teacher, there is a very high probability that you are a part of the mainstream society on many of the criteria listed above. The journey to becoming a critical and reflexive educator requires teachers to examine their positionality. Your positionality should drive you to consider your role in preparing students for "the richness of living in an increasingly diverse national community" (Delpit, 2006, p.67), creating equitable learning experiences for all students, and creating a community of learners who celebrate and not just tolerate diversity.

Interrogation. *What are my beliefs about race, class, and culture? What cultural messages will I need to unlearn and relearn?*

Our personal histories, social conditioning, classroom experiences as a student, cultural assumptions, and stereotypes, all contribute significantly to beliefs about who does and does not belong in classrooms. Personal histories and experiences directly inform how practitioners teach, who we see as "capable" and deserving of our time and effort, and how we accommodate the needs of students. Consider this: If a teacher thinks a student would be better served somewhere else, what are the chances that the teacher will attempt to design their classroom space and instruction to accommodate the needs of that student? Remember the biopsychosocial model from Chapter 1? This is an example of how we may be limiting people with disabilities. We must unlearn assumptions about which behaviors, personalities, learning styles, dis/abilities, cultures, and ethnicities are "fit" and "unfit" for classroom instruction, and these ideas may be more entrenched than we would like to admit.

Table 2.2 Examine Who (and What) is Present and Missing
Imagine for a moment your ideal classroom. You have all the options you can imagine for location. Visualize the classroom setup, including the arrangement of furniture. Your budget is generous, and space is not an issue. All forms of technology are available upon request and there are no applications, letters, or petitions involved. Everything works. Explore your classroom. Open the cabinets stocked with all the desired supplies. Your creativity is unlimited; you can decorate the room anyway you like.
Have you clearly visualized your ideal classroom? Now let us go a step further. Who are your students? Scan the room. Look at their faces. What do they look like? Who is present? Who is absent? How do they learn best? How have you provided a means for them to express what they know?
Both who (and what) is present and who (and what) is missing should help you begin to identify your beliefs about race, class, culture, and disability. Examine the demographics of your ideal classroom and consider the origins of your views for why this configuration is your "ideal."

If you think back to your own schooling (or to the classrooms you encounter presently), students are often tracked along very different trajectories. The racial configuration of college preparation or advanced courses compared to those of special education or remedial classes illustrate how race and disability intertwine in the social context of education (Erevelles, 2017), and are used to segregate and oppress students based on their difference from some hypothetical norm (i.e. something perceived as typical or standard). The configuration of these classes has for decades sent a strong message about diverse students and where they belong in school settings. Practitioners will better serve all students if we unlearn the assumptions we have developed as a result of these perceptions and practices. Although academic tracking often masquerades as being purely about achievement, to adopt this view is to ignore the diverse structural and systemic disadvantages many students face, leading us to accept, rather than challenge, these socially constructed hierarchies.

To provide a more equitable learning experience for all students, we must learn/relearn to create school and classroom cultures that ensure full citizenship and belonging for all students. Classroom citizenship is a right and not a privilege that must be earned on the grounds of "good" behavior or academic achievement.

Students should not need to prove themselves to be included in the classroom. Federal regulation mandates students be placed in the least restrictive educational environment (LRE). It states, "To the maximum extent appropriate, children with disabilities, including children in public or private institutions or other care facilities, must be educated with children who are nondisabled" (Office of Special Education and Rehabilitative Services, 1997).

The concept of LRE highlights the importance of presuming competence of all students, another practice we must learn/relearn. Blatt (1999), one of the first scholars to illustrate the significance of presuming competence points out that Helen Keller, despite her international fame as a writer and speaker was initially believed to be "retarded." Only with the help of an optimistic teacher did Helen Killer demonstrate that she could be educated. Consider this in light of her teacher, Anne Sullivan, having no way of knowing that Helen Keller would ever learn to read or write, yet she remained committed to Keller's education. Anne Sullivan must have presumed Keller was competent and that reading and writing was possible (Blatt, 1999). As teachers we have the ethical responsibility to assume that all students possess knowledge and are capable of learning.

To presume competence means that:

> ...educators must assume students can and will change and, that through engagement with the world, will demonstrate complexities of thought and action that could not necessarily be anticipated. Within this frame, difficulties with performance are not presumed to be evidence of intellectual incapacity (Biklen, 2000, cited in Biklen & Burke, 2006, p.168).

As practitioners we have an obligation to unlearn the habit of projecting negative assumptions about students' ability to possess and acquire knowledge based on disability labels, race, class, and culture. Instead, we must learn/relearn to presume competence in the absence of any advance "evidence" to suggest our efforts will be successful and take action to create contexts in which students can demonstrate their full capabilities.

Interrogation. *What are my beliefs about disability and how did I learn or acquire these beliefs? What are the cultural messages about disability that I will need to unlearn and relearn?*

Case Study: Beth

My (Beth's) very first teaching position after graduating from university was in a remote area in West Virginia. I was hired to start a brand-new program for students aged 5-23 who had been labeled with what we would now call moderate intellectual disabilities. At that time students in my classroom were not even deemed "educable," which tells you quite a bit about low expectations and why labels matter.

Over the course of that first year, I would come to learn just how inaccurate the quite limited view of my students' capacities and talents were. I recall so many stories where students demonstrated many of the abilities that they were deemed deficient in based on standardized measures of ability. In what we would surely recognize as entrepreneurship, environmental science, and math, students would tell me when it was time to harvest black walnuts or why the price for fox pelts had gone down. They had knowledge about what kinds of fish and game were most prized for eating and why. They were also charmingly funny—often making fun of my limited fund of knowledge when it came to West Virginia life, language, and culture. My students also demonstrated a high level of emotional intelligence—several older students would comfort a student who had a seizure disorder—taking turns sitting with him when he was having a bad day with multiple seizures or when he was sleepy from his medication. These were all highly prized abilities that somehow did not translate to any of the clinical assessments that cemented the student's educational placements. I remember thinking if the tables were turned, just how deficient I would be in the kinds of intelligence most prized in their communities.

Think back for a moment to recall your earliest memories of disability. Were you a very young child or perhaps older? Maybe you had a friend in your neighborhood who had a disability or perhaps you remember going to school with someone who was disabled. Perhaps you have a member of your family or maybe you were born with or acquired a disability yourself. Maybe you can't recall ever meeting anyone with a disability and so your earliest memory of disability came from watching a Disney movie, like the Hunchback of Notre Dame, or a cartoon or children's television show. In sharing our collective stories about coming to know disability, several common themes would likely emerge from our stories. These themes tell us a lot about the cultural messages about disability that we likely learned and will now need to unlearn as we try to envision more inclusive and socially just schools and classroom communities.

If you are reading this chapter, it is likely that you grew up after the passage of a landmark education law, which mandated that students with disabilities were entitled to a free and public education. This law, the Individuals with Disabilities Education Act (IDEA), was passed in 1975. Prior to IDEA, students with disabilities were often excluded from public schools completely, particularly if school officials believed they could not benefit from instruction. Currently, about 14 percent of students receive special education services, as outlined in their Individualized Education Program (IEP) plan. However, this percentage can vary across states or even districts. As stated above, a provision of this law mandates that all students be educated in the "least restrictive" environment (LRE)—or the most inclusive classroom. Yet, students with disabilities still experience significant levels of segregation within schools when they are pulled out of the general education classroom for instruction. Moreover, the law only requires that students be educated in general education classrooms for 80 percent of their school day to be considered fully included. Does 80 percent seem like a low bar? Would 80 percent of anything feel like something was missing?

Growing up after the passage of this landmark legislation, we should be able to assume that students with disabilities went to your school and were included in your classroom for at least some part of the school day. We can also assume that you teach (or will teach) in inclusive classrooms. Currently, more than 60 percent of students with disabilities are included for at least 80 percent of the school day, although the percentage for students with autism is slightly less than 40 percent and for students labeled with intellectual disabilities it is less than 20 percent. The majority of students with these labels are regularly excluded from general education classrooms and curriculum (USDOE, 2019). Do we think of this kind of segregation as discrimination, a necessary and beneficial practice, or "just the way things are?"

The first cluster of cultural messages we must unlearn include ableism, deficit thinking, and normalcy. Ableism is a concept that is similar to other forms of oppression like racism and sexism. Ableism is a discriminatory attitude that suggests that typical ways of being in the world (e.g. neurotypical; able bodies) are inherently better than disabled ways of being in the world. Ableism is grounded in deficit thinking. When we think of our students in deficit ways, we misplace our efforts and attention, focusing on fixing students, rather than removing barriers or ensuring full access to our instruction. When we reject ableism and deficit thinking, we become more open to thinking about our students with disabilities as complex and unique individuals with a range of strengths and needs (like any other student). We shift our focus from locating deficits in students or thinking they need to conform to what we perceive as "normal," to thinking about how we can actively remove barriers to learning for all students. Of course, this doesn't mean that we don't "see" disability (which like race, gender, or sexuality, is an important part of a person's identity), but that we don't perceive those differences as deficits.

Related to "seeing" disability we also need to reject silences around disability. Young children, in particular, are naturally curious about disability. They may be fascinated by an assistive device or mobility aide. They may have questions about people they perceive as having interesting differences. Often parents will be embarrassed when their child asks questions about disabilities. Similarly, students in a classroom might wonder why a child is being sent out or pushed in or they may wonder about a child who uses a communication device. When we fail to talk about disability, we make it a secret or a taboo topic in ways that are unhelpful and lead to misunderstandings and feelings of shame. Like any valued difference, we should "see" disability in all aspects of our schools—from including students with disabilities in our classrooms, to including disability in our curriculum. After all, inclusion isn't just about *who* we teach, but also *what* we teach—as well as who teaches. If we think about disability from a cultural or identity-based perspective, then we can begin to think about ways to infuse our curriculum with disability centric content and examples. Students with disabilities, like all students, should see their experiences mirrored back to them in the stories we read, the histories we learn, and the lives we center.

Finally, given the fact that many students with disabilities are excluded for significant parts of the school day, another cultural message you might have received is what we might call conditional inclusion or provisional membership. This occurs when students with disabilities are only included some of the time or in very superficial ways. Perhaps you recall a student being "sent out" for speech class or "pushed into" social studies class. Maybe there were a few kids who sat with an aide on their own island in the back of the room. You probably weren't sure why these kids were coming and going, and likely made you a bit uneasy because no one talked about it. After all, how are you supposed to think about a child who suddenly appears in your art class or who disappears after the homeroom period? The messages we receive suggest that some students are not full members of the class, but are like squatters or guests (Kliewer, 1998). If we are to relearn more welcoming and inclusive cultural messages, we must refocus our attention from fixing the child to fixing our mode of instruction and our ideas about belonging. Like any other child, no child should have to earn their way into the classroom, they simply belong. Thus, as teachers, we do not ask *whether* a child belongs or *whether* they should be in our classroom, but instead we focus on *how* we can ensure that all children can fully and meaningfully participate as full and active members of our classroom community because that is the definition of a community! The rest of this book continues to explore how we can better create these communities.

Interrogation. *What assumptions do I hold and enact about autism, intellectual and developmental disability, and other students with complex support needs? How do/could these assumptions impact my planning and instruction?*

Case Study: Christy Part 1

Like many people of my generation, my (Christy's) first exposure to autism in the media came from watching the movie "Rainman." Dustin Hoffman's portrayal of Raymond Babbit drew on deeply entrenched stereotypes of the autistic savant, able to count cards and memorize obscure facts, but unable to engage socially, and "safely" returned to the institution at the conclusion of the movie, after he helped to humanize his nondisabled brother, played by Tom Cruise. This two-dimensional representation became the backdrop for my teacher education related to autism. As a preservice teacher candidate in the early 1990s, my teacher training, while inclusive in orientation, was not guided by disability studies theoretical framing. Instead, I learned diagnostic criteria and strategies for support that assumed commonalities across labels. In other words, my training was guided by a medical model approach to education. And while autism was part of that education, our understandings of the spectrum were far different than today. I learned that only 1 in 10,000 children were labeled with autism, over 75% of all children with autism were also cognitively delayed. Building on my earlier learnings from "Rainman," my coursework seemed to confirm that children with autism were in a "world by themselves" and generally preferred objects to people. I wrote papers on the topic and entered my first years of teaching assuming there was a limit on what students with autism could learn, viewing children with autism as outsiders, the ultimate "other."

I believed strongly that all children, regardless of disability, deserved access to rich, rewarding, and inclusive school experiences, but I didn't challenge the definitions of disability I had been taught as an undergraduate. I didn't question why students of color were more likely to be labeled with intellectual disabilities, while more White students acquired labels of autism. I learned how to administer achievement tests, but I didn't have the tools yet to fully question the meaning and usefulness of the results. When I was told that a student had an IQ of 46, I assumed that told me something important about their potential for success in learning. I believed that all students belonged, but I wasn't always asking the right questions about their opportunities for meaningful engagement or my role in hindering or facilitating access. In my early years of teaching, I focused on making sure all kids had access to general education spaces and instruction, but didn't sufficiently challenge the assumptions about competence and performance.

But as I started reading books that challenged the usefulness of IQ, I began to question its authority in classification and constructions of disability. Trent (1994) and Gould (1996) provided nuanced analyses of the fallacies of IQ, with specific attention to the intersections with race and eugenics (i.e., the study of how to arrange reproduction to increase the occurrence of heritable characteristics within humans).

In *Smart Culture,* Hayman (1998) argues for the socially constructed nature of "smartness" and competence:

> Intelligence does not exist in a vacuum. Rather, "intelligence" is defined by the relevant context, principally by the demands of the environment and the perspective of the observer. Intelligence thus is not absolute, but contingent or situational; it is not general, but local or specific; and it is not abstract, but practical or experiential. Intelligence, like beauty, is truly in the eyes of the beholders…(p. 270)

In other words, intelligence and smartness are contextual. So, what does that mean in terms of practice? It tells us that smartness or competence are not things that reside in a person—either they have it or they don't. Rather, a student's ability or competence depends on many factors, like what we define as "smartness," the opportunities we provide the student, the meaning we chose to make of their performance and participation. In other words, we as practitioners play a vital role in constructing competence—smartness is, as they say, in the eye of the beholder! Let's imagine you have a student in your class who has been labeled intellectually disabled. What might you presume about that student's likelihood of success in the class? What kinds of books and materials would you provide? How would you envision this student participating during group discussions? Too often labels, especially developmental disability labels, become lenses we see students through. And sometimes this leads teachers to limit the resources, materials, and opportunities made available to that student. Then, when that student isn't successful, we blame the student or their label, rather than the lack of opportunity or appropriate support we've provided.

This is especially important to keep in mind when we are talking about autism or other developmental disabilities that impact performance. For centuries, educators and philosophers have equated speech with intellect. Many individuals with unreliable communication have been considered incompetent and denied access to rich and rewarding school experiences (Ashby & Woodfield, 2019; Biklen & Kliewer, 2006; Donnellan, 1984). Building on what we said above about presuming competence, we need to presume that all students are capable of more than they are currently demonstrating if they provided with the right support and instruction. Thus, we need to ensure that all students have reliable means of communicating and ways of participating in class. We can never truly know what someone is thinking or what they know—we can only assess and evaluate what they are able to demonstrate. This is one of the reasons why many students with autism struggle on traditional aptitude tests but do better on those that do not require speech or pointing on demand in a timed setting (Dawson, et al., 2007). Therefore, if we consider autism and other developmental disabilities as differences in performance rather than simply cognition or understanding, that shifts the onus of responsibility to practitioners to keep asking different questions and trying different methods and technologies. And all of this should be guided by the voices and perspectives of people with disabilities themselves.

Interrogation. *Who is an expert on disability? How does it shift my understanding of autism and developmental disability to apply the language/lens of neurodiversity?*

Case Study: Christy Part 2

Several years ago, I (Christy) submitted a manuscript for potential publication in a prominent special education journal. My co-author and I had conducted a textual analysis of autobiographies written by people with autism that focused on themes of social interaction and constructions of competence. It was our intention to de-center the role of the "expert" and stated in our introduction that as researchers without disabilities we considered people with autism to be the real experts on autism. We didn't think that was a controversial statement, nor were we expecting resistance to this seemingly logical (at least to us) positioning. In our rejection letter, the editor took umbrage to our claim and insisted that people with autism are only experts on their own experience, they can't speak for others. For this and other reasons outlined in the letter, the manuscript was deemed unsuitable for publication in that journal. We sent it elsewhere and it was published with the original statement about expert status. But I thought about that editor's response for years afterwards. Who is authorized to tell the story of disability? Whose perspective should be privileged? Would they have questioned my ability, as a researcher without autism, to speak to the experience of autism? Does researcher or educator status supersede personal experience?

One of the tenets of disability studies is the importance of privileging the voices of people with disabilities as the experts on the experience of disability. Too often the story of disability has been told by a nondisabled voice, often with dangerous results. Blatt argued, "We tell stories about people who can't tell stories, who can't stop us from telling our stories about them." These stories have been known to "kill" people with intellectual disabilities. Blatt wrote those chilling words in 1981, during the height of the deinstitutionalization movement. He knew that the books, articles, labels, reports, etc. written by so-called professionals about people considered to be intellectually disabled have done terrible harm—segregation, sterilization, institutionalization, abuse. He further argued that one of the only ways to address this problem is to listen to the voices of people we have historically silenced. The mantra, "Nothing about us without us" has been a rallying cry of the disability rights movement for decades. People with disabilities are taking on self-advocacy roles asserting their right to define their experience, seek the support and services they deem helpful, and not be subjected to "treatments" aimed to eradicate difference or enforce normalcy. They are actively claiming their disabled identity and their membership as part of a cultural group. When we view disability as culture, this helps us decenter the able-bodied experience as the norm against which all other experiences and ways of being are compared and judged. Disability stops being an imperfect or incomplete approximation of humanity, but rather part of humanity itself.

The neurodiversity movement builds on this legacy and asks us to consider autism as a neurological difference, rather than a deviance or deficiency.

> Neurodivergent, sometimes abbreviated as ND, means having a brain that functions in ways that diverge significantly from the dominant societal standards of "normal" (Walker, 2014). The term neurodivergent, coined by Kassiane Asasumasu, reflects a recognition of autism, as well as other diverse neurologies and ways of being, as variation of human experience, rather than a deficiency in need of remediation or cure. (Ashby & Woodfield, 2019, p. 153)

When we shift our lens from remediation of deviance to recognition and celebration of divergent ways of being, when we view the autistic or disabled experience as one of value, we can more easily attend to the meaning of that experience to the person. We can push against assumptions that speech is the preferred mode of communicative interaction, that sitting still in one's seat demonstrates active listening in class; in other words, that looking indistinguishable from non-disabled peers should be the goal for students with disabilities.

But many of the pervasive cultural messages reinforce deficit and ableist perspectives. Take, for example, the puzzle piece image so frequently used to represent autism. What does that image signify or elicit? Is the puzzle portraying autism as something unknowable, enigmatic, mysterious? There is something insidious and problematic with this representation. Until the missing piece clicks into place, the puzzle is not complete, not whole, not fully realized, not fully human. What message does that send to a student on the autism spectrum?

We need more diverse representations of the disabled experience as guideposts and cultural signifiers. Just as we need to ensure that our classroom curriculum, materials, and practices are culturally responsive and sustaining of students from diverse racial, ethnic, linguistic and religious backgrounds, we need to ensure access to diverse experiences and representations of disability. And we need to ensure that our pedagogical approaches and class activities do not unintentionally privilege particular, non-disabled ways of being and performing, particularly those that prioritize spoken speech. In the early 20th century oralists discouraged deaf children from using sign language as they feared it would hinder development or verbal speech, but they also argued that use of sign language was too animalistic, not human enough. Insistence on oral methods of communication in the name of normalcy hindered full and meaningful engagement in schooling and robbed deaf children of cultural and linguistic connection with deaf peers. Similarly, Bureau of Indian Affairs schools forcibly removed indigenous children from their families and forbade them from speaking their home languages. We see these actions as related to communicative ableism enacted today when children are denied access to preferred modes of alternative communication, assistive technology and when activities are structured in ways that prohibit non-speech access.

Interrogation. *What are some of the shared histories and ideologies of race, culture and disability and the culture, and what is my role as a general or special educator in perpetuating inequities?*

Part of being a reflective practitioner involves asking some of the types of questions you have engaged with thus far in this chapter. In addition to self-reflection, it is also important to critically reflect on the field you are entering (or currently working in), as well the role you will likely play in it. If we think about the present moment we find ourselves in as a field, we must first acknowledge the role that special education has played in disproportionately identifying students of color as disabled, placing them in more restrictive/segregated settings than White peers, and subjecting them to more severe disciplinary sanctions, such as suspensions and expulsions (Losen & Orfield, 2002; U.S. Department of Education, 2016). The problem of overrepresentation of students of color has been documented since the 1970s (when we first began collecting data on the problem). Acknowledging a problem is a necessary first step toward making change. Beyond acknowledging the problem of disproportionality, we must also understand how we got to this moment, which entails reckoning with the past. Tracing these historical roots of the problem can help us to trace a different and more equitable future.

If we were to trace the history of race, culture, and disability, we would find many instances in which those histories overlapped or collided in troubling ways. These shared histories would include histories of segregation and discrimination. Importantly, we would also find examples of resistance where oppressed groups demanded their right to equity, inclusion, and respect. You might ask yourself, "What does the past have to do with the present?" Of course, one reason to study history is to think about how many of our present practices contain seeds of the past. Another reason to pay attention to the past is that histories always reveal underlying ideologies. Moreover, how we think about difference influences how we act toward those who we see as embodying those differences. Changing outcomes requires us to rethink our assumptions.

The shared ideologies of race and disability have most often relied upon deficit thinking, othering, segregation, and dehumanization. Tracing the history of race and disability also reveals the often overlooked or taken-for-granted concept of normal—a concept that is only made real by creating a denigrated and abnormal other. Although we don't have the space to trace the entire history of race and disability, we highlight several snapshots that reveal key moments in which these histories overlap in ways that continue to reverberate in terms of educational practice.

Snapshot 1

Eugenics and biological determinism. In the first decades of the 20th century eugenicists promoted the racist idea of racial hierarchies, in which individuals from southern and eastern Europe, African countries, and indigenous groups were believed to be less intelligent than those from northern European and Nordic countries (Trent, 1998; Gould, 1996). Immigrants from less desirable countries were often labeled as unfit or feebleminded to justify their exclusion from citizenship, to rationalize marriage restrictions, and promote sterilization and segregation (Baynton, 2001; Connor & Ferri, 2013). The development of intelligence tests would be put into service to codify these perceived differences, a history that has legacies in some recent and culturally biased interpretations of achievement gaps (e.g. Morgan et al, 2012, 2015).

Snapshot 2

Segregation. By the mid-20th century, advocates in the United States began to push to overturn longstanding Jim Crow laws and to desegregate schools. This push led to the historic *Brown v. Board of Education* (1954) decision. Even after this Supreme Court decision declaring segregated schools unconstitutional and unequal, school districts around the nation instituted tactics to delay and refuse to comply. Federal troops were brought into places like Little Rock, Arkansas to force the issue, so schools found ways to segregate students within otherwise integrated schools. Tools that we take for granted today, such as academic tracking, remedial classes, special education, and gifted classes were all tactics designed to keep racial groups separate. Decisions about student placement were often based on psychometric tests that were culturally biased (Giordano, 2005), yet made to appear objective and neutral. If we look at enrollment patterns of today's schools, we continue to see disproportionate numbers of White and Asian-American students in gifted classes and higher tracks and disproportionate numbers of Black and Brown students in remedial and special education classes.

Snapshot 3

Inclusion and Equity. Building on the legacy of *Brown*, other civil rights cases pushed for educational rights of minoritized students and questioned the supposed fairness of intelligence tests. Decisions such as *PARC v. Pennsylvania (1971)* and *Mills v. Board of Education of the District of Columbia (1972)* borrowed some of the legal strategies of *Brown* to demand that students with disabilities had the right to a free and appropriate public education for the first time. *Diana v. State Board of Education* (1970) required that testing be done in the child's first language and *Larry P. v. Wilson Riles* (1971-1982) first acknowledged the disproportionate labeling of Black students as intellectually disabled. Each of these decisions expanded educational access and challenged the logics of exclusion and racial bias.

This very abbreviated history lesson holds several important lessons. First, science and educational practice are always inside culture. What we mean by that is that all ways of knowing reflect the underlying logics of the time and context that they are situated within. Our ideas about constructs such as intelligence or ability reflect our working assumptions about how the world works and how we think about difference. This is not to discount science, but to consider how our everyday assumptions and scientific truths provide a window into history and culture. Why, for instance, have we spent so much time trying to locate racial categories in the body, rather than recognizing race as a social construct that reflects geography, rather than biology? How have ideas about ability and intelligence been used to reify and justify racial inequality? This history teaches us that when we notice racialized differences in achievement or behavior, we would be wise to look to the social context of our schools and classrooms, rather than look to any inherent differences within students.

Interrogation. *How am I not recognizing this child's ability? What is it about the task or instructional context that is not allowing this child to demonstrate their smartness? How can I presume competence and create conditions that allow students to express their competence* (Ashby & Woodfield, 2019; Ashby & Kasa, 2013)*?*

The second lesson is that special education services historically and presently have played an important role in removing students who are seen as outside the norm from general education classrooms. Too often, those students placed in special education have been from poor and minoritized groups, leading Harry and Klingner (2006) to ask the question, "Why are there so many minority students in special education?" Even more telling, why do the most disproportionate special education classifications happen to be those that are also the most subjective and reliant on intelligence testing and clinical judgement?

Interrogation. *How can I use my role as a special education teacher to expand access and ensure equity? How can I combine culturally sustaining teaching, universal design, and inclusive practice to ensure that all students can meaningfully participate in ways that are most efficient and equitable? What does it mean to be an anti-ableist and anti-racist ally in my role as a special educator? How can I push colleagues to promote equitable and inclusive schools? What are the habits of mind and ethical considerations* *that I must adopt and enact as a critical and reflexive practitioner? How can I begin to develop habits of cultural reflexivity and critical consciousness and maintain these as part of my teaching practice?*

We envision the list found in Table 2.3 helping practitioners examine their own beliefs and practices related to the issues raised in this chapter. This list is not meant to be a set of items you can check off. Instead, these questions are meant to spur your thinking and encourage reflection. As you assess your teaching practice and reflect on the content of this chapter, we hope you experience a renewal in your commitment to inclusive practices and engaging in cultural reflexivity. By so doing, we hope we can teach, learn, and engage in our classrooms in more culturally sustaining and inclusive ways. Start your reflection by examining the following:

Table 2.3 Key Considerations to Examine and Reflect on Your Development of Cultural Reflexivity and Critical Consciousness
I have thought about my own positionality and privilege and that of my students.
I am aware of the stereotypes, cultural biases, and ableist attitudes I bring to my teaching practice and to my assumptions about my students, families, and communities (adapted from the Multicultural Teaching Competencies Inventory).
I have reviewed my curriculum and teaching materials to ensure representation of diverse perspectives and identities.
I have ensured that all students have ways to meaningfully access and engage in instruction and communicate with peers and teachers.
I have identified books and resources to develop my cultural consciousness and reflexivity and have a plan for personal development.
I communicate an unequivocal presumption of competence to all students through my actions in the classroom.
I actively create opportunities and contents for students to demonstrate their competence and make their understanding available to others.
I promote neurodivergent and disability specific ways of being in the world and ensure that class materials and activities incorporate neurodivergent perspectives.
I actively reflect on and interrogate taken for granted assumptions and practices in my field and my role within that field.
I advocate for students, families and communities and find ways to work in solidarity with them.

Summary

In this chapter, we challenged practitioners to situate themselves in terms of identity and culture and interrogate how those positionalities may align with or differ from those of students with disabilities and from minoritized populations. Understanding our assumptions about disability and cultural identity can impact the provision of responsive and sustaining education for individuals with disabilities. It is important to examine how cultural identity informs internalized ways of knowing, being, and acting, which influence views about disability and diversity. Utilizing the interrogation questions in this chapter can contribute to practitioners developing habits of cultural reflexivity and critical consciousness. As you move forward, consider the questions outlined below.

Guiding Questions

1. How are you situated in terms of identity and culture and how do those positionalities align with or differ from those of individuals with developmental disabilities including autism and intellectual disability?

2. What are your cultural assumptions about disability and culturally responsive and sustaining education for individuals with developmental disabilities including autism and intellectual disability?

3. How does your cultural identity inform your "habitus" (internalized ways of knowing, being, and acting), which influence your views about disability and neurodiversity?

4. Explain how you could develop cultural reflexivity and critical consciousness.

References

Artiles, A. J. (2011) Toward an interdisciplinary understanding of educational equity and difference: The case of the racialization of ability. *Educational Researcher, 40*(9),431-445. https://doi.org/10.3102/0013189X11429391

Artiles, A. J. (2015). Beyond responsiveness to identity badges: future research on culture in disability and implications for response to intervention, *Educational Review, 67*(1), 1-22. https://doi.org/10.1080/00131911.2014.934322

Ashby, C. & Kasa, C. (2013). Pointing forward: Supporting academic access for individuals that type to communicate. *ASHA Perspectives on Augmentative and Alternative Communication, 22*(3), 143-156. https://doi.org/10.1044/aac22.3.143

Ashby, C. & Woodfield, C. (2019). Honoring, constructing and supporting multi-modal voices: Making space for diverse communicators in inclusive classrooms. In K. Scorgie & C. Forlin (Eds.) *Promoting Social Inclusion: Co-Creating Environments that Foster Equity and Belonging.* Emerald Group Publishing.

Baynton, D. C. (2013). Disability and the justification of inequality in American history. *The disability studies reader, 17*(33), 57-59.

Biklen, D. & Burke, J. (2006) Presuming competence, *Equity & Excellence in Education, 39*(2), 166-175. https://doi.org/10.1080/10665680500540376

Biklen, D. & Kliewer, C. (2006). Constructing competence: Autism, voice and the 'disordered' body. *International Journal of Inclusive Education, 10*(2), 169-188. https://doi.org/10.1080/13603110600578208

Bishop, S., Richler, J., Cain, A., & Lord, C. (2007). Predictors of perceived negative impact in mothers of children with autism spectrum disorder. *American Journal on Mental Retardation, 112*(6), 450-461.

Blanchett, W. J., Klingner, J. K., & Harry, B. (2009). The intersection of race, culture, language, and disability: Implications for urban education. *Urban Education, 44*(4), 389-409. https://doi.org/10.1177/0042085909338686

Blatt, B. (1999) Man through a turned lens. In S. J. Taylor & S. D. Blatt (Eds.), *In search of the promised land: The collected papers of Burton Blatt* (pp. 71–82). American Association on Mental Deficiency.

Brown v. Board of Education, 347 U.S. 483 (1954).

Cochran-Smith, M. (2004). *Walking the road: Race, diversity, and social justice in teacher education.* Teachers College Press.

Connor, D. J., & Ferri, B. A. (2013). Historicizing dis/ability: Creating normalcy, containing difference. In M. Wappett & K. Arndt (Eds.), *Foundations of disability studies* (pp. 29-67). Palgrave Macmillan.

Dawson, M., Souliere, I., Gernsbacher, M. A., & Mottron, L. (2007). The level and nature of autistic intelligence. *Psychological Science, 18*(8), 657-662.

de Brey, C., Musu, L., McFarland, J., Wilkinson-Flicker, S., Diliberti, M., Zhang, A., ... & Wang, X. (2019). Status and Trends in the Education of Racial and Ethnic Groups 2018. NCES 2019-038. *National Center for Education Statistics*. Downloaded from https://nces.ed.gov/pubs2019/2019038.pdf

Delpit, L. (2006). *Other people's children: Cultural conflict in the classroom.* New Press.

Dewey, J. (1933). *How we think: A restatement of the relation of reflective thinking to the educative process.* Henry Regnery.

Diana v. State Board of Education, No. C-67-RFP (N.D. Cal. 1970).

Donnellan, A. M. (1984). The Criterion of the Least Dangerous Assumption. *Behavioral Disorders, 9*(2), 141–150. https://doi.org/10.1177/019874298400900201

Ervelles, N. (2017). Disability and race. In L. Davis (Ed.), *Beginning with Disability* (1st ed., pp. 129-136). Routledge. https://doi.org/10.4324/9781315453217

Fish, R. E. (2019). Standing out and sorting in: Exploring the role of racial composition in racial disparities in special education. *American Educational Research Journal, 56*(6), 2573-2608.

Giordano, G. (2005). *How testing came to dominate American schools: The history of educational assessment.* Peter Lang.

Gould, S.J. (1996). *The mismeasure of man.* W.W. Norton and Co.

Hayman, R. L. (1998). *The Smart Culture: Society, intelligence and the law.* New York University Press.

Huer, M., Saenz, T., & Doan, J. (2001). Understanding the Vietnamese American community: Implications for training educational personnel providing services to children with disabilities. *Communication Disorders Quarterly, 23*(1), 27-39.

Jordan-Irvine, J.J. 2003. *Educating teachers for diversity: Seeing with a cultural eye.* Teachers College Press.

Kliewer, C. (1998). *Schooling children with down syndrome: Toward an understanding of possibility.* Teachers College Press.

Ladson-Billings, G. 2001. *Crossing over to Canaan: The journey of new teachers in diverse classrooms.* Jossey-Bass.

Larry P. v. Riles, 343 F. Supp. 1306 (N.D. Cal. 1972).

Losen, D. J., & Orfield, G. (2002). *Racial inequity in special education*. Harvard Education Publishing Group.

Mills v. Bd. of Educ. of District of Columbia, 348 F.Supp. 866 (D.D.C. 1972).

Morgan, P. L., Farkas, G., Hillemeier, M. M., Maczuga, S. (2012). Are minority children disproportionately represented in early intervention and early childhood special education? *Educational Researcher, 41*(9), 339–351. https://doi.org/10.3102/0013189X12459678

Morgan, P. L., Farkas, G., Hillemeier, M. M., Mattison, R., Maczuga, S., Li, H., & Cook, M. (2015). Minorities are disproportionately underrepresented in special education: Longitudinal evidence across five disability conditions. *Educational Researcher*, *44*(5), 278-292.

National Collaborative on Diversity in the Teaching Force. 2004. *Assessment of diversity in America's teaching force: A call to action.* Washington, DC: National Collaborative on Diversity in the Teaching Force.

Office of Special Education and Rehabilitative Services, Education. (1997). 34 CFR 300.550, 20 U.S.C.§§1412(a)(5).

Pennsylvania Association of Retarded Citizens (PARC) v. Pennsylvania, 343 F.Supp. 279 (E.D.Pa. 1972).

Picower, B. (2009). The unexamined Whiteness of teaching: How White teachers maintain and enact dominant racial ideologies. *Race Ethnicity and Education: Critical Race Praxis, 12*(2), 197-215. https://doi.org/10.1080/13613320902995475

Prasse, D., & Reschly, D. (1986). Larry P.: A case of segregation, testing, or program efficacy? *Exceptional Children*, *52*(4), 333-346.

Prieto, L. R. (2012). Multicultural Teaching Competencies Inventory [Database record]. Retrieved from PsycTESTS. doi: https://doi.org/10.1037/t07775-000

Rocha, R. R., & Hawes, D. P. (2009). Racial diversity, representative bureaucracy, and equity in multiracial school districts, *Social Science Quarterly*, *90*(2), 326-344. https://doi.org/10.1111/j.1540-6237.2009.00620.x

Rogers-Adkinson, D., Ochoa, T., & Delgado, B. (2003). Developing cross-cultural competence: Serving families of children with significant developmental needs. *Focus on Autism and Other Developmental Disabilities*, *18*(1), 4-8.

Skiba, R. J., & Williams, N. T. (2014). Are Black kids worse? Myths and facts about racial differences in behavior. *The Equity Project at Indiana University*, 1-8.

Thoma, C., Agran, M., & Scott, L. (2016). Transition to adult life for students who are Black and have disabilities: What do we know and what do we need to know. *Journal of Vocational Rehabilitation, 45*(2), 149-158.

Tincani, M., Travers, J., & Boutot, A. (2009). Race, culture, and autism spectrum disorder: Understanding the role of diversity in successful educational interventions. *Research and Practice for Persons with Severe Disabilities, 34*(3-4), 81-90. https://doi.org/10.2511/rpsd.34.3-4.81

Trent, J. (1994). *Inventing the feeble mind: A history of mental retardation in the United States.* The University of California Press.

Trent Jr, J. W. (1998). Defectives at the World's Fair: Constructing disability in 1904. *Remedial and Special Education, 19*(4), 201-211.

U.S. Department of Education, National Center for Education Statistics. (2019). *The Digest of Education Statistics, 2019* (NCES 2020-009), Table 204.60. Downloaded from https://nces.ed.gov/programs/digest/d18/tables/dt18_204.60.asp

U.S. Department of Education, Office of Special Education and Rehabilitative Services. (2016). *Racial and ethnic disparities in special education a multiyear disproportionality analysis by state, analysis category, and race/ethnicity.* Retrieved from https://www2.ed.gov/programs/osepidea/618-data/LEA-racial-ethnic-disparities-tables/disproportionality-analysis-by-state-analysis-category.pdf

U.S. Department of Education, Office of Special Education and Rehabilitative Services, Office of Special Education Programs. (2018). 40th annual report to Congress on the implementation of the Individuals with Disabilities Education Act. Retrieved from https://www2.ed.gov/about/reports/annual/osep/2018/parts-b-c/index.html

Walker, N. (2014). Neurodiversity: Some basic terms and definitions. *Retrieved from http://neurocosmopolitanism.com/neurodiversity-some-basic-terms-definitions/*

Welterlin, A., & LaRue, R. (2007). Serving the needs of immigrant families of children with autism. *Disability & Society, 22*(7), 747-760.

Chapter 3

Acknowledging other cultural identities and their beliefs around culture and disability

Tracy McKinney, Nigel P. Pierce, and Nanette Missaghi

> **Objectives**
> - Summarize key terms associated with one's beliefs and practices around acknowledging cultural identities and beliefs different from one's own.
> - Develop an understanding of culturally responsive acknowledgment.
> - Generate skills for navigating multiple perspectives regarding beliefs different from one's own.
> - Describe interventions related to increasing ones acknowledgement of representation and culturally relevant pedagogy.
> - Review case study through the use of key terms and interventions.

The purpose of this chapter is to examine several unfavorable constructs and how they are based on one's cultural beliefs and are ingrained in policies and practices. In this chapter we offer knowledge and skills related to acknowledging one's own cultural identity, the identities of the students and families we work with, and how to learn to accept the differing beliefs related to disability that are different than one's own. While the role of one's racial identity, racism, and one's beliefs around skin color and ability are critical for a practitioner as well, it will not be examined in this chapter. Rather, we aim to provide practical skills to learn how to acknowledge the cultural beliefs of others different from one's own around culture and disability. Additionally, we will discuss the impact of these beliefs on their interactions with individuals of other cultures including individuals with disabilities. Finally, we will examine the ways an individual with a disability is viewed by various cultures. Practitioners will be able to use this chapter as a guide to navigate and challenge their thoughts surrounding cultural and ability diversity. The question at hand is it the cultural mismatch or is it racism? We believe the answer is both.

Table 3.1 Key Terminology	
Assimilation	The act of fitting into a set of norms while diminishing one's own authenticity (Emdin, 2016).
Culture	Socio-demographic markers such as race and ethnicity are often taken as proxies for culture, yet culture is dynamic, multidimensional, and imbued with power and complexity. Student identities reflect strategic sampling of multiple identity and cultural resources, yet because of reductionist and problematic views of culture, culturally diverse students are often seen through a deficit lens (Artiles, 2014).
Culturally Relevant Pedagogy	A pedagogical strategy that "uses the cultural knowledge, prior experiences, frames of reference, and performance styles of ethnically diverse students to make learning more relevant and effective" (Gay, 2010).
Tradition	The passing down of opinions or practices (Hiroa & Buck, 1926).
Value	The esteem you hold regarding an item, idea, or person (Hiroa & Buck, 1926).

As the number of people from diverse cultural backgrounds and diverse abilities continues to expand (Kraus et al., 2018; McKinnon, 2001), our society must shift from its exclusionary ideology cloaked under the shroud of what is viewed as "normalcy" to the more equitable treatment of all people regardless of culture, race, or ability. In the United States, workplaces and educational arenas continue to be integrated as the rise of diverse ethnic groups bombard the existing White cultural majority. Throughout history, major events demonstrated a level of cultural diversity, inclusion, and moral progress as a society. The election of the first Black president, Barack Obama, was a huge indicator that the United States has made some progress regarding racial and cultural challenges that stymied this nation. This was an event that many before him dreamt of, but never thought would come to fruition. Additionally, those in political office such as governors, mayors, and local officials are more racially and culturally diverse than ever before (Krostad, 2015).

In the disability arena, individuals with various learning abilities and physical abilities have held numerous public political offices. These events would not be possible if large portions of our society continuously held on to negative beliefs regarding diversity. This is not to insinuate that we have abolished racial, cultural, and ability inequality or inequities. Quite the contrary. Currently in the United

States, there are many instances of injustice against people of color. In 2020, Ahmaud Arbery was gunned down by White men, while George Floyd was suffocated by a White police officer, and Breonna Taylor was shot in her own home. Since the Civil Rights Act of 1964 and the passing of the Americans with Disabilities Act (ADA) in 1990, it would appear we have regressed in the acceptance of differences. There is a breach in our humanity and ethical treatment of one another. These events occurred while the individual who held the U.S. Presidency said insulting and insensitive things towards people with disabilities (Harnish, 2017).

In these times we must continue to institute honest self-examination about who we are, who we support, where our allegiances lie, and what our true beliefs are if we intend to continue to see, acknowledge, and accept more diversity in all segments of our lives. The reflective suggestions from Chapter 1 can help you start. If we hear derogatory or racist conversations or jokes in the practitioner's lounge or if we are sitting through a curriculum adoption proposal where the content is culturally insensitive, we must speak out against it. Silence is complicity. Geneva Gay shares, "Whether in education, law, politics, or economics, too often techniques are used that reinforce rather than transform the status quo" (Gay, 2004, p. 193). We must continue to examine policies that consistently work to perpetuate the marginalization through harm and denial of access (to education, housing, opportunities, etc.) to those who are culturally and linguistically different and who have disabilities, while examining our own beliefs if we honestly want our schools and nation to be more equitable as it relates to diversity and inclusion in its many forms.

Acknowledging the cultural identity of others (or students) must first begin with an individual's (or practitioner's) understanding of historical context—whether good or bad—about their own culture and how these experiences have shaped belief. To "acknowledge" means "to accept, admit, or recognize something, or the truth or existence of something" (Merriam-Webster, 2020). If someone does not understand the history of their own culture, they can easily be misguided about the history and culture of others. Having the ability to acknowledge the cultural identity of others in relation to one's own is an obtainable endeavor but the realization is that everyone matriculates through the process differently and at a different pace. Hence, what should be emphasized about acknowledgement of cultural differences is that learning and understanding different cultures is more than a few workshops, professional development courses, or training modules about cultural diversity.

Culture describes the backgrounds of students and how they learn. It should also take into consideration student's implicit and explicit funds of knowledge, ways of speaking, traditions, and backgrounds. Culture is defined "...as a way of life of a group of people. We have come to know that it is more than a way of life" (Missaghi, 2017). James Banks (2010) explains, "the essence of a culture is not its artifacts, tools, or other tangible cultural elements but how the members of the group interpret, use, and perceive them. It is the values, symbols, interpretations, and perspectives that distinguish one people from another in modernized societies; it is not material objects and other tangible aspects of human societies. People within a culture usually interpret the meaning of symbols, artifacts, and behaviors in the same or in similar ways" (Banks).

> **Interrogation:** *Take a moment and reflect on who you are as a cultural being. Think about who you are in relation to your family and friends. How do you identify? What is your cultural identity? The lens by which people identify others is greatly impacted by their own beliefs or biases.*

There has been a growing amount of research in education that focuses on how practitioner biases (implicit or explicit) impact how they interact with students (Staats, 2016). Similarly, the interactions between practitioners and students with disabilities are based on the practitioner's cultural lens, whether it is in an inclusive or self-contained setting. All these factors must be considered using an analysis of intersectionality. This concept at its core suggests that you cannot look at various constructs in isolation. For example, someone who is Hispanic and identifies as a female could possibly be marginalized across two different social constructs: race and gender. The root of this marginalization stems from historical racism and sexism and is fueled by power and privilege (Crenshaw, 1989). This concept of intersectionality can be applied to the marginalization of individuals identified as having a disability who are also culturally and ethnically diverse. This overlap is evident given the history of overrepresentation and underrepresentation in schools.

Culture

It is our intent to analyze practitioner beliefs and how such beliefs impact generalized perceptions and attitudes toward cultural acceptance often manifested in various ways. In Chapter 2, belief(s) is defined as...*an idea about some part of the natural or social world or a view of reality*. We extended that definition with another description that closely aligns with the scope of this chapter. Hachfeld and colleagues (2011) describe beliefs as the attitudes, views, ideologies, or models that practitioners hold about students with a different cultural background from their own. Therefore, the lack of understanding of other cultures is problematic when there is an unwillingness to learn about cultural differences. Pajares (1992) suggests that individuals tend to hold on to beliefs based on incorrect or incomplete knowledge. Incorrect knowledge becomes the catalyst that fuels many of the stereotypes and prejudices that one culture or race holds against another (Chang & Demyan, 2007) making it difficult for individuals to reestablish learned beliefs.

The following section provides a synopsis of practitioner beliefs, attitudes, and practices that shape the acceptance of other cultures when it differs from that of the practitioner. Culture is a multidimensional and dynamic construct. Within the classroom, understanding the differences about someone's culture is usually reinforced by the views of practitioners who are the gatekeepers of knowledge and information. We must engage in reflective practices (see Chapter 1) to better understand our roles in this process. How practitioners view cultural differences are often guided by social underpinning established by educational policies in the United States that perpetuate cultural hegemony (Borden, 2014). Therefore, regardless of any ethnic congruency between student and practitioner research suggests that practitioners are inclined to teach based upon a Eurocentric model (West-Olatunji et al., 2008). Other examples of the larger cultural disconnect often found between practitioner and student can be ascribed to the broader institutional construct that promotes individualistic over collectivistic learning discourse (Garrity et al., 2019).

Practitioners, particularly those who are White who have minimal exposure to other cultures, often default to the socio-demographic markers like race and ethnicity that are often taken as proxies for culture (Chang & Demyan, 2007). This narrow understanding of student cultural norms reinforces stereotypes with respect to factors such as ability level, motivation, and behaviors. The perspective of behaviors for children of color can be misleading if practitioners have limited prior access with the culture of the student and may fail to differentiate between culturally specific behaviors or other underlying issues (Robinson-Ervin et al. 2011). See Chapter 7 for more information about how that can affect family dynamics.

The authors speculate that the cultural disconnect between practitioners and students, which are well documented in previous research (Blanchett, 2006; Gay, 2000; Sleeter, 1993), continues to shape the attitudes and beliefs of practitioners regarding their level of cultural acceptance. To remedy this problem, Boveda and Aronson (2019) assert that practitioners must be competent in intersectionality. The two created a tool to examine intersectional competence through a conceptual review as it relates to special education and summarized that intersectionality can bridge gaps between diverse areas such as culture and ability.

While thinking of intersectionality between culture and ability, consider that disabilities are perceived differently throughout various cultures, although there generally seems to be a sense of mourning from their initial expectations (Harry, 2002). While there are some noted cultural differences related to disabilities, disability as a headlining category has taken precedence and has often left other identity areas, such as the cultural identity realm, untapped (Harry, 2002). Some cultures believe a disability is a gift (Fadiman, 1997), while others struggle to see a silver lining. Some cultures boast with pride, while others blame themselves or ignore the disability. Still there are also some preferences within the broad category of disability as it relates to specific disability categories. Harry (2002) explains that among different cultural groups, parental levels of expectations vary. For example, a child may be labeled as having an intellectual disability at school, but the parents did not necessarily believe that label to be valid based on the child's interactions at home.

The approach to providing educational services has evolved over time. Historically, special education was mandated in 1975, although each state had the ability to implement their own policies prior to the passing of the Education for All Handicapped Children Act (Kauffman et al., 2020). Many of the early special education services followed the medical model which suggested that *dis*-ability deficits were within the children and were able to be fixed (Rees, 2017). Children with disabilities were also supported by practitioners and those who provided services using a moral model lens. Both models share the perspective that individuals identified as having a disability are flawed carrying with them a degree of stigma and pathology (Olkin, 2002). More recently, a shift in special education has guided practitioners to consider a social model approach in providing special education to those in schools. This approach emphasizes how society along with prevailing culture should include individuals with disabilities and that the educational system must accommodate the needs of all children regardless of their disability (Olkin, 2012; Rees, 2017; Robinson & Summers, 2012). Conversely, it has been suggested that a social model approach to special education has its own challenges based upon how it identifies individuals with disabilities as part of an underrepresented group who experience similar prejudice and discrimination associated with race, ethnicity, gender, and sexual orientation (Olkin, 2002).

Acceptance in the context of the aforementioned instructional models depends upon a socialized hierarchy which allows those who provide educational means to shape the outcomes of those individuals who are in need. Therefore, practitioners must recognize that the current institutional practices in special education, though well intentioned, have devalued the cultural identity of thousands of students when the system fails to prioritize cultural prominence of diverse students and their families. In the words of Ladson-Billings (2009), culturally relevant pedagogy empowers students intellectually, socially, emotionally, and politically by using cultural referents to impart knowledge, skills, and attitudes. Currently students across the United State face limited access to public school practitioners who identify or fully understand their cultural heritage. Practitioners enter the workforce lacking knowledge of how to incorporate culturally relevant pedagogy that makes learning more relevant and effective (Gay, 2010). This will be discussed further in Chapter 8.

Irrespective of the practitioner's cultural background, many have a less favorable view of individuals with disabilities and are less likely to appropriately incorporate these students in the classroom due to a lack of training. General education practitioners are often faced with numerous challenges when working with students with disabilities due to a lack of support in the classroom by school administrators and other specialists (Hodge et al, 2009). The difficulty in the acceptance of others and understanding the historical context rests in embracing truths about the educational system, the truths about the roles those in power have held, and how it has played a pivotal role in minimizing the cultural heritage of non-Whites. The overwhelming majority of public elementary and secondary school practitioners are White, although there has been an overall decline based on data from the National Center for Education Statistics (U.S. Department of Education [NCES], 2017). The need for more cultural awareness is critical in the years ahead if practitioners in the United States plan to truly embrace the concept of inclusivity. This may be a difficult task for practitioners who do not want to disrupt the status quo by bringing up or discussing controversial issues associated with education and diversity (Liggett & Finley, 2009). However, it is necessary for progress.

Based on the data from the NCES (2017), over a 12-year period the total percentage of White practitioners declined slightly. It would not be uncommon to find practitioners who work in school districts where they are ethnically and culturally different from their students or reside in communities where they may be considered an outsider when bearing in mind socio-economic factors. This could present itself as a problem when practitioners are trying to have meaningful relationships with students, community members, and parents if the practitioner has never engaged with other cultural or ethnic groups.

Christophen Emdin encourages creating a classroom community where practitioners are comfortable taking the role of facilitators at times (2016). He acknowledges that while practitioners are frequently leading the education process, they also continue to learn from the students' experiences. Allowing students to lead groups or even take on the role of the teacher is a great way for the teacher to take note in the sometimes unconventional ways the students describe concepts based on their experiential lens. Students connect with each other in a way that is often different from the practitioner-student connection. This may be in part due to students living in the same community, attending the same boys and girls club after school, or worshipping at the same place. This connects nicely with concepts explored in Chapter 9.

Emdin recalled teaching a lesson on Newton's Laws of Motion using marbles as a point of reference. His students were not enthused with this description. What Emdin does next is noteworthy. He gives two students a chance to teach the same lesson. He provides them with his lesson plan and all of the resources he had on the topic. He was amused to see how involved the peers were watching their fellow students teach the lesson. He also noticed how the student teachers used a more relevant example related to the subway and someone pulling the emergency brake. The entire class let out an audible "ahhhhhh," which was not what Emdin experienced when he taught the lesson. That's when it clicked. It was then he realized even though he was the certified teacher he did not always have to be the only person teaching.

While observing the lesson he learned from the students, he learned about different ways to connect with the students and how to present different content to them in a way that would be meaningful. Emdin went on to encourage teachers to bring the students' culture into the classrooms in subtle and not so subtle ways.

Interrogation: *As you consider creating your classroom environment, including your table names or team names, one way to incorporate the culture of the students is to name the groups or areas in your classrooms with names that students are familiar with in their culture. So perhaps instead of the "Red Team" or "The Bluebirds," you create "Team Mo" and "Team Luther," named after the community barbershop and corner store. In addition to using this noninvasive strategy, you could also invite Mo and Luther into the classroom to lead a lesson on budgeting or another subject they have mastery in that ties to both their real life and the students' lives. This will help make the content relevant and give the practitioner an opportunity to connect with the community members.*

These strategies will not cost money and will not take very much effort, but they are likely to increase student buy-in as well as build community within your classroom and spill over into the neighborhood. As members of the neighborhood become more aware of the ways in which you are attempting to bridge the school-community gap, they may begin to see you as a less of an outsider. Further, parents will be more likely to get involved once they see you take the first step. Emdin mastered building a strong classroom community and at one point he realizes that the bond he had created was so solid that a student was willing to miss out on a trip to Disney World to fulfill a commitment that she had made to her classmates (2016). While this may be an extreme example, this is the type of buy-in you get when you have successfully created a classroom community.

Classrooms today are very diverse and may be composed of many different cultures, so practitioners should be able to adapt. The main idea is for practitioners to learn the general patterns of how the culture of their students interpret and address disabilities so they can more effectively serve their students. For example, families may have different views of disability that could be related to cultural and/or religious beliefs. Jegatheesan and colleagues (2010) documented the experiences of three South Asian families living in the United States. It was noted that these families stressed their concern for their child speaking the families' primary language of Arabic as a part of their culture and religious belief. Practitioners must be aware of the child and family beliefs while connecting the academic content to the culture of the student.

It is also important that practitioners recognize that historic events are intertwined with some cultural nuances. Studies such as the Tuskegee Experiment, where approximately 600 Black Americans were never adequately treated for syphilis even when a treatment was available, has had a lasting cultural impact

(Green et al., 1997). Likewise, medical studies such as those conducted at Johns Hopkins laboratory which included tissue samples from Henrietta Lacks—an African American woman—were scrutinized because the family was never made aware of the research that included Henrietta's tissue until over 20 years after her death (Lucey, Nelson-Rees, & Hutchins 2009).

Such events, coupled with the horrific treatment of slaves throughout American history, might explain Black Americans' cynicism toward the medical field, and in some regards could be warranted (DeGruy, 2005). It may further provide some cultural context when examining the underrepresentation of African American children diagnosed with autism. There are cases, however, of African American families who enthusiastically participate and engage in the diagnostic process (Hilton et al. (2010), while there are other instances of African American families who are reluctant or skeptical of any medical treatment, including those associated with autism diagnoses (Wetherby et al., 2008). In all, these are just some of the many experiences of African American culture that practitioners need to consider and know about.

Understanding the cultural and historical relevance associated with health disparities for Black Americans can have an impact on the diagnosis and/or treatment for youth with autism. Currently there is a 1.5 year difference in diagnosis between Black and White children with autism (Mandell et al., 2002) and when Black children are diagnosed, there is a significant likelihood of them being misdiagnosed or identified as having a more severe case of autism than White children (Burkett et al., 2015). Researchers and those in the educational field must continue to address the level of cultural competence needed by every practitioner throughout the United States.

Practitioners should also note that perception of the same disability can vary among families of different cultures. For example, an American family who has a child with epilepsy may think of it as a medical condition to monitor and treat. However, the Li family, who are Hmong, felt it was a gift to have a child with epilepsy. They felt it was a spiritual blessing and they were concerned with her safety, but honored that she had been chosen (Fadiman, 1997).

> **Interrogation:** *Imagine having both these children in your classroom. Without considering cultural differences, practitioners may attempt to address the needs of the child without considering the cultural-family factors. This may negatively impact how the Li family is viewed by the school staff. After having a seizure, you may call the parents very concerned. The parents may not be concerned at all. This could cause confusion on your end because the parents did not react in the way you anticipated. They may not believe or react in ways that you feel are appropriate. You may want them to support their child based on the current legal mandates (IDEA, 2004) and assimilate to the "traditional American cultural" way of thinking about seizures.*

Cultural assimilation is rooted in American history, with many examples at the forefront. A salient example is the boarding schools created in the 19th century to "kill the Indian and save the man," as articulated by Captain Richard Pratt in 1892. He created the Carlisle Indian School as a mechanism to forcibly assimilate American Indian children and youth to eliminate their cultures. Brenda Child concluded, "Boarding school history offers a plausible explanation for how and why colonialism has been destructive to American Indian community life, with the resulting losses to tradition and especially to the Native languages of North America" (p. 282, 2018).

Cultural assimilation continues in classrooms across America when practitioners do not understand their students' culture and teach using Eurocentric American educational models that touts one culture as dominant and superior. As a result, students may get punished or even misdiagnosed as having a disability. For example, if a student comes from a culture where it is disrespectful to look adults in the eye when being punished and the practitioner is expecting the student to provide eye contact during discipline, there is certainly a mismatch. This is the point where one must pause. It is important to take a minute here and reflect on one's expectations and think about what the parents' beliefs entail.

Generating skills for navigating multiple cultural perspectives regarding beliefs different from one's own can be very difficult. However, the first step is self-work. *How do you identify culturally? What is your culture? Do you expect others to assimilate or do you practice acknowledgement as a culturally responsive practice?* Dr. Terry Cross describes a continuum towards cultural proficiency (1989) that can be a helpful resource for practitioners to complete a self-analysis of reflection of mindset. Upon that continuum there are six points: cultural destructiveness, cultural incapacity, cultural blindness, cultural precompetence, cultural competence, and cultural proficiency. Individuals are asked to honestly reflect where one might be on the continuum. For example, someone may be at the beginning, cultural destructiveness, where one actively participates in the destruction of a student's or family's belief, tradition, or practice that is different than one's own. Perhaps one finds themselves at the midpoint, cultural blindness, where one believes all people are the same and that ability, cultural practice, or color do not make people different. Or a person may be at the opposite end, cultural proficiency, where one is an expert at cultural competency. It is important to be honest. It is nearly impossible to do the work if one is not transparent. The Cultural Continuum (Cross, 2012) is a helpful strategy to use as one encounters and wants to navigate cultural differences; it nicely connects with the reflective practices described in Chapter 1. When used, it is critical to create reflection time for one self and seek out allies and colleagues to assist in unpacking one's beliefs and behaviors towards accepting cultural beliefs that are counter to one's own cultural views on disability.

Another important analysis to conduct is a classroom environment analysis. How does the classroom reflect other cultures? Can students see themselves positively represented in the space where they spend a very large portion of their day? It is critical for students to see themselves positively represented in the classroom. When we look back at the civil rights movement, it is often omitted that there was also a focus on the underrepresentation and misrepresentation of other cultures in the curriculum. There were numerous ethnic groups advocating for the accurate inclusion of their respective cultures (Gay, 2004). While we may have some inclusion of cultures in today's curriculum, we need to evaluate whether the information is accurate, redundant, and thorough. Is the information that is provided regarding different cultures the same year after year? Are the same notable individuals recycled year after year? Is there comprehensive information provided about different cultures throughout the year or is it only in the Black History Month curriculum or the Latino History Month curriculum? Adding to the analysis is to ensure one's instruction is also culturally responsive and equity minded. As shared in this chapter, the practitioner's mind set informs instruction and outcomes.

It is not surprising that in America, societal norms around the rights for individuals identified with disabilities occurred at approximately the same time as the civil rights movement occurred in the early 1960s (Karger & Rose, 2010). Many of the leaders in the disability rights movement acknowledge they were called to action by watching some of the civil rights leaders. There are certainly parallels between the rights of Black Americans and those in the disability community. Disability rights centered on the equitable treatment of those who seemingly did not have the rights of all Americans. Further, they sought inclusive schools and classrooms. Researchers noted there was a marked difference in acceptance of inclusion in multicultural neighborhoods versus neighborhoods that were not multicultural (Carrington, 1999).

Practitioners' mindsets related to inclusion can also be impacted by the school administration. Conversely, practitioners' mindsets can also have a strong impact on the students they teach. In fact, there is emerging research that focuses on the effect and role that a practitioner's mindset has on student beliefs and performance. In a recent teacher STEM study (Canning, et al., 2019), it was found that a teacher's belief in the intellectual ability of their student--high or low--directly impacted how a student performed. If a student believed in themselves to complete challenging work or meet standards, as demonstrated by the mindset and behaviors of their teacher, they were more likely to perform at higher levels. The beliefs of the teachers who had fixed mindsets correlated to having a negative impact on student performance which, in turn, increased the achievement gap. Stereotype threat is another layer of mindset. A person's mindset influences how one perceives people of other races and cultures by treating them in stereotype mode or treating them as human beings with great capacity for excellence. A practitioner has the power to frame their instruction in non-stereotypical ways that encourage students to perform at higher levels as opposed to when students feel threatened and perform in fear (Steele 2002).

Case Study: Susan

Susan is a White, culturally European American cis-gendered person, who teaches third grade in a very diverse elementary school in San Diego, California. She values diversity, advocates for her culturally diverse students, and holds the highest expectations of them. She adores her classroom, which is composed of many different cultures. Susan recognizes that cultural diversity exists but hasn't taken the time to learn the specific cultures of her students. For example, she knows Latinx students are present because she hears them speak Spanish, but she lacks curiosity to go deeper to learn their cultural identities. She is aware of the presence of Somali students due to their Arabic names and that the girls wear head coverings, but Susan stays in the surface of a deeper cultural understanding. She doesn't know the word for head coverings in Arabic.

After the school year started, Susan noticed that her Somali students did not listen to her rules and expectations even though she used the "Morning Ritual" strategy every day. She believed by repeating the rules every morning that all the children would adhere and honor them just like she honored them. One student, Abdi, was not responding in ways that she understood to be engaging, such as following her rules, walking in a straight line, being quiet when instructed, and speaking English in class. A major issue is that Abdi does not communicate with his schoolmates in group work and will get up and go to a corner to be by himself when there is a lot of activity or chatter. Susan and the class must wait for him to go from activity to activity. When Susan corrects him, he will have an outburst of emotions and runs away. For example, when he would skip out of the lunch line, she would call out in the lunchroom, "Abdi, you know the rules. Get back in the line." Abdi didn't like this and he would talk back to her. After several different incidents, she began to send him to the principal's office.

The principal visits prompted a special education inquiry led by the school's behavior team. They did an informal assessment and believe that Abdi may have autism. They decided that a formal assessment should be undertaken so the Team lead, Vanessa, contacted Abdi's mother, Fadumo Omar. They needed to get her permission. Mrs. Omar had not visited the classroom and was unaware of the Behavior Team. Vanessa introduced herself and told Mrs. Omar that they thought Abdi may have a disability and should undergo an assessment. They also asked her to come to the school to sign paperwork that would give the school permission to do the assessment. Mrs. Omar became upset and said, "How can you tell me that Abdi, my firstborn son, is disabled? I do not give permission and do not call me again!"

Vanessa conveyed this information back to the Team and Susan. They were in a state of disbelief and did not know what they should do next. Meanwhile Abdi continued to be a disruption in the class and Susan continued to feel unsupported and wanted Abdi removed from her classroom.

Chapter 3

Case Study Activity

- What are your observations of this case study?
- What culturally responsive strategies could be used to mitigate a more effective outcome that meet the needs of Abdi and Mrs. Omar?
- Using the Cultural Continuum, think about what the cultural issue, practice, belief, or behavior that Susan is struggling with and where she is on the continuum with her mindset.

Table 3.2 Cultural Continuum Activity
In this activity it is useful for the educator to try and identify the culture of the student. In many cases, practitioners may lump everyone together and assume all Africans or Arabs, for example, have the same culture. Next it is important for the educator to isolate the practice, belief, tradition, or behavior that one is experiencing challenges and difficulties accepting or addressing positively. The next step is to compare and contrast that element with one in their culture. Isolate the issue Susan is experiencing. What is it? Next, assess where Susan is on the continuum (options listed below) with the issue that is different. What is her mindset? Write a statement of the observation. Take an opportunity to reflect and discuss with colleagues and cultural allies.
Cultural destructiveness: See the difference, stomp it out
For example, a practitioner may notice a cultural difference of engagement such as talking during work time. In some cultures, talking during work time is normal because of the collective nature of that culture. The practitioner thinks that is wrong and seeks to stop it. In time, the student may be referred to special education if they don't comply.
Cultural incapacity: See the difference, make it wrong
Continuing with the above example, the practitioner tells the students from the other culture that it is wrong to speak to others during work time because it is cheating. The practitioner makes it wrong. The student will be penalized and punished.
Cultural blindness: See the difference, act like you don't
Continuing with the first example, the practitioner is afraid of the culture of the student and/or may be blind that it is a cultural practice different from their own. In this case, the practitioner tells the students to be quiet because they just like to talk. The practitioner may also be afraid if race is involved and/or has low expectations. The behavior may be ignored because the practitioner is avoiding potential conflict or really doesn't care about the intellectual growth of the students.

Table 3.2 Cultural Continuum Activity, (continued)
Cultural precompetence: See the difference, respond inadequately Continuing with the first example, the practitioner is aware that culture is playing a role in the work time chatter but may lack the schema or understanding of the culture. The practitioner may stumble by saying, "students, remember that all cultures have different ways of acting during work time. I respect that but in my classroom we must remain silent to ensure we are all learning."
Cultural competence: See the difference, understand the difference that difference makes Continuing with the first example, the practitioner is aware that culture is playing a role in the work time chatter. They notice what is happening and take the time to do research and connect with colleagues who come from the student's culture to understand how talking during work time might be a cultural norm. This is the stage of trying to figure things out.
Cultural proficiency: See the differences and respond positively and affirmingly Continuing with the first example, once understanding is ascertained, the practitioner makes adjustments in their teaching style to figure out when they want silent time and when the talking during work time is cherished and built for further student engagement. This is acceptance.
Cultural adaptation: See the difference and adapt Continuing with the first example, the practitioner is fully committed to how this cultural element of working on lessons in the classroom is practiced across the students in their classroom. They spend the time to adapt when necessary and build on new cultural understandings of the range of how their culturally diverse students want to learn. For example, the practitioner learns that students from more collective cultures like Dine, African American, and Ojibwe will gravitate to more group work where students can share, talk, and help each other learn. This is not cheating. Cultures that are more individualistic in nature and taught to work independently, such as European American children, will thrive in situations where they can work autonomously. The practitioner knows when and where to adapt.

(Dr. Terry Cross, Adapted by Nanette Missaghi)

Summary

While perfection isn't expected, effort is necessary and that begins with acknowledgement. This chapter began by explaining the purpose of the chapter and bringing to light many of the unjust and horrific events of 2020. It continued to explain how these and many other incidents can be traced to racists and inequitable beliefs and why it is imperative that individuals acknowledge their role in this system. The brief literature review discussed culture and how it relates to families and disabilities. We shared how intersectionality plays a role in our lives and we also discussed how practitioner beliefs impact student achievement. As the chapter progressed there were discussions surrounding the disparity among Black Americans and how that plays a role in the delayed diagnoses of autism. There were also specific examples provided of how practitioners can connect with their students by researching cultures and disabilities and what that might actually look like in a classroom setting. The chapter ended with strategies to become more aware of your acknowledgment of other cultural identities and beliefs. We leave you with this charge: we must all do our part and that may mean we will be a bit uncomfortable or even embarrassed at times, but in the end it will be worth it.

Guiding Questions

1. What are your beliefs and practices around acknowledging cultural identities and beliefs different from your own?
2. What is culturally responsive acknowledgment?
3. How can you navigate multiple perspectives regarding beliefs different from your own?
4. How can you increase your acknowledgement of representation and culturally relevant pedagogy?

References

Acknowledge (2020). In Merriam-Webster.com. Retrieved June 1, 2020 from https://www.merriam-webster.com/dictionary/acknowledge

Americans With Disabilities Act of 1990 (1990). Pub. L. No. 101-336, 104 Stat. 328.

Banks, J.A. & Banks, C. A. (2010). *Multicultural Education: Issues and Perspectives.* New York, NY: John Wiley and Sons (page 8).

Blanchett, W. J. (2006). Disproportionate representation of African American students in special education: Acknowledging the role of White privilege and racism. *Educational Researcher, 35*(6), 24–28. https://doi.org/10.3102/0013189X035006024

Borden, R. S. (2014). The English only movement: Revisiting cultural hegemony. *Multicultural Perspectives, 16*(4), 229–233.

Boveda, M., & Aronson, B. A. (2019). Special education preservice teachers, intersectional diversity, and the privileging of emerging professional identities. *Remedial and Special Education, 40*(4), 248-260.

Burkett, K., Morris, E., Manning-Courtney, P. et al. (2015). African American families on Autism diagnosis and treatment: The influence of culture. *J Autism Dev Disord 45*, 3244–3254. https://doi.org/10.1007/s10803-015-2482-x

Canning, E.A., Muenks, K., Green, D.J., and Murphy, M.C. (February 15, 2019). STEM faculty who believe ability is fixed have larger racial achievement gaps and inspire less student motivation in their classes, *Science Advances, 5*(2). DOI: 10.11261/sciadv.aau4734.

Carrington, S. (1999). Inclusion needs a different school culture. *International Journal of Inclusive Education, 3*(3), 257-268.

Chang, D. F., & Demyan, A. L. (2007). Teachers' stereotypes of Asian, Black, and White students. *School Psychology Quarterly, 22*(2), 91–114.

Civil Rights Act of 1964 (1964). Pub.L. 88-352, 78 Stat. 241.

Crenshaw, K. W. (1989). Demarginalizing the intersection of race and sex: a black feminist critique of antidiscrimination doctrine, feminist theory and antiracist politics. *University of Chicago Legal Forum,* 139–167.

Cross, T. L. (2012). Cultural competence continuum. *Journal of Child and Youth Care Work.* 24, 83-85.

Emdin (2016). *For White folks who teach in the hood... and the rest of y'all too: Reality pedagogy and urban education.* Beacon Press.

Fadiman, A. (1997). *The spirit catches you and you fall down: A Hmong child, her American doctors, and the collision of two cultures.* New York: Farrar, Straus, and Giroux.

Garrity, S., Shapiro, A., Longstreth, S., & Bailey, J. (2019). The negotiation of Head Start teachers' beliefs in a transborder community. *Early Childhood Research Quarterly*, 47, 134–144.

Gay, G. (2000). *Culturally responsive teaching.* New York: Teachers College Press.

Gay, G. (2004). Beyond brown: Promoting equality through multicultural education. *Journal of Curriculum & Supervision, 19*(3), 193–216.

Gay, G. (2010). Acting on beliefs in teacher education for cultural diversity. *Journal of teacher education, 61*(1-2), 143-152.

Gramsci, A. (1971). *Selections from the prison notebooks* (Q. Hoare & G. Nowell-Smith, Eds., Trans.). New York: International Press.

Green B.L., Maisiak R., Wang M.Q., Britt, M.F., & Ebeling, N. (1997). *Participation in health education, health promotion, and health research by African Americans: Effects of the Tuskegee Syphilis Experiment. J Health Education, 28*(4): 196–201.

Hachfeld, A., Hahn, A., Schroeder, S., Anders, Y., Stanat, P., & Kunter, M. (2011). Assessing teachers' multicultural and egalitarian beliefs: The Teacher Cultural Beliefs Scale. *Teaching and Teacher Education, 27*(6), 986–996.

Harnish, A. (2017). Ableism and the Trump phenomenon. *Disability & Society, 32*(3), 423-428.

Harry, B. (2002). Trends and issues in serving culturally diverse families of children with disabilities. *The Journal of special education, 36*(3), 132-140.

Hodge, S., Ammah, J. O. A., Casebolt, K. M., LaMaster, K., Hersman, B., Samalot-Rivera, A., & Sato, T. (2009). A diversity of voices: Physical education teachers' beliefs about inclusion and teaching students with disabilities. *International Journal of Disability, Development and Education, 56*(4), 401–419

Individuals with Disabilities Education Act of 2004, P.L. 108-446.

Karger, H., & Rose, S. R. (2010). Revisiting the Americans with Disabilities Act after two decades. *Journal of Social Work in Disability & Rehabilitation, 9*(2-3), 73–86

Kauffman, J. M., Ahrbeck, B., Anastasiou, D., Badar, J., Felder, M., & Hallenbeck, B. A. (2020). Special education policy prospects: Lessons from social policies past. *Exceptionality*. DOI: 10.1080/09362835.2020.1727326

Kraus, L., Lauer, E., Coleman, R., and Houtenville, A. (2018). 2017 Disability Statistics Annual Report. Durham, NH: University of New Hampshire

Krogstad, J.M. (2015). 114th Congress is most diverse ever. Retrieved from http://www.pewresearch.org/facttank/2015/01/12/114th-congress-ismost-diverse-ever/

Ladson-Billings, G. *The dreamkeepers: Successful teachers of African American Children*, 2nd ed.; Jossey-Bass: San Francisco, CA, USA, 2009.

Liggett, T., & Finley, S. (2009). "Upsetting the Apple Cart": Issues of Diversity in Preservice Teacher Education. *Multicultural Education, 16*(4), 33–38.

McKinnon, J. (2001). 'The black population: 2000', Census 2000 Brief, US Census Bureau, Washington, DC.

Missaghi, Nanette (2017). The Relevance of Culture and Identity: Why it Matters in Waldon,

K.A. & Baxley, T. P (Eds.) *Equity Pedagogy: Teaching Diverse Student Populations.* Dubuque, IA. Kendall Hunt.

Olkin, R. (2002). Could you hold the door for me? Including disability in diversity. *Cultural Diversity and Ethnic Minority Psychology, 8*(2), 130–137

Pajares, M. F. (1992). Teachers' beliefs and educational research: Cleaning up a messy construct.

Review of Educational Research, 62(3), 307–332.

Rees, K. (2017). Models of disability and the categorisation of children with severe and profound learning difficulties: Informing educational approaches based on an understanding of individual needs. *Educational and Child Psychology, 34*(4), 30–39.

Robinson, S., & Summers, K. (2012). An evaluation of the educational support for teachers who teach children with life-limiting illness in schools. *Pastoral Care in Education, 30*(3), 191–207.

Robinson-Ervin, P., Cartledge, G., & Keyes, S. (2011). Culturally responsive social skills instruction for adolescent Black males. *Multicultural Learning and Teaching, 6*(1).

Sleeter, C. E. (1993). How White teachers construct race. In C. McCarthy & W. Crichlow (Eds.), *Race identity and representation in education* (p. 157–171). New York: Routledge.

Staats, C. (2016). Understanding implicit bias: What educators should know. *American Educator, 39*(4), 29–33.

Steele, C. M., Spencer, S. J., & Aronson, J. (2002). Contending with group image: The psychology of stereotype and social identity threat. In M. P. Zanna (Ed.), Advances in experimental social psychology, Vol. 34, 379-440. Academic Press.

U.S. Department of Education, National Center for Education Statistics, Schools and Staffing Survey (SASS), "Public School Teacher Data File," 2003–04; and National Teacher and Principal Survey (NTPS), "Public school teacher data file," 2015–16. See Digest of Education Statistics 2017, table 209.10.

West-Olatunji, C. A., Behar-Horenstein, L., Rant, J., & Cohen-Phillips, L. N. (2008). Enhancing cultural competence among teachers of African American children using mediated lesson study. *Journal of Negro Education, 77*(1), 27–38.

Chapter 4

Working with diverse languages and disability

Diana Baker, Tian (Jessie) Jiang, Hyejung Kim, Helen McCabe, and Calvin Stanley

---

Objectives

- Explore the benefits of multilingualism for students with developmental disabilities including autism and intellectual disability (ID).

- Learn about challenges associated with educating multilingual students with developmental disabilities including autism and ID.

- Gain strategies for working effectively with multilingual students with developmental disabilities and their families.

Chapter 4 provides information for working with students with disabilities from diverse language backgrounds. Often, practitioners and clinicians advise families to speak just one language to multilingual children with autism and/or intellectual disabilities (ID). As both neurodevelopmental disabilities present communication-related challenges in early childhood and often co-occur, many practitioners assume that navigating multiple languages would be too confusing for children who have been working so hard to communicate at all. In fact, research shows that many children with autism and ID can and do learn more than one language (Baker, 2017; Ware, Lye, & Kyffin, 2015), that interventions that incorporate a student's heritage language may be more effective than monolingual instruction (Lim et al., 2019), and that familiarity with languages spoken at home and in the community supports inclusion for neurodiverse children who in turn feel less isolated (Yu, 2013). Yet, the American special education model presents an array of challenges for multilingual children with autism and ID and their families. This chapter aims to: 1) inform practitioners about the benefits of multilingual exposure and interventions for students with autism and ID and their families; 2) outline the current challenges impeding effectiveness in working with multilingual students with autism and ID; and 3) provide practical tools and strategies for working with linguistically diverse children with autism and ID and their families.

Table 4.1 Key Terminology	
Bilingualism or Multilingualism	The "dynamic process in which at least two languages are used in an individual's life to some degree." (American Speech-Language-Hearing Association, 2004 as cited in Yu, 2018, p. 146) Speaking two or more languages.
Bilingual Education	"[H]igh quality education programs that include the home and second language" (Cheatham et al., 2021, p. 8). A range of models exist, including transitional bilingual education, maintenance bilingual education, dual immersion.
Emerging Bilinguals (EBs)	Individuals who speak a language other than English at home. "[t]his term highlights their linguistic resources" (García, et al., 2008 as quoted in Martinez-Alvarez, 2019, p. 174).
Interpreter or Translator	Professionals who "convert information from one language into another language. Interpreters work in spoken or sign language, whereas translators work in written language" (Acar & Blasco, 2018, p. 170).

Many children around the world, and increasingly in the United States, are growing up in households where multiple languages are spoken or attend schools where the language of instruction is not their first language (L1). This chapter uses the term "emerging bilingual" (EB) to highlight the linguistic resources possessed by this group of students and to avoid positioning English as superior to the other languages that students speak (Columbo, Tigert, & Leider, 2019; Martinez-Alvarez, 2014). Even with expanding bilingual educational options across the United States, students with developmental disabilities such as autism and ID are almost always channeled into monolingual (i.e., English-only) educational settings with limited, if any, learning support in their home language (Kangas, 2014). In some cases, families of children with language and learning-related disabilities are advised to refrain from exposing the child to the family's first language (L1) (Ware, et al., 2015; Yu, 2013).

In this chapter, readers will meet Xiao Ming, a fictional kindergartener who recently moved to the United States from China. This student was diagnosed with a developmental delay and is learning both Mandarin Chinese and English. The experiences of this student and her family illustrate the complex relationships between bilingualism, disability, and education and highlight promising practices for educating EBs with disabilities.

Case Study Part 1: Introduction to Student's Educational Journey

Xiao Ming (5 years old) and her parents arrived in their rural community four months ago. The family was sponsored by her uncle, who has been living in town for nearly a decade and owns an auto body shop. Her uncle was eager for Xiao Ming to come to the United States in time to start kindergarten, where she could receive the special education services he knew she needed for her developmental disability.

Once in the United States, Xiao Ming started Kindergarten with a veteran kindergarten teacher and a teaching assistant. Unfortunately, no one in the primarily White school spoke Mandarin. Her parents noticed that sometimes she would say something (in either Mandarin or emerging English) that her teachers could not decipher. Although it was hard to see their child struggling to communicate, her parents did not want to interfere.

Xiao Ming is working on early academic skills such as 1:1 correspondence and letter identification and her expressive communication is starting to emerge. She occasionally utters two or three words, mostly to make requests or refusals (e.g., "More water" or "No bath"). However, she still tends to use behaviors rather than words to make her desires known (e.g., dropping down to the floor when she is asked to come to the table or taking a crayon from another child).

Benefits of Bilingualism and Bilingual Instruction

Although negative attitudes toward bilingualism for students with neurodevelopmental disabilities persist (Martinez-Alvarez, 2019), emerging scholarship illustrates the ways in which these students may benefit from being raised in bilingual settings. Potential advantages include positive multicultural identity development (Edgin et al., 2011; Yu, 2013), increased verbal fluency (Gonzalez-Barrero & Nadig, 2017), expanded expressive vocabulary (Jegatheesan, 2011), and listening comprehension (Spooner et al., 2009). In fact, being bilingual may instead *offset* challenges typically associated with disabilities in areas such as non-verbal intelligence (Petersen et al., 2012), adaptive functioning (Hambly & Fonbonne, 2012), and working memory (Pinto-Cardona, 2017).

Home language maintenance has also been shown to increase parent-child interactions (Hampton et al., 2017) and facilitate participation in religious and cultural activities (Jegatheesan, 2011; Lim et al., 2019). Furthermore, families are able to communicate more easily and with more emotional openness when the household language is their L1 (Fernadez y Garcia et al., 2012), and familial stress levels may drop when special education services are provided in children's home languages (Seung et al., 2006).

Case Study Part 2: Contemplating Bilingual Exposure

> The teacher and teaching assistant are both advocates of inclusion and experienced in working with students with disabilities. They recently attended a professional development workshop about the benefits of bilingual instruction and are eager to support Xiao Ming. They designed the classroom to provide as much structure and consistency as possible, with a visual daily schedule and clearly defined areas. In addition, they have labeled each area of the classroom in both English and Mandarin corresponding pictures to draw on Xiao Ming's visual strengths.
>
> The teacher and teaching assistant want to collaborate with both the ESL teacher and the parents to help the student build English and Mandarin skills. But the speech therapist believes that targeting two languages simultaneously would confuse the student. Her parents also wonder if they should wait until she had a stronger English foundation before reintroducing Mandarin, especially since special education services were only available in English.
>
> However, the teacher suggests that it is important for the parents to speak to her in Mandarin since it is the language they are most comfortable with and that improving her Chinese will allow Xiao Ming to communicate with her relatives and other Chinese-speakers in the community. The teacher explains that ultimately, Xiao Ming will be able to communicate better – not worse – if she has the opportunity to develop both languages.

Challenges

Despite mounting evidence that bilingualism is not detrimental and indeed advantageous to children, including those with autism and ID, many challenges remain. These include misconceptions about the impact of being educated in and using two languages, and the lack of bilingual service providers and highly qualified interpreters with sufficient content knowledge (Cho & Gannotti, 2005).

Uncertainty About How Language Exposure Impacts Learning and Relationships

While evidence-based research indicates that bilingualism is an asset for many students with disabilities, confusion remains among parents and practitioners. Families of children with autism are advised by professionals to speak only English at home to avoid confusing their children (Baker, 2017; Kay-Raining Bird et al., 2005). Many parents prioritize English acquisition based on the belief that this will allow the child to access higher quality special education services and be more integrated into the school and the broader community (Fernandez y Garcia et al., 2012; Hampton et al.; Lim & Charlop, 2018; Soto & Yu, 2014; Yu, 2013).

When children from multilingual backgrounds are educated in English-only environments, one important cost is that they may lose facility in their family's primary language, thereby limiting interactions, relationships, and cultural attachment with family members who are not proficient in English, such as with grandparents and other family caregivers (Fahim & Nedwick, 2014; Medina & Salamon, 2012; Wang et al., 2019; Yu, 2013). Additionally, when parents have limited English proficiency, restricting all home communication to English stifles natural communication and negatively influences parent-child interactions and family relationships (Lim & Charlop, 2018; Wang et al., 2019; Yu, 2013).

The Need for Linguistically Qualified Professionals: Practitioners and Translators

Even when practitioners and parents are eager for their children to learn both English and their home language, in most regions of the United States, logistical realities prevent EB students with disabilities from receiving support for their disability- and language-development-related needs simultaneously (Kay-Raining Bird et al., 2012). Obstacles include special education services being offered in English only (Soto & Yu, 2014), insufficient or inappropriate training and resources for teachers (Rivera et al., 2019), and a shortage of multilingual service providers (Dennison et al., 2019; Lang et al., 2011). The lack of English proficiency among the child's family makes access to resources more challenging (Cho & Gannotti, 2005).

When the ideal situation of all service providers being able to communicate directly with their students and families in L1 is not available, another option is to employ an interpreter. However, this option presents its own set of challenges. According to Cho and Gannotti (2005), it is important for the interpreter to have "requisite knowledge of disability and special education terminology as well as bilingual proficiency" (p. 7). Certified interpreters, without experience or knowledge of the field of special education, may struggle to both understand and communicate the technical content accurately, resulting in frustrating miscommunication between the professionals and family (Accar & Blasco, 2016; Cheatham, 2011). Although the Individuals with Disabilities Education Improvement Act (IDEA, 2004) mandates that interpreters must be provided, the reality is that one is not always present when educational decisions are made. Reasons may include the lack of an available interpreter, the family declining to employ one from the outset, or perhaps the family ending the relationship with the interpreter during the process due to dissatisfaction (Cho & Gannotti, 2005; Wolfe & Duran, 2013). In smaller communities, where there is a chance that the family and interpreter may know each other, confidentiality concerns may influence how much personal information the family wishes to share with their community (Accar & Blasco, 2016).

Case Study Part 3: Trouble at Xiao Ming's IEP meeting

Xiao Ming's family also struggles with communication at formal educational meetings. At the student's individualized education program (IEP) meeting, the teacher noticed that the parents' answers didn't match her questions. The bilingual interpreter had traveled over an hour to attend the meeting and struggled to keep up with the fast-paced conversation. It was clear that he didn't understand all of the technical jargon that the practitioners were using. Additionally, both the teachers and the parents directed questions to the interpreter ("What are their goals for their child?" and "What do they want us to do with her homework?") rather than speaking directly to each other, adding to the already difficult atmosphere.

After struggling through several meetings where communication was especially challenging, the school found a bilingual special educator who had graduate degrees in special education and applied behavior analysis. She agreed to serve as an interpreter. During their first meeting, the interpreter explained to the school staff that they should speak directly to the parents. She was simply a tool to facilitate their communication.

Though a little awkward at first, at the end of the meeting, the practitioners commented on how well it went. They felt like they learned a lot about the student, her family, and their goals and concerns. The parents and teachers were able to have substantive conversations about how to best support her learning needs. The speech therapist had begun to understand the value of supporting bilingualism and was completely on board. One decision made was that they would use consistent communication techniques so that she could generalize skills across environments. For example, the practitioners would pair the English words "all done" with the corresponding ASL sign. While at home, her parents would say "完成了" in Chinese, while simultaneously signing "all done" (using the same ASL sign as at school). Everyone was surprised by how quickly Xiao Ming caught on. Not only that, but her maladaptive behaviors, such as dropping to the floor became noticeably less frequent.

Strategies: Working with EB Students at the Intersection of Disability and Language

The case study illustrates that evidence-based techniques can be very effective in helping EB students with disabilities develop communication skills in both languages. Moreover, incorporating families' home languages in their children's education facilitates home/school collaboration. The following section provides a compilation of research recommendations to offer practical guidance to schools and practitioners working with EB students with disabilities.

Collaboration and Professional Development

Although dually-identified students are best served when they are viewed holistically with all of their strengths and needs are considered together, more often than not, schools adopt a "divide and conquer approach," with individual practitioners attending only to the learning needs that fall within their own specialization (e.g., special education, or English language development; Kangas, 2018, p. 31). To address this dilemma, tools were developed to facilitate collaboration among practitioners who work with EB students with disabilities (Kangas, 2018). For example, because IEPs for such students rarely address goals related to English language development, Kangas offers a checklist designed to encourage practitioners to "co-create" IEPs.

Collaborations across English language learners (ELL) and special education departments are relatively new; therefore, practitioners may need guidance on how to consult more effectively with one another (Kangas, 2018). ELL teachers can ask special educators questions (e.g., "How can I modify and/or adapt my instruction to support the student's special needs?) and, in return, special educators can ask questions of ELL teachers, (e.g., "What are the student's strengths in the English language?") (Kangas, 2018, p. 36). These types of questions are designed to spark conversations between practitioners from different departments so that they can learn from one another and meet the students' needs more seamlessly.

We extend the discussion by showing the ways in which *both* special educators and ELL teachers can collaborate not only with each other but also with families across all phases of the IEP process (see table 4.2).

Table 4.2 IEP Meeting Checklist for Educating EB Students With Autism and ID and Their Families

Before IEP meetings
- Family interview
  - Ask the family about their preferred language (PL).
  - Interview the family about educational, social, developmental/medical, and family history in their preferred language.
  - Acknowledge the family's preference of linguistic environment at school.
  - Understand the family's goals on areas of communication development that are important at home (e.g., functional communication, social interaction).
- Information to share
  - Provide a brief list of typical special education services and parental rights in both L1 and L2.
- IEP meeting preparation
  - Be aware of the benefits and challenges of multilingual environments.
  - Schedule sufficient time considering the interpretation process.
  - Make sure that the parents have appropriate communication means (e.g., inviting an L1 interpreter).
  - Invite ESL or bilingual teachers.
  - Include information obtained from family interviews when writing a draft of the present level of performance and annual goals section in IEPs.

⬇

During the meeting
- Review the written information verbally in both L1 and L2.
- IEP document writing
  - Include the child's communication skills in both L1 and L2 in the present level of performance.
  - Set communication goals in both school and home in annual goals.
  - Specify instructional language for each special education service to be provided.
  - Provide a summary of the meeting in the family's PL.

⬇

After the meeting
- Share the entire document with the summary in PL.
- Provide an example of weekly schedules that includes general education, English language services, special education services with instructional language in each setting.

One simple way to empower families during the IEP process is to provide translations of key educational terms (see Table 4.3 for example terms).

Table 4.3 Typical Special Education Services Terms in L1 and L2 (Example for Case Study)

Chinese	English
言语语言治疗	Speech and language therapy (SLT)
职能治疗	Occupational therapy (OT)
心理 / 精神健康服务 (例如, 评估, 咨询服务)	Psychological/mental health services (e.g., assessment, counseling)
行为管理服务和计划	Behavior management program
学习策略 / 学习能力支持	Learning strategies/study skills support
服务协调 / 个案管理	Service coordination/case management
辅助技术 / 辅助性和替代性沟通	Assistive technology/augmentative and alternative communication
沟通软件或程序	Communication software or apps
特别化的交通	Special transportation
家庭培训 / 家庭咨询	Family training or counseling
转衔服务 / 职业服务 (必须的)	Transition services/vocational services (required)

(Levine, Marder, & Wagner, 2004; Wei, Wagner, Christiano, Shattuck, & Yu, 2014)

In addition to the importance of collaboration across fields, pre- and in-service training for practitioners promises to be one of the most effective avenues for preparing practitioners to teach EB students with disabilities. Teachers have reported needing more knowledge about language development and culturally relevant practices for the students they are teaching (Hammer et al., 2004; Wolfe & Duran, 2013). See Chapter 6 to explore this further.

Communicating with EB Students and Their Families

School districts should strongly consider the importance of direct communication with *all* families as they plan to recruit, hire, and retain personnel. In addition to the benefits of incorporating students' first languages and making connections to their home culture, EB students and families also benefit when practitioners and service providers come from similar ethnic and linguistic backgrounds (Rivera et al., 2014; Rohena et al., 2002).

Where multilingual/multicultural professionals are not available, districts should strive to hire interpreters who are proficient in both the family's L1 *and* the special education processes and associated terminology (e.g., ABA, push-in services, executive functioning; Soto & Yu, 2014). Cheatham (2011) stressed the importance of "frequent and on-going training" (p. 84) for both interpreters and practitioners. Responding to the complex nature of clinical interpretation, Messent (2003) proposed that training might entail applied activities like interpreters collectively reviewing videotaped meetings and discussing how they would interpret the content. Practitioners and team members find that having practitioners who are familiar with both the educational setting and the language and culture of the child's family enhances communication with EB students and their families.

During meetings, the IEP team leaders should encourage interpreters and family members to request clarification if they are unfamiliar with any technical terms or concepts. Additionally, practitioners should use terms that are accessible to laypeople and avoid technical jargon where possible. It is also important to foster an atmosphere that welcomes casual conversations and observations rather than relying solely on professional perspectives and formal contributions (Baker, et al., 2019). Practitioners and interpreters should speak at a reasonable rate, and practitioners should use second-person pronouns (e.g., "How do *you* help your child adjust to unexpected changes at home?" versus "How does *she* help her child adjust to unexpected changes at home?"), and make eye contact with the family member rather than directing questions to the interpreter. Interpreted meetings will take longer than meetings in which all members speak the same language, so districts will need to allow additional time accordingly (Cheatham, 2011; Cho & Gannotti, 2005). Table 4.4 presents practical strategies for collaboration between practitioners and interpreters.

Intervention Strategies

Another area of need regards how to adapt intervention strategies for EB students with disabilities. As with TD bilingual students, current research highlights the importance of using a student's first language to support learning (Cheatham et al., 2012; Rivera et al., 2019; Seung, et al., 2006). One strategy that enables families and practitioners to bridge language development simultaneously is to introduce signs (e.g., ASL) that are consistently paired with both languages (Fahim & Nedwick, 2014). When the student in the case study's family and teachers consistently used the "all done" sign paired with English at school and Mandarin at home, they noticed that she caught on quickly, and after just a couple weeks, she was more likely to communicate "all done" to get out of a non-preferred activity rather than dropping to the ground as she has been doing. Inviting families to learn how to implement interventions with their children is an effective method for generalizing the skill

Table 4.4 Suggestions for Practitioners When Working With an Interpreter

Always speak in the direction of the family member, not toward the interpreter. • Use second person language ("you," not "she" or "he"). • Make eye contact with the family member and speak directly to him/her.
Speak at a measured pace and pause to allow time for the interpreter to interpret for the family. • Do not respond to something someone has said in English until the interpreter has interpreted to the family.
Allow extra time for a meeting that includes an interpreter.
Use less technical jargon and break down technical terms to ensure they are being interpreted correctly.
Collaborate with the interpreter to create simple written materials for in-home-language. • Create a glossary with common special education terms (see, e.g., Table 4.3).

across home and school settings (Dalmau et al., 2011; Mitchell, 2016; Olvera & Olvera, 2015; Thordardottir et al., 2015).

Although more research is needed, some preliminary studies have demonstrated other ways in which the students' L1s can be incorporated into interventions alongside English. Wang and colleagues (2019) proposed two relatively simple strategies to incorporate the students' first language by embedding L1 vocabulary into instructive feedback. For example, if a child labels a word in English, such as "milk," the instructor could provide feedback while modeling the child's native language equivalent: "Yes, 牛奶!" Similarly, the authors suggest if a child is learning to identify the word "*dog*," the teacher could follow the correct response with feedback and an additional bilingual component (e.g., "That's right. What is it?" and immediately prompt "狗") (p. 800).

Practitioners face many challenges in appropriately supporting EB students with disabilities. However, there are specific steps that districts, schools, and individual teachers can take to create a supportive multilingual environment for students and promote open communication with their families. First, it is critical that districts prioritize recruiting, hiring, and retaining multicultural/multilingual staff who are qualified in educating students with disabilities. Ongoing opportunities for in-service training and cross-departmental collaboration can help practitioners learn from one another and hone their skills while increasing the retention of qualified staff. See Chapter 9 to explore how this pertains to coaching. When it is not possible to employ practitioners who speak the same language as a student's home language, effective interpreters are needed to support educational decision-making. Adopting intervention strategies to meet the unique learning needs of EB students with ASD and ID is feasible and essential to creating the best learning environment possible.

Summary

Even though accommodating families' language preferences and abilities is required by IDEA, oftentimes students with disabilities are educated in English-only special education settings without support in their home languages. This chapter challenged the assumption that this is the best course of action, suggesting that students with developmental disabilities can be well served in multilingual settings such as dual-immersion programs. The research found that systematically incorporating students' L1s in literacy interventions can help them develop a better command of *both* languages. Best practices for facilitating bilingual learning environments for EB students and their families include scaffolding for collaboration between practitioners including interpreters, especially during IEP meetings (see Table 4.4); tools to empower EB students and their family members during education decision-making process (see Table 4.2 and Table 4.3); and evidence-based interventions that incorporate students' home languages along with English.

By assembling practical suggestions in an accessible format, we hope practitioners can push the conversation forward and explore ways to incorporate their students' home languages into IEP goals, intervention strategies, and classroom practices. Teachers can learn and share techniques for helping their students to become increasingly competent at navigating bilingual environments based on their individual learning profiles and needs.

Guiding Questions

1. What are the benefits of multilingualism for students with autism and ID?
2. Discuss the challenges associated with educating multilingual students with autism and ID.
3. What are effective strategies for working with multilingual students with autism and ID?

References

Accar, S., & Blasco, P.M. (2016). Guidelines for collaborating with interpreters in early intervention/early childhood special education. *Young Exceptional Children, 21*(3), 170-184.

Baker, D. (2017). The language question: considering three Somali American students with Autism. *Multiple Voices for Ethnically Diverse Exceptional Learners, 17*(1), 20-38.

Baker, D., Ackerman, L., Pohl, P., & Kim, H. (2018). Somali American Boys with Autism: Examining Three Educational Transitions Through Capital Theory. *Journal of International Special Needs Education*.

Bretherton, I., & Beeghly, M. (1982). Talking about internal states: The acquisition of an explicit theory of mind. *Developmental psychology, 18*(6), 906.

Cheatham, G.A. (2011). Language interpretation, parent participation, and young children with disabilities. *Topics in Early Childhood Special Education, 31*(2) 78–88.

Cheatham, G. A., Santos, R. M., & Kerkutluoglu, A. (2012). Review of comparison studies investigating bilingualism and bilingual instruction for students with disabilities. *Focus on Exceptional Children, 45*(3), 1-12.

Cho, S.J., & Gannotti, M.E. (2005). Korean-American mothers' perception of professional support in early intervention and special education programs. *Journal of Policy and Practice in Intellectual Disabilities, 2*(1), 1-9.

Colombo, M., Tigert, J. M., & Leider, C. M. (2019). Positioning teachers, positioning learners: Why we should stop using the term English learners. *TESOL Journal, 10*(2), e00432.

Dalmau, Y. C. P.,Wacker, D. P., Harding, J.W., Berg,W. K., Schieltz, K. M., Lee, J. F., et al. (2011). A preliminary evaluation of functional communication training effectiveness and language preference when Spanish and English are manipulated. *Journal of Behavioral Education, 20*(4), 233–251.

Dennison, A., Lund, E. M., Brodhead, M. T., Mejia, L., Armenta, A., & Leal, J. (2019). Delivering home-supported applied behavior analysis therapies to culturally and linguistically diverse families. *Behavior Analysis in Practice, 12*(4), 887-898.

Edgin, J. O., Kumar, A., Spanò, G., & Nadel, L. (2011). Neuropsychological effects of second language exposure in Down syndrome. *Journal of Intellectual Disability Research, 55*(3), 351-356.

Fahim, D. & Nedwick, K. (2014). Around the world: Supporting young children with ASD who are dual language learners. *Young Exceptional Children, 17*(2), 3-20.

Fernandez y Garcia, E. F., Breslau, J., Hansen, R., & Miller, E. (2012). Unintended consequences: An ethnographic narrative case series exploring language recommendations for bilingual families of children with autistic spectrum disorders. *Journal of Medical Speech-Language Pathology, 20*(2), 10-17. org/article/risk-learners-and-bilingualism-it-good-idea.

Geurts, H. M., Verté, S., Oosterlaan, J., Roeyers, H., & Sergeant, J. A. (2004). How specific are executive functioning deficits in attention deficit hyperactivity disorder and autism?. *Journal of child psychology and psychiatry, 45*(4), 836-854.

Gonzalez-Barrero, A. M., & Nadig, A. (2017). Verbal fluency in bilingual children with Autism Spectrum Disorders. *Linguistic Approaches to Bilingualism, 7*(3-4), 460-475.

Hambly, C., & Fombonne, E. (2012). The impact of bilingual environments on language development in children with autism spectrum disorders. *Journal of Autism and Developmental Disorders, 42*(7), 1342-1352.

Hammer, C. S., Miccio, A. W., & Rodriguez, B. L. (2004). Bilingual Language Acquisition and the Child Socialization Process.

Hampton, S., Rabagliati, H., Sorace, A., & Fletcher-Watson, S. (2017). Autism and bilingualism: A qualitative interview study of parents' perspectives and experiences. *Journal of Speech, Language, and Hearing Research: JSLHR, 60*(2), 435-446. doi:10.1044/2016_JSLHR-L-15-0348

Jegatheesan, B. (2011). Multilingual development in children with Autism: Perspectives of South Asian Muslim immigrant parents on raising a child with a communicative disorder in multilingual contexts. *Bilingual Research Journal, 34*, 185–200. doi: 10.1080/ 15235882.2011.597824

Kangas, S. E. (2014). When special education trumps ESL: An investigation of service delivery for ELLs with disabilities. *Critical Inquiry in Language Studies, 11*(4), 273-306.

Kangas, S. E. (2018). Why working apart doesn't work at all: special education and English learner teacher collaborations. *Intervention in School and Clinic, 54*(1), 31-39.

Kay-Raining Bird, E., Cleave, P., Trudeau, N., Thordardottir, E., Sutton, A., & Thorpe, A. (2005). The language abilities of bilingual children with Down syndrome. *American Journal of Speech-Language Pathology, 14*, 187-99.

Kay-Raining Bird, E., Lamond, E., & Holden, J. (2012). Survey of bilingualism in autism spectrum disorders. *International Journal of Language & Communication Disorders, 47*, 52–64. doi: 10.1111/j. 1460-6984.2011.00071.x.

Levine, P., Marder, C., and Wagner, M. (2004). Services and supports for secondary school students with Disabilities. A special topic report from the National Longitudinal Transition Study-2 (NLTS2). Menlo Park, CA: SRI International.

Lim, N. & Charlop, M.H. (2018). Effects of English versus heritage language on play in bilingually exposed children with autism spectrum disorder. *Behavioral Interventions, 33,* 339-351. https://doi.org/10.1002/bin.1644

Lim, N., O'Reilly, M. F., Sigafoos, J., Ledbetter-Cho, K., & Lancioni, G. E. (2019). Should heritage languages be incorporated into interventions for bilingual individuals with neurodevelopmental disorders? A systematic review. *Journal of Autism and Developmental Ddisorders, 49*(3), 887–912. https://doi.org/10.1007/s10803-018-3790-8[HH43]

Martínez-Álvarez, P. (2014). Reconceptualizing what counts as language and learning in bilingual children with disabilities. *NYS TESOL Journal, 1*(2), 39-58.

Martínez-Álvarez, P. (2019). Dis/ability labels and emergent bilingual children: current research and new possibilities to grow as bilingual and biliterate learners. *Race Ethnicity and Education, 22*(2), 174-193.

Medina, A. M., & Salamon, J. T. (2012). Current issues in teaching bilingual children with autism spectrum disorder. *Journal of the American Academy of Special Education Professionals, 69,* 75.

Messent, P. (2003). From postmen to makers of meaning: A model for collaborative work between clinicians and interpreters. In R. Tribe & H. Raval (Eds.), *Working with interpreters in mental health* (pp. 135–150). New York, NY: Routledge.

Mitchell, D. B., Szczerepa, A., & Hauser-Cram, P. (2016). Spilling over: Partner parenting stress as a predictor of family cohesion in parents of adolescents with developmental disabilities. *Research in Developmental Disabilities, 49,* 258-267.

Olvera, P., & Olvera, V. I. (2015). Bilingual school psychology: challenges and opportunities. *Contemporary School Psychology, 19*(3), 165-172.

Petersen, J. M., Marinova-Todd, S. H., & Mirenda, P. (2012). Brief report: An exploratory study of lexical skills in bilingual children with autism spectrum disorder. *Journal of Autism and Developmental Disorders, 42,* 1499–1503. doi:10.1007/s10803- 011-1366-y.

Pinto-Cardona, E. I. (2017). Effects of bilingualism in short-term memory in individuals with Down syndrome. FIU Electronic Theses and Dissertations. 3362. https://digitalcommons.fiu.edu/etd/3362

Rivera, C. J., Baker, J., Tucktuck, M. N., Rüdenauer, H., & Atwell, N. (2019). Based practices for emergent bilinguals with moderate intellectual disability: A review of literature. *Journal of Latinos and Education*, 1-15 (online first) (DOI: 10.1080/15348431.2019.1609478

Rohena, E. I., Jitendra, A. K., & Browder, D. M. (2002). Comparison of the effects of Spanish and English constant time delay instruction on sight word reading by Hispanic learners with mental retardation. *The Journal of Special Education, 36*(3), 171-186.

Seung, H., Siddiqi, S., & Elder, J. H. (2006). Intervention outcomes of a bilingual child with Autism. *Journal of medical speech-language pathology, 14*(1), 53-64.

Soto, G., & Yu, B. (2014). Considerations for the provision of services to bilingual children who use augmentative and alternative communication. *Augmentative and Alternative Communication, 30*(1), 83-92.

Spooner, F., Rivera, C. J., Browder, D. M., Baker, J. N., & Salas, S. (2009). Teaching emergent literacy skills using cultural contextual story-based lessons. *Research and Practice for Persons with Severe Disabilities, 34*(3-4), 102-112.

Thordardottir, E., Cloutier, G., Ménard, S., Pelland-Blais, E., & Rvachew, S. (2015). Monolingual or bilingual intervention for primary language impairment? A randomized control trial. *Journal of Speech, Language, and Hearing Research, 58*(2), 287-300.

Yu, B. (2013). Issues in bilingualism and heritage language maintenance: Perspectives of minority-language mothers of children with autism spectrum disorders. *American Journal of Speech Language Pathology, 22*, 10–24. doi: 10.1044/1058- 0360(2012/10-0078)

Wang, Y., Kang, S., Ramirez, J., & Tarbox, J. (2019). Multilingual diversity in the field of applied behavior analysis and Autism: A brief review and discussion of future directions. *Behavior Analysis in Practice, 12*(4), 795-804.

Ware, J., Lye, C. B., & Kyffin, F. (2015). Bilingualism and students (learners) with intellectual disability: A review. *Journal of Policy and Practice in Intellectual Disabilities, 12*(3), 220-231.

Wei, X., Wagner, M., Christiano, E. R., Shattuck, P., & Yu, J. W. (2014). Special Education Services Received by Students with Autism Spectrum Disorders from Preschool through High School. The Journal of special education, 48(3), 167–179. https://doi.org/10.1177/0022466913483576

Wolfe, K., & Duran, L.K. (2013). Culturally and linguistically diverse parents' perceptions of the IEP process: A review of current research. *Multiple Voices for Ethnically Diverse Exceptional Learners, 13*(2), 2013, 4–18.

Chapter 5

Supporting the right to gender and sexuality diversity and disability

Meaghan M. McCollow, JoDell R. Heroux, and Talya Kemper

Objectives

- Explore how a rights-based model of disability can be used to understand issues related to sexual identity and disability.
- Rationalize the importance of sexuality education as a right for individuals with developmental disabilities including autism spectrum disorder and intellectual disability.
- Develop an understanding of issues related to the intersection of sexual identity and disability.
- Explain and dispel common myths related to sexuality education and developmental disabilities including autism spectrum disorder and intellectual disability.
- Define key terms in regard to sexuality and gender identity.

Chapter 5 focuses on the intersection of gender identity and sexuality and disability. Many continue to hold the belief that individuals with developmental disabilities (DD), including autism and intellectual disability (ID), do not have sexual identities (Swango-Wilson, 2011). Individuals with developmental disabilities face many barriers to accessing their own sexuality. One barrier is the common misconception that individuals with disabilities are incapable of being sexually active, incapable of understanding the complexities of gender identity and sexuality or deny the existence of sexuality as part of their lives (Murphy & Elias, 2006). This leads to the sexual and gender identities of this population being ignored or overlooked (Löfgren-Mårtenson, 2008), and to the erroneous conclusion that sexuality and gender identity are irrelevant to this population. This chapter begins with a rights-based perspective and then discusses the ways in which gender and sexual identity intersect with disability, focusing on those with developmental disabilities. Implications for practice will then focus on providing appropriate information to this population and strategies for ensuring all identities are recognized.

Table 5.1 Key Terminology

Sexual health	"A state of physical, emotional, mental and social well-being in relation to sexuality; it is not merely the absence of disease, dysfunction or infirmity. Sexual health requires a positive and respectful approach to sexuality and sexual relationships, as well as the possibility of having pleasurable and safe sexual experiences, free of coercion, discrimination and violence. For sexual health to be attained and maintained, the sexual rights of all persons must be respected, protected, and fulfilled" (WHO, 2006)
Sexuality	"Sexuality is experienced and expressed in thoughts, fantasies, desires, beliefs, attitudes, values, behaviors, practices, roles and relationships… Sexuality is influenced by the interaction of biological, physiological, social, economic, political, cultural, legal, historical, religious and spiritual factors" (WHO, 2006)
Sexual rights	"The fulfillment of sexual health is tied to the extent to which human rights are respected, protected and fulfilled. Sexual rights embrace certain human rights that are already recognized in international and regional human rights documents and other consensus documents and in national laws" (WHO, 2010)
Sex assigned at birth	"The sex (male or female) given to a child at birth, most often based on the child's external anatomy" (HRC, nd)
Gender expression	"External appearance of one's gender identity; frequently expressed through behavior, clothing, haircut, voice; may or may not conform to socially defined behavior or characteristics associated with being masculine or feminine" (HRC, nd)
Gender identity	"One's innermost concept of self as male, female, a blend of both, or neither. One's gender identity can be the same or different from their sex assigned at birth" (HRC, nd)
Sexuality education	"Sexuality education is a lifelong process of acquiring information and forming attitudes, believes, and values about such important topics as identity, relationships, and intimacy" (SIECUS, 2004)
Cisgender	"A term used to describe a person whose gender identity aligns with those typically associated with the sex assigned to them at birth" (HRC, nd)

Table 5.1 Key Terminology, (continued)	
Non-binary	"An adjective describing a person who does not identify exclusively as a man or a woman. Non-binary people may identify as being both a man and a woman, somewhere in between, or as falling completely outside these categories. While many also identify as transgender, not all non-binary people do" (HRC, nd)
Queer	"A term people often use to express fluid identities and orientations. Often used interchangeably with 'LGBTQ'" (HRC, nd)
Transgender	"An umbrella term for people whose gender identity and/or expression is different from cultural expectations based on the sex they were assigned at birth. Being transgender does not imply any specific sexual orientation. Therefore, transgender people may identify as straight, gay, lesbian, bisexual, etc." (HRC, nd)
Asexual	"The lack of a sexual attraction or desire for other people" (HRC, nd)
Bisexual	"A person emotionally, romantically or sexually attracted to more than one sex, gender or gender identity though not necessarily simultaneously, in the same way or to the same degree" (HRC, nd)
Genderqueer	"Genderqueer people typically reject notions of static categories of gender and embrace fluidity of gender identity and often, though not always, sexual orientation. People who identify as 'genderqueer' may see themselves as both male and female, neither male or female, or as falling completely outside these categories" (HRC, nd).
Rights-based model of disability	A framework for understanding disability as an important dimension of human culture, [recognizing that] all human beings, including those with disabilities, have certain inalienable rights (Degener, 2014).

The World Health Organization (WHO, 2018) states that "the sexual rights of all persons must be respected, protected, and fulfilled (p. 4); this includes the sexual rights of individuals with disabilities." While it is a basic human right for all people to receive accurate information related to sexual health and relationships (WHO, 2018), many individuals with disabilities have limited, if any, access to this information. One reason for this might be that sexuality education is incredibly complex and multifaceted. It involves more than biological explanations of sexual development; it includes social, psychological, spiritual, ethical, and cultural aspects (Gougeon, 2009), which are often challenging to address in any educational situation. While this is a plausible explanation, it is more likely the result of an ableist society that perpetually underestimates and devalues disabled people.

Ableism (defined in Chapter 1 and Chapter 3) is rooted in deficit assumptions of disability as a problem in need of fixing or curing and perpetuates myths and stereotypes of disability. These myths, stereotypes, and false assumptions have fostered negative attitudes towards individuals with disabilities and limited their access to a free and adequate expression of their sexuality (Franco, Cardoso, & Neto, 2012). Understandings of disability have historically been informed by a medical model, viewing disability as abnormal and in need of remediation or fixing. Individuals with intellectual developmental disabilities are often perceived stereotypically as less capable of independence and self-determination and in need of guidance and support for making life decisions. From this orientation, service providers and education professionals are empowered and elevated as the experts in identifying and addressing the needs of those with disabilities. This positions disabled individuals as passive recipients of services rather than agents of their own lives.

The preparation of professionals in human services (i.e. healthcare, education, and service organizations) remains heavily influenced by the medical model of disability, which offers some explanation for the limited attention to issues of disability and sexuality. From this orientation, individuals with intellectual disability (ID) and developmental disabilities (DD) are often perceived as incapable of understanding the complexities of human sexuality and being sexually active (Murphy & Elias, 2006). Other myths include the belief that individuals with ID/DD are asexual, should only have intimate relationships with other disabled people, and should avoid having children (Sexuality and Disability Consortium, 2015). At the core of these myths is the overarching assumption that individuals with disabilities vary so dramatically from nondisabled individuals that they could not possibly understand or experience sexuality in meaningful ways. This has significant implications for disabled people's access to, and experience of, sex, sexuality, and gender identity. Therefore, any attempts to address these issues must begin with a systematic dismantling of these medically influenced myths. First, we need to uncover the myths associated with disability and sexuality. Then we need to examine them from a rights-based model of disability if we are to achieve the ultimate goal of promoting a paradigm shift toward a perspective that views disabled people as full human beings, capable of the entire range of human experiences (Di Giulio, 2003).

Myths of Disability and Sexuality

The medical model has been the primary foundation for making meaning of disability and this meaning is derived from seemingly objective comparisons of bodies and minds to a statistically identified norm. From this perspective, the more quantifiably deviant an individual is from the norm, the more disabled they are, and the more disabled they are, the less capable they must be. While this is widely understood, and accepted, as an objective way to determine the presence of disability, many argue that disability is actually socially, rather than medically, constructed, as explained in Chapter 1. Dray (2009) asserted, "disability can be explained as an objective, medically based phenomenon or as a subjective, socially constructed phenomenon" (p. 722). This means disability must be understood within a complex web of social relations and shared activity (Gergen, 1990) rather than something medically or psychologically wrong within an individual.

A social construct is something that exists as a result of human interaction and society's collective agreement on its existence. For example, race and gender are not biological and genetic traits; rather they are socially constructed identities with variable meanings across contexts (see Howard & del Rosario, 2000 for a definition of race). These socially constructed concepts overlap and intersect in complex ways, particularly in regard to sexuality. Access to sexuality and sexuality education is challenging for individuals with ID/DD and even more so for those who are non-White and/or non-binary and/or homosexual. Medical and scientific explanations of race, gender, and disability have a long history and remain incredibly influential in society's perceptions and treatment of individuals with disabilities. They perpetuate the idea that an incredibly complex concept, such as disability, can be understood simply as the difference between normal and abnormal and fosters negative stereotypes of disability. Stereotypes such as, the object of pity, the subhuman organism, and the eternal child (Baglieri, 2017) perpetuate implicit biases and pose significant barriers to sexuality and sexuality education for individuals with ID/DD.

The Object of Pity

The object of pity stereotype reinforces the notion that disabled people are tragic, pitiable, and in need of considerable care and support. This perspective has led many individuals to pursue careers in human services where the focus is on fixing, curing, or supporting disabled people to live more "normal" lives. Language is a powerful indicator of how pervasive this stereotype is. For example, phrases such as "wheelchair bound," "suffers from," "special needs," and "handicapped," reflect an underlying assumption that disability is tragic (Ralph, 2017). Consider for a moment, the likelihood that individuals with ID/DD would have access to sexuality education or the ability to freely express themselves as sexual beings if programs and services operate from this assumption. This stereotype is deeply rooted in societal understandings of disability and will continue to limit access to sexuality and sexuality education for those with ID/DD unless it is replaced by a rights-based model of disability that promotes agency and self-determination.

The Subhuman Organism

The stereotype of the subhuman organism characterizes disabled individuals as less human, as animal-like, and even "vegetative" (Baglieri, 2017). Nowhere is this assumption more clearly reflected than through the practice of institutionalization. Exposés and documentaries such as *Christmas in Purgatory* (Blatt & Kaplan, 1966) and *Willowbrook: The Last Great Disgrace* (Rivera, 1972) raised public awareness of the horrific abuse and neglect disabled people experienced as a result of the widespread assumption that moderately and/or profoundly disabled people are subhuman. From this perspective, forced sterilization and growth attenuation therapy are rationalized as appropriate practices. "If growth could be permanently arrested while the child was still small, both child and parent would likely benefit because this would facilitate the option of continued care in the home" (Gunther & Diekema, 2006, para. 1). Growth attenuation therapy involves the administration of high doses of estrogen for a short period of time to halt bone growth while rapidly advancing maturation of the epiphyseal growth plates results in permanent attenuation in size (Gunther & Diekema, 2006). Forced sterilization, which was legalized through the U.S. Supreme Court in Buck v. Bell (Holmes & U.S. Supreme Court of the United States, 1926), allowed states to perform procedures on individuals who were deemed as having ID/DD that would prevent these individuals from having children. Buck v. Bell has never been overturned by the U.S. Supreme Court, though subsequent cases have challenged the authority of the ruling.

Professionals, organizations, and systems that operate from the assumption that individuals with moderate to profound ID/DD are sub-human are not likely to consider whether they have sexual needs or desires nor promote their right to experience/express sexuality. Indeed, from this perspective, this may lead to operating under the assumption that interventions must be used to stop sexual needs or desires.

The Eternal Child

The eternal child stereotype presents individuals with ID/DD as perpetually naive and child-like. This perspective has been reflected in films and literature across cultures and eras (Baglieri, 2017) and reinforces the myth that individuals with ID/DD are incapable of navigating life's complexities without constant supervision. Disabled individuals perceived this way are generally considered to be harmless children regardless of their chronological ages (Baglieri, 2017). One can see this perspective being used in discussion, for example, when a professional or other refers to an individual with ID/DD as having the "mental age of" followed by an age much younger than the individual's chronological (e.g., mental age of 5, or mental age of a kindergartener, when referring to a teenager or young adult). This "mental age" perspective harms individuals with ID/DD by failing to recognize their life history, their developmental growth, and the experiences they have had.

Families, caregivers, and professionals holding this belief are less likely to acknowledge a disabled individual's sexuality or need for sexuality education. This is especially problematic given that adults with ID/DD "experience the same emotions as non-disabled people, are capable of a broad range of behaviors, and possess individual and complex personalities" (Biklen, 1981, p. 5). The perception of the "eternal child" leads to withholding information on sexuality and sexual health from individuals with ID/DD (Lesseliers & Van Hove, 2002; Swango-Wilson, 2008). Preventing access to this information harms individuals with ID/DD by keeping individuals from appropriate information, such as health information, body awareness and care, access to care, and knowledge of their rights.

Rights-based Model of Disability and Sexuality

The medical model of disability does little in the way of promoting self-determination for individuals with disabilities and actually perpetuates negative stereotypes. The ability to freely experience and express sexuality is a human right, yet this right remains elusive for individuals with ID/DD due in large part to attitudinal barriers based on stereotypical understandings of disability. The rights-based model of disability offers a more nuanced approach to understanding and supporting individuals with disabilities by focusing on the issue of dignity. "Human dignity is the anchor norm of human rights. Each individual is deemed to be of inestimable value and nobody is insignificant" (Quinn & Degener, 2002, p. 14). The human rights model focuses on the inherent dignity of the human being and places the individual at the center of all decisions and locates the "problem" outside the individual and in society (Quinn & Degener, 2002).

For professionals, caregivers, and service providers, the human-rights model offers a strengths-based approach to disability. From this perspective, impairment does not hinder one's capacity to exercise their human rights, rather impairment is viewed as a natural part of human diversity. This model clarifies that impairment does not diminish human dignity nor does it impinge upon the disabled person's status as a rights-bearer (Degener, 2014). It also acknowledges the importance of identity and recognizes that identity may be shaped by impairment, gender, race, sexual orientation, age, or religion. Intersectionality is an important concept and has critical implications related to disability and sexuality. Disability does not occur in isolation and the experience of disability is different for individuals who hold multiple identities such as disabled, non-White, non-binary, or homosexual. Remember the term intersectionality from Chapter 1? Crenshaw (1989) coined this term as a way to understand how multiple oppressions are not suffered separately but as a single, synthesized experience. When addressing issues of disability and sexuality, it is critical to draw from a human-rights framework that acknowledges and embraces intersectionality. From this perspective, we can begin to dismantle negative assumptions of disability and other marginalized identities and more effectively address access to sexuality education and expression.

Dispelling Myths on Sexuality and Disability

The stereotypes listed above and the possible effects on sexuality education for individuals with ID/DD provide a platform to work toward dispelling myths around sexuality and disability. In the following section, we will present a number of myths that have been created and perpetuated, and facts that clarify the myths. To clarify terminology, we will begin this section by defining what is meant by "sexuality."

Defining Sexuality

While many assume that by talking about sexuality, one is talking about the act of sex, that is not the true definition of sexuality. *Sexuality* is "experienced and expressed in thoughts, fantasies, desires, beliefs, attitudes, values, behaviors, practices, roles and relationships... Sexuality is influenced by the interaction of biological, physiological, social, economic, political, cultural, legal, historical, religions and spiritual factors" (WHO, 2018). In other words, sexuality is much more than the act of intercourse; sexuality is derived from the human experience. When discussing *sexuality education*, it is the "lifelong process of acquiring information and forming attitudes, beliefs, and values about such important topics as identity, relationships, and intimacy" (SIECUS, 2004). Thus, sexuality and sexuality education are intertwined in the human experience where we learn about ourselves and our sexuality, develop relationships, and discover intimacy with others. While frequently presented in a binary format (e.g., gay or straight), sexuality is a spectrum. This means that individuals can identify across the spectrum of sexuality and do not fall neatly into binary categories. For example, an individual may identify as *bisexual*, which means that they are romantically attracted to more than one gender. Further in this chapter, we will discuss gender identity and its relation to attraction, gender expression, and sex.

Common Myths on Disability and Sexuality

There are several myths, or assumptions, that are generally held around the topic of disability and sexuality. We will highlight those that relate generally to individuals with ID/DD and autism and will then work through dispelling these myths. Some common myths are that individuals with ID/DD and autism are:

- Asexual
- Incapable of understanding sexual orientation
- Incapable of understanding sexuality education
- Incapable of informed consent
- Incapable of appropriate sexual expression or romantic relationships

Assumptions About Sexual Identity

Assumptions about sexual identity are pervasive in society. The "norm" of society is to operate from a heteronormative viewpoint. That is, in general, representations of heterosexuality are considered normal and part of everyday life. The default, in most cases, is to assume that relationships occur between individuals of the opposite sex. This assumption carries into myths we see regarding individuals with disabilities and their sexuality (see Rembis, 2010 for discussion on a social model of disabled sexuality).

The assumption of asexuality for individuals with ID/DD and autism is related to other myths. This myth requires further clarification to distinguish between the actual definition of asexuality, and how others use the term asexual. An individual who identifies as *asexual* (which falls under the LGBTQ+ umbrella) does not have sexual attraction or desire for other individuals (HRC, nd). This lack of attraction is related to romantic attraction and does not mean an individual does not form other types of connections to others (e.g., emotional attraction, physical attraction). Asexuality also does not mean that a person does not have a libido, or sex drive. The identity of asexual has been placed upon individuals with ID/DD and autism, however, without considering those individuals actual identities. In this way, the identity of asexual has been transformed to mean no sexual attraction and no libido. And this is where the myth creates the assumption that individuals with ID/DD and autism are asexual and, therefore, are uninterested in romantic attraction or in sex. Dispelling this myth is not intended to minimize those with ID/DD and autism who do identify themselves as asexual, rather, it is meant to call out the myth that *all* individuals with ID/DD and autism must be asexual and do not need sexuality education due to being uninterested in sex (Milligan & Neufeldt, 2001). The dispelling of this myth is also intended to correct the assumption that individuals who identify as asexual do not have libido.

Even when there is not an assumption that individuals with ID/DD and autism are asexual, or, rather, uninterested in romantic attraction, there is still the assumption of heterosexuality. The reality, however, is that individuals with (and without) ID/DD and autism, identify across the spectrum of sexual orientation and gender identity (Bedard, Zhang, & Zucker, 2010). Individuals with ID/DD and autism are capable of learning about their own sexual orientation and have the right to identify their own sexual orientation. Later in this chapter, we will dedicate a space to discussing queerness and disability in further detail.

Assumptions About Understanding and Decision-Making

Another pervasive assumption about the capabilities of individuals with ID/DD and autism is that they lack the ability to understand concepts related to and ability to make decisions regarding sexuality. This assumption goes against the concept of presuming competence and honoring the experiences and abilities of individuals with ID/DD and autism. Concepts related to sexuality and gender identity can be taught, including the concepts of consent, *sexual health*, *sexual rights*, and relationships. By approaching sexuality and gender identity for individuals with ID/DD and autism from a rights-based perspective, one can begin to address the assumptions made about the capabilities of these individuals and work toward providing the appropriate information. Individuals with ID/DD and autism, just like any other individual, have *sexual rights* that include access to appropriate and correct information, opportunities to explore their own identities, and access to information about their own sexual health and development.

Gender Identity

Gender identity goes beyond the binary it is frequently watered down to, such as the demographic information collected in the U.S. Census 2020 (U.S. Census Bureau, 2019) and used by many other applications and surveys. Gender is a spectrum, not an either/or binary of male/female, and is not determined by physical anatomy (Prince, 2005). Gender identity, rather, is "one's innermost concept of self as male, female, a blend of both, or neither" (HRC, nd). Individuals may choose to express their gender identity in many ways, from the clothes they choose to hairstyles to behavior (HRC, nd). Gender expression may not conform to the ways in which society perceives an individual's gender to be (e.g., a masculine-appearing individual wearing skirts or dresses). Just as individuals with ID/DD and autism may have different sexual identities, they also have different gender identities. Frequently, though, individuals with ID/DD/autism do not have access to opportunities to explore or establish or express their gender and sexual identities (Niles & Harkins Monaco, 2017).

There are common terms used referring to different gender identities. The term *cisgender* refers to those whose gender identity matches the sex they were assigned at birth. An individual who identifies as *transgender* has a gender identity that differs from the sex they were assigned at birth. Individuals who identify as *non-binary* do not identify exclusively as male or female, rather, they "may identify as being both a man and a woman, somewhere in between, or as falling completely outside these categories" (HRC, nd). *Genderqueer* is another identity others may recognize in themselves, where they embody gender fluidity in their identity and expression.

The Gender Unicorn

Understanding gender identity and sexual identity can be complicated. Many times, people confuse these identities or assume a direct correlation between them. Reality is, though, that humans are complicated and have different identities and ways of expressing themselves. The Gender Unicorn (Figure 5.1) provides an illustration of gender identity, gender expression, and sexuality (Pan & Moore, nd), showing how these aspects are "interrelated rather than interconnected" (Burdfield, 2017, p. 195).

Figure 5.1 The Gender Unicorn

Double-Rainbow

Individuals with autism may be seven times more likely to be gender non-conforming than neurotypical individuals (Janssen, Huang, & Duncan, 2016). This means individuals with autism may identify under what is referred to as the "double-rainbow," indicating their autism identity along with their identity in the LGBTQ+ community (Narby, 2012). This identity can lead to unique issues for individuals with autism as they navigate social situations, seek to understand their gender identity, gain access to services and support, or receive gender affirming treatments (Rudacille, 2016). Several studies have explored the intersection of gender identity and autism identity that include the voices of individuals who identify within the double-rainbow (see Davidson & Tamas, 2016; Kallitsounaki & Williams, 2020; Kourti & MacLeod, 2019).

Sexuality Education and Practitioners

Practitioners need to be responsible for building skills and removing barriers for individuals with ID/DD and autism. This chapter began by addressing some of the assumptions and stereotypes individuals with ID/DD and autism face related to their own sexuality. Practitioners need to first address their own biases and assumptions about disability and sexuality and come to a place of being willing to learn and to teach their learners. In some cases, practitioners may also need to set aside their own values and beliefs to be an open-minded and accepting presence to others. Practitioners do not have to know everything to begin addressing sexuality education, but willingness and openness to understanding are key. Other qualities and dispositions include giving positive, inclusive messages, being willing to say, "I don't know, let me find out," give facts and a range of opinions, and be specific in language (i.e., avoid euphemisms and indirect language).

Sexuality Education Is...

It is important for practitioners to recognize that sexuality education is an important component of the development of all individuals and take responsibility for providing appropriate education, along with a team that centers the rights and interests of the individual with ID/DD or autism. Sexuality education covers a broad understanding of sexuality and gender and is not simply about the act of intercourse itself. A rights-based sexuality education includes these components:

- It values the human rights of all individuals.
- It is scientifically accurate information.
- It addresses gender identity and expression.
- It provides a safe and healthy learning environment.
- It utilizes effective instructional approaches that include participation.
- It empowers learners and promotes self-advocacy.
  (Berglas et al., 2014)

For individuals with ID/DD and autism, sexuality education can be made more difficult because of language, social, and communication differences. Individuals with ID/DD and autism have sexual feelings, however, may be out of sync with abilities within social awareness, skills, and development (Volkmar & Wolf, 2013). While practitioners do need to keep in mind age-appropriateness, for adolescents and young adults having an interest in romantic relationships, in the act of sex, in flirting, etc. are appropriate behaviors. It is not inappropriate for individuals with ID/DD and autism to be interested in these aspects of humanity. The difference is that these individuals may need more explicit instruction related to these behaviors because they typically have a lower level of sexual knowledge and experience when compared to neurotypical peers (Volkmar & Wolf, 2013). It is important to keep in mind that sexual awareness and interest varies across individuals, which is true in any given context whether we are speaking about individuals with ID/DD and autism or about neurotypical individuals, however, this does not mean that sexuality education should not be provided.

Practical Steps for Practitioners

There are practical steps practitioners can take to address sexuality education, regardless of the age group they work with. First, gaining some knowledge and understanding of normal stages of child and adolescent sexual development allows practitioners to provide age-appropriate sexuality education. Resources such as the Sexual Information and Education Council of the United States (SIECUS) provide guidelines of key concepts across ages (www.siecus.org). Practitioners should also consider priority skills and skills that will lead to the development of other skills (i.e., pivotal behaviors; Cooper et al., 2007). Targeting pivotal skills allows practitioners to maximize impact and the limited teaching time that is felt by so many practitioners. Other instructional strategies practitioners can use to teach behaviors and skills related to sexuality education include task analysis, video modeling, and self-management.

Task analysis, breaking down complex tasks into a sequence of smaller steps, can be used to teach a variety of skills, including hygiene-related skills, asking someone on a date, or purchasing a condom. Video modeling can be used to teach skills as well, though care should be taken for creating and selecting appropriate videos. Video modeling could model a wide range of skills including hygiene skills, how to take birth control pills, what to do on a date, how to say no, or how to give consent. A resource of already-made video models that practitioners might consider is www.amaze.com. These videos address topics that fall under sexuality education such as puberty, sexual orientation, gender identity, and personal safety. Finally, self-management is another strategy practitioners can use to teach skills. Self-management supports independence in skills and promotes self-determined behaviors. Self-management strategies could be used to develop a daily hygiene checklist, a checklist of health-related tasks, and a flowchart on how to ask someone out on a date.

Family involvement is important. It is worth noting, however, that there may be cases in which the values and beliefs of the family clash with the rights, identities, and interests of the individual with ID/DD/autism. *In these instances, it is important to center the rights of and the safety of the individual with ID/DD/autism.*

Risk and Vulnerability

What happens if sexuality education is not provided for individuals with ID/DD/ASD? What happens if the assumptions about sexuality and the abilities or interests of youth with developmental disabilities (DD), including those with autism and intellectual disability (ID), are perpetuated? There are consequences, whether intentional or not.

Exploitation and Abuse

Individuals with DD, including those with autism and ID, are at increased risk for sexual abuse and assault at a rate nearly three times that of the rest of the population (Balderian et al., 2013; Harrell, 2014; Krohn, 2014), though the rate of sexual abuse may be underreported due to communication and cognitive abilities (Dion et al., 2013). A 2018 investigation by National Public Radio brought to light an epidemic of sexual assault being perpetuated on individuals with ID/DD across the United States (Shapiro, 2018). The series included highlighting the importance of providing sexuality education and teaching about healthy relationships (Shapiro, 2018).

There are many reasons that individuals with DD, including those with autism and ID, are at risk for sexual abuse and exploitation. One reason is that for some, the need for assistance in daily living activities (e.g., toileting, hygiene, dressing) puts them in situations where abuse may occur. Often, too, these individuals have a noted lack of privacy; not just when attending to personal hygiene and needs, but also in living spaces. Not having access to appropriate terms and information also leaves individuals with DD, including those with autism and ID, vulnerable to abuse, particularly abuse that goes unreported. While it may make others more comfortable to teach individuals euphemisms for body parts and sexual acts, this leads to confusion when an individual tries to communicate. For example, consider an individual who has been taught the word "cookie" in place of the word "vulva" or "hot dog" in place of "penis," trying to communicate to someone outside of their immediate family an event that has occurred and made them feel uncomfortable.

Multiple Marginalization

A risk for individuals with DD, including those with autism and ID includes a risk for multiple marginalization. Research indicates that, for individuals with DD, including those with autism and ID who identify themselves as part of the LGBTQ+ community, there is an increased risk for having bad school experiences, poor quality of life outcomes, rejection, and bullying (Gutmann Kahn & Lindstrom, 2015).

Sexual Health and Sexual Rights

Overall, it is important to address the sexual health and sexual rights of all individuals, including individuals with DD, including those with autism and ID.

Sexual health goes beyond preventing infection and disease, and preventing unwanted pregnancies, and promotes the "physical, emotional, mental and social well-being [of individuals] in relation to sexuality" (WHO, 2018). By promoting the sexual health of individuals with DD, including those with autism and ID, we can work toward ensuring their sexual rights.

Case Study: Dana

Dana is a 16-year-old cisgender female in the tenth grade. Dana is fully included in all academics at her high school. She has a moderate intellectual delay that impacts her learning, independent living skills and social emotional intelligence. In addition, Dana struggles with impulse control and anger. Dana lives with her mother, her stepfather and her two younger sisters. On her support team is her regional social worker, her mental health therapist, her inclusion teacher and her mother and stepfather. In middle school Dana came out to her family as a lesbian. Her family wants to support her but do not believe she is capable of understanding sexual orientation or that she fully understands what identifying as a lesbian means. Her parents believe that she thinks being a lesbian means having a best friend who is also a woman. Dana's parents stated at the most recent IEP meeting that they do not want her to continue thinking about sexuality or sex. They spoke with her doctor and their minister and both told them that Dana is not capable of understanding such complex emotions as sexuality (due to her disability) and the best thing to do is to stop talking about it as she will only become more confused. They both add that even though Dana is chronologically 16 she still has emotions and intellect similar to a child and should therefore be treated like a child when it comes to sexuality. At this same IEP meeting when Dana was asked what clubs she would like to join at the school, she stated she wanted to join the Gay Straight Alliance that her English teacher advises. Her parents were very upset and did not want her to join the club and said they wanted her to have a new English teacher. The social worker was supporting the parents, the therapist was supporting Dana's wishes, and the inclusion teacher was trying to mediate. As the discussion became heated, everyone decided to take a pause and reconvene in a week. The IEP meeting is tomorrow. *What would you do as the inclusion teacher to support the parents but also help Dana keep her autonomy and make her own decisions? What type of myths are impacting the thinking of Dana's IEP team? What type of myths are being promoted by Dana's doctor and the family's minister? Would dispelling the myths help the parents understand Dana's sexuality?*

Summary

This chapter provided a foundation in the rights-based model for discussing the rights of individuals with DD, including those with autism and ID, related to sexuality and to gender identity. There are many misconceptions regarding how individuals with DD, including those with autism and ID experience and relate to sexuality and how individuals with DD, including those with autism and ID express their sexual and gender identities. Through the lens of the rights-based model and by dispelling myths and misconceptions, this chapter laid the groundwork for understanding the ethics of sexuality education for individuals with DD, including those with autism and ID and how ignoring their sexual and gender identities denies their intersecting identities. While it may be uncomfortable (for some) to discuss sexuality for individuals with DD, this doesn't mean it's not the right of the individual with DD, including those with autism and ID, to receive sexuality education. Being denied access to this information violates human rights for these individuals (Stein & Dillenburger, 2017). Rather than ignore the sexuality and gender identities of individuals with DD, including those with autism and ID, appropriate information should be provided that allows them to be safe and to live their full lives.

Guiding Questions

1. How can a rights-based model of disability be used to understand issues related to sexual identity and disability?
2. What is the importance of sexuality education as a right for individuals with developmental disabilities?
3. Describe the intersection of sexual identity and disability.
4. Explain and dispel common myths related to sexuality education and developmental disabilities including autism spectrum disorder and intellectual disability.

References

Baglieri, S. (2017). *Disability studies and the inclusive classroom: Critical practices for embracing diversity in education*. Taylor & Francis.

Baladerian, N. J., Coleman, T. F., & Stream, J. (2013). A report on the 2012 national survey on abuse of people with disabilities. *Los Angeles: Spectrum Institute*.

Bedard, C., Zhang, H. L., & Zucker, K. J. (2010). Gender identity and sexual orientation in people with developmental disabilities. *Sexuality and Disability*, *28*(3), 165-175.

Berglas, N. F., Constantine, N. A., & Ozer, E. J. (2014). A rights-based approach to sexuality education: Conceptualization, clarification and challenges. *Perspectives on Sexual and Reproductive Health*, *46*(2), 63-72.

Blatt, B., & Kaplan, F. (1966). *Christmas in purgatory*. Boston: Allen & Bacon.

Biklen, D. (1981). The Supreme Court v. retarded children. *Journal of the Association for the Severely Handicapped*, *6*(2), 3-5.

Burdfield, C. (2017). SpongeBob SquarePants and gender identity. *Heroes, Heroines, and Everything in Between: Challenging Gender and Sexuality Stereotypes in Children's Entertainment Media*, 195.

Cooper, J. O., Heron, T. E., & Heward, W. L. (2007). Applied behavior analysis.

Crenshaw, K. (1989). Demarginalizing the intersection of race and sex: A black feminist critique of antidiscrimination doctrine, feminist theory and antiracist politics. *u. Chi. Legal f.*, 139.

Davidson, J., & Tamas, S. (2016). Autism and the ghost of gender. *Emotion, Space and Society*, *19*, 59-65.

Degener, T. (2014). A human rights model of disability. *Disability social rights*, 1-30.

Dray, B. J. (2009). Social construction of disability. In Provenzo, E. F., Renaud, J. P., &

Provenzo, A. B. (Eds.). *Encyclopedia of the Social and Cultural Foundations of Education: AH; 2, IZ; 3, Biographies, visual history, index* (Vol. 3). Sage.

Di Giulio, G. (2003). Sexuality and people living with physical or developmental disabilities: A review of key issues. *Canadian Journal of Human Sexuality*, *12*(1).

Dion, J., Paquette, G., Tremblay, K. N., Cyr, M., & Dionne, C. (2013). Sexual abuse of intellectually disabled youth: a review. *The Prevention Researcher*, *20*(3), 14-16.

Franco, D. G., Cardoso, J., & Neto, I. (2012). Attitudes towards affectivity and sexuality of people with intellectual disability. *Sexuality and Disability*, *30*(3), 261-287.

Gergen, K. J. (1990). Social understanding and the inscription of self. *Cultural psychology: Essays on comparative human development*, 569-606.

Gougeon, N. A. (2009). Sexuality education for students with intellectual disabilities, a critical pedagogical approach: outing the ignored curriculum. *Sex Education*, *9*(3), 277-291.

Gunther, D. F., & Diekema, D. S. (2006). Attenuating growth in children with profound developmental disability: A new approach to an old dilemma. *Archives of Pediatrics & Adolescent Medicine*, *160*(10), 1013-1017.

Gutmann Kahn, L., & Lindstrom, L. (2015, October). "I just want to be myself": Adolescents with disabilities who identify as a sexual or gender minority. In *The educational forum* (Vol. 79, No. 4, pp. 362-376). Routledge.

Harrell, E. (2014). *Crimes against persons with disabilities, 2009-1012 statistical tables.* Washington, DC: U.S. Department of Justice.

Holmes, O. W. & Supreme Court Of The United States. (1926) U.S. Reports: Buck v. Bell, 274 U.S. 200.

Howard, T. C., & del Rosario, C. D. (2000). Talking race in teacher education: The need for racial dialogue in teacher education programs. *Action in Teacher Education*, *21*(4), 127-137.

Human Rights Council (n.d.). *Glossary of Terms*. HRC. https://www.hrc.org/resources/glossary-of-terms?utm_source=GS.

Janssen, A., Huang, H., & Duncan, C. (2016). Gender variance among youth with autism spectrum disorders: A retrospective chart review. *Transgender Health*, *1*(1), 63-68.

Kallitsounaki, A., & Williams, D. (2020). A relation Between autism traits and gender self-concept: Evidence from explicit and implicit measures. *Journal of Autism and Developmental Disorders*, *50*(2), 429-439.

Kourti, M., & MacLeod, A. (2019). "I Don't Feel Like a Gender, I Feel Like Myself": Autistic Individuals Raised as Girls Exploring Gender Identity. *Autism in Adulthood*, *1*(1), 52-59.

Krohn, J. (2014). Sexual harassment, sexual assault, and students with special needs: Crafting an effective response for schools. *U. Pa. JL & Soc. Change*, *17*, 29.

Lesseliers, J., & Van Hove, G. (2002). Barriers to the development of intimate relationships and the expression of sexuality among people with developmental disabilities: Their perceptions. *Research and Practice for Persons with Severe Disabilities*, *27*(1), 69-81.

Milligan, M. S., & Neufeldt, A. H. (2001). The myth of asexuality: A survey of social and empirical evidence. *Sexuality and disability*, *19*(2), 91-109.

Murphy, N. A., & Elias, E. R. (2006). Sexuality of children and adolescents with developmental disabilities. *Pediatrics*, *118*(1), 398-403.

Narby, C. N. (2012, January 3). *Double Rainbow: Navigating Autism, Gender, and Sexuality*. Bitch Media. https://www.bitchmedia.org/post/double-rainbow-navigating-autism-gender-and-sexuality-feminism

Niles, G., & Harkins Monaco, E. A., (2017). Gender identity and sexual diversity: Supporting individuals with an intellectual or developmental disability, *DADD Online Journal*, *4*, 177-189.

Quinn, G. (2016). i Degener, T.(2002): The moral authority for change: Human rights values and the worldwide process of disability reform. *Human Rights and Disability: The current use and future potential of United Nations human rights instruments in the context of disability.* New York, Geneva: United Nations.

Pan, L., & Moore, A. (n.d.). The Gender Unicorn [Illustration]. In *Trans Student Educational Resources*.

Prince, V. (2005). Sex vs. gender. *International Journal of Transgenderism*, *8*(4), 29-32.

Ralph, N. (2017, April 13). *Understanding Disability*. Drake Music. https://www.drakemusic.org/blog/nim-ralph/understanding-disability/

Rembis, M. A. (2010). Beyond the binary: Rethinking the social model of disabled sexuality. *Sexuality and Disability*, *28*(1), 51-60.

Rivera, G. (investigative reporter). (1972). Willowbrook: The last great disgrace. In A. T. Primo (executive producer). WABC-TV Channel 7. New York, New York.

Rudacille, D. (2016). Living between genders. *UMBC Faculty Collection*.

Shapiro, J. (2018, January 1). For some with intellectual disabilities, ending abuse starts with sex ed. Morning Edition

Sexuality and Disability Consortium (2015.). Myths and misperceptions of disability and sexuality. https://sdc.ahslabs.uic.edu/wp-content/uploads/sites/19/2015/12/MythsAndMisperceptionsOfDisabilitySexuality.pdf

Sexuality Information and Education Council of the United States (SEICUS). (2004). *Guidelines for comprehensive sexuality education (3rd ed.)*. Retrieved from www.siecus.org

Swango-Wilson, A. (2011). Meaningful sex education programs for individuals with intellectual/developmental disabilities. *Sexuality and Disability*, *29*(2), 113-118.

Volkmar, F. R., & Wolf, J. M. (2013). When children with autism become adults. *World Psychiatry, 12*(1), 79.

U.S. Census Bureau (2019). U.S. Census 2020. https://2020census.gov/en/about-questions.html

World Health Organization. (2018, February 5). *Defining sexual health*. Sexual and reproductive health. https://www.who.int/reproductivehealth/topics/sexual_health/sh_definitions/en/.

Chapter 6

Creating positive relationships with diverse students with disabilities and ensuring academic success through culturally sustaining pedagogies

Shelley Neilsen Gatti, Martin Odima Jr., and Kathlene Holmes Campbell

Objectives

- Unpack the importance of building authentic relationships with students with developmental disabilities including autism and intellectual disability through culturally sustaining pedagogy.
- Describe the contributing factors promoting and interfering with building effective relationships with students with developmental disabilities including autism and intellectual disability.
- Apply relationship strategies and academic frameworks to ensure social emotional learning (SEL) and academic success for diverse students with developmental disabilities including autism and intellectual disabilities.

I have come to a frightening conclusion. I am the decisive element in the classroom. It is my personal approach that creates the climate. It is my daily mood that makes the weather. As a teacher I possess tremendous power to make a child's life miserable or joyous. I can be a tool of torture or an instrument of inspiration. I can humiliate or humor, hurt or heal. In all situations it is my response that decides whether a crisis will be escalated or de-escalated, and a child humanized or de-humanized (Ginott, 1972, p. 15).

Chapter 6 provides an overview of how students rely on teachers and school communities to create and sustain effective, caring, and engaging classroom communities where all students are valued, accepted, loved, and are learning. The research is clear that the single greatest effect on student achievement is the effectiveness of the teacher (Goodlad, 1990; Marzano, Pickering, & Pollock, 2001) and having a great teacher is the single most important school-based factor in closing the student opportunity gap (Master, Loeb, & Wyckoff, 2014). Effective and culturally relevant teaching starts with relationship building (Gay, 2010). When students feel a greater sense of belonging and connecting to the classroom and school community, they are more likely to be engaged and academically successful (Hammond, 2015). According to Alim and Paris (2017) it is also centrally about love, a love that can help us see our young people as whole versus broken when they enter schools and a love that can work to keep them whole as they grow and expand who they are and can be throughout education (p. 14).

This chapter will take a deeper look at relationships, why they matter for youth with autism and intellectual disabilities (ID), how they are pivotal to student success, barriers to developing student relationships, and ways practitioners develop relationships in culturally sustaining ways to influence academic success and social emotional well-being.

Table 6.1 Key Terminology	
Cognition	Cognition is generally referred to as learning and processing of information and involves the integration of different developmental domains, such as social, communication, and motor. In this chapter, we use Yvette Jackson's application of cognition and cognitive skills believing that Intelligence is modifiable, all students benefit from a focus on high intellectual performance, and learning is influenced by the interaction of culture, language and cognition (Jackson, 2011, p. 71 & 89).
Opportunity Gap	The opportunity gap is the disparity in access to resources inside the school (e.g., materials, curriculum opportunities, quality teachers) and outside the school (e.g., socioeconomic status, English proficiency, safety, healthcare) needed for all children to be successful (Schott Foundation).
Social Emotional Learning	Social and emotional learning (SEL) is the process through which children and adults understand and manage emotions, set and achieve positive goals, feel and show empathy for others, establish and maintain positive relationships, and make responsible decisions (CASEL).
TPACK	TPACK is a framework designed around the idea that content (what you teach) and pedagogy (how you teach) must be the basis for any technology that you plan to use in your classroom to enhance learning (Mishra & Kohler, 2006).

Table 6.1 Key Terminology, (continued)	
Trauma	Trauma is a psychological injury that causes damage or harm and varies in permanency, severity, and longevity (Kerns, Newschaffer, & Berkowitz, 2015). It occurs as a result of violence, abuse, neglect, loss, disaster, war and other emotionally harmful experiences and has immediate and/or lasting adverse effects on the individual's functioning (SAMHSA 2014).
Universal Design for Learning (UDL)	Universal design for learning (UDL) is a framework to improve and optimize teaching and learning for all people based on scientific insights into how humans learn so that all learning environments are accessible and effective for all. The three essential elements of UDL include multiple means of representation, multiple means of engagement, and multiple means of action and expression (CAST).

Impact of Student–Teacher Relationships

There continues to be a growing body of research demonstrating the importance of student-teacher relationships (STRs) for students and teachers (Cornelius-White, 2007; Hamre & Pianta, 2001; Kincade, Cook, & Goerdt, 2020; Quin, 2016). In this chapter, relationships are defined as repeated and reciprocal interactions (Scott, 2017) across the day and throughout the school year where students and teachers share mutual communication, positive emotions, and trust (Pianta, 1999). The Student–Teacher Relationship Scale (Pianta, 2001) is the most commonly used measure in studies examining STRs and defines relationships based on the teacher's perspective of closeness, conflict, and dependency (Cederlund, Hagbern, Billstedt, Gillberg, & Gillberg, 2008; Murray & Pianta, 2007). Positive student-teacher relationships impact student engagement, behavior, predict both short- and long-term academic success (Pianta, Hamre, & Allen, 2012), mental health (Wit, Karioja, Rye, & Shain, 2011), placement in special education (Pianta, Steinberg, & Rollins, 1995), teacher well-being (Spilt, Hoomen, & Thijs, 2011), and can serve as a protective factor for students experiencing learning and behavior challenges (Baker 2006; Bierman, 2011).

While there is nearly 50 years of research on relationships and the majority of teachers recognize the significance of creating a positive relationship with students, there continues to be a lack of intentional approaches to build relationships with all students and especially for students who engage in challenging behavior (Duong et al., 2018). Instead, some teachers may rely on reactive and punitive responses, which cause harm to the student's sense of belonging, motivation, and relationship with the teacher (Jennings & Greenberg, 2009). This has important implications for students with disabilities who may be at risk for greater difficulties in social-emotional domains (Ashburner, Ziviani, & Rodger, 2010) and significant behavior problems (Dekker, Koot, VanderEnde & Verhulst, 2002), creating less likelihood that they will access the benefits of close student–teacher relationships (Eisenhower, Blacher, & Bush, 2015).

The available research on STRs for students with autism and ID is limited. McIntyre, Blacher and Baker (2006) examined adaptation to kindergarten and found that children with intellectual disability had poorer STRs as compared to their typically developing peers. Blacher, Baker, and Eisenhower (2009) followed this group of children over two years and found that these students continued to have poorer quality STRs and experienced less closeness and more conflict and dependency each year. One important finding is that children with intellectual disability continue to be most hindered by behavioral and social factors more so than academic issues and needs when it comes to building relationships with teachers (Blacher et al., 2009).

The studies on STR quality for students with autism yield similar results, yet students with autism may have even greater levels of conflict and less closeness with teachers as compared to children with typical development (Longobardi, Prino, Pasta, Gastaldi, & Quaglia, 2012) and children with intellectual disability (Blacher et al., 2014). Blacher and colleagues (2014) examined STRs with elementary age students with autism educated in a private, specialized school for students with autism and compared these results to students with typical development and intellectual disability. They found that STRs for children with autism were qualitatively different with less closeness and more conflict than the other groups of students. Furthermore, this pattern persisted across classrooms and teachers from one year to the next (Eisenhower et al., 2015). Caplan, Feldman, Eisenhower and Blacher (2016) found similar results and that STR quality for young students with autism remains moderately stable over time. Collectively, this research points to the importance of effective intervention and professional development for teachers to understand the characteristics of these disabilities and implement specific relationship-based interventions, including social emotional and positive behavioral interventions in culturally sustaining ways.

In addition to disability characteristics impacting STRs, other risk factors implicated include gender, race, and socio-economic status (SES). Student–teacher relationships have been reported to be poorer with boys than girls and economically and racially diverse students (Hughes & Kwok, 2006; Saft & Pianta, 2001). In fact, some have argued that student–teacher relationships can partially explain opportunity gaps (Cohen, Garcia, Apfel, & Master, 2006). This has important implications considering the intersectionality of disability, race, gender, SES, and the potentially multiplicative educational and social inequities for students and their families (Gillborn, Rollock, Vincent, & Ball, 2012).

Barriers Impacting Student–Teacher Relationships

There is a consensus about the importance of practitioners developing meaningful relationships with students, however, students with disabilities and students of color may be disadvantaged when it comes to accessing and benefiting from the positive outcomes of STRs. In this section we describe some of the barriers impacting the development of STR for students of color with autism and intellectual disability.

Behavior and Reciprocal Social Skills Associated With the Disability

The most reliable predictor of the quality of STRs is behavioral challenges posed by the child (Blacher et al., 2009; Eisenhower, Baker, & Blacher, 2007; Hamre, & Pianta, 2009; Serpell & Mashburn, 2012). Common characteristics of students with autism and intellectual disability include externalizing and internalizing challenging behaviors, using challenging behavior to communicate needs, social difficulties, and for students with autism, unique symptomatology, such as repetitive movements and restricted interests (Blancher et al., 2014; Robertson, Chamberlain, & Kasari, 2003). Externalizing and internalizing behavior problems pose a risk for STRs, and the severity of the autism characteristics contributes to the quality of STRs (Caplan et al., 2016). These characteristics alone set students up for fewer quality interactions with teachers that decline over time (Eisenhower et al., 2015) and relate to concurrent and long-term liabilities of poor STRs (Blancher et al., 2014). Furthermore, students with disabilities and of color may face structural inequities and interpersonal violence, causing a host of emotions about those inequities (Annamma & Morrison, 2018). These feelings may manifest and be viewed as challenging behavior further impacting STRs.

Professional development on the characteristics of the disabilities is a good start. As noted in several chapters in this book, practitioners also need to understand how their own race, racialized backgrounds, and experiences influence student interactions. Teachers need to empathize with what students face in terms of systemic oppression and how it may affect their interactions with others. It is important that practitioners allow students space to own their emotions, unpack where they may be coming from while concurrently using that passion to change the system (Annamma & Morrison, 2018), and expand their own critical consciousness (Ladson-Billings, 2017). These types of support can be crucial to students and teachers' long-term success in school communities.

Trauma

When children experience trauma, it impacts their relationships; their sense of trust and safety with others, especially adults; and leads to difficulty with emotional regulation (Koerner, 2012). Children with disabilities and of color may be at greater risk for experiencing trauma in their childhood (Hibbard & Desch 2007; Kerns et al. 2015). When students experience trauma, it requires adults to use more persistent and systematic ways to build relationships. Positive STRs help students develop emotional connection and a sense of safety that serves to enhance engagement in academic pursuits and as a buffer against risk (Cook, Coco, Zhang, Duong, Renshaw, & Frank, 2018).

As described above and in Chapter 1, students experience racism and ableism (i.e. assertion that systems and interactions privilege some and exclude and otherize other students while reproducing inequities based on race and ability status) in the school community and according to Gorski, these systemic injustices in our school communities retraumatize students (as cited in Gaffney, 2019). Systems of oppression that show up in schools, such as interactions with students, bias, lack of and misrepresentation in the curriculum, discipline policies that advantage White students over students of color, and special education identification and placement all have the potential to cause trauma for students and families (Gaffney, 2019). These school-based traumatic events accumulate to cause structural and interpersonal forms of discrimination and potentially contribute to academic disparities (e.g., dropout, suspensions/expulsions) and opportunity gaps (e.g., gifted and talented programs) (Liang et al., 2020).

Intersectional Systemic Injustice: Bias and Systemic Racism and Ableism

Bias, systemic racism, and ableism cause trauma and create barriers to the student-teacher relationships for the teacher, student, and family. By examining the intersectionality of racism and ableism using disability critical race theory (see Chapter 1) scholars can describe how they are socially constructed, interdependent, and how students are simultaneously profiled by race and disability (Annamma, Connor & Ferri, 2013) to deny the rights of some students and families (Migambi & Neal, 2018) and create a significant education deficit. According to Annamma and Morrison (2018), "Once individuals or groups of students are positioned as less desirable, they are barred access to: 1) curriculum that is engaging and accurate; 2) pedagogy that is responsive and ingenuous; and 3) relationships that are authentic and hopeful" (p. 72).

Intersectionality of race and ability create barriers not only to student–teacher relationships, but significant inequities for students and families. These issues show up in special education identification, placement, and exclusionary discipline practices (Skiba, Artiles, Kozleski, Losen, & Harry, 2016). Fish (2019) describes status associated with different disabilities and how intellectual disabilities have greater social stigma and less status due to perceptions of deficits in the subjective constructs of intelligence and challenging behavior. This underlying racial bias embedded in systems places students of color at a disadvantage, plays a role in how teachers treat boys of color, and results in lower status, which impacts how teachers, peers, and administrators view these students (Fish, 2019).

Implicit bias and racialized conceptions of ability continue to allow parents and practitioners to use certain special education categories as a tool for continued racial segregation. Research suggests that families with more resources may advocate for labels such as autism over other disability categories (Eyal, 2013; Liu, King, & Bearman, 2010; Ong-Dean, 2009). These categorical processes that sort students into different disability categories, create and reinforce racialized categories of disability and reinforce racial inequity (Domina, Penner, & Penner, 2017; Fish, 2019) and the closer students are to the desired norm (e.g., White, male, cis-gender, heterosexual), the more likely they are to be imagined as capable, regardless of behavioral and academic interactions (Broderick & Leonoardo, 2016).

For families of color, these social status outcomes may be delayed. Delay of accurate diagnosis has important implications for early intervention, accessing a variety of services, and are another way systemic racism and bias impact families and children. Once identified as having a disability, students of color are more likely to be segregated than their White peers with the same label in special education classrooms (Fierros & Conroy 2002). These special education identification and placement practices continue to position some students as deserving and worthy of educating in classrooms, alongside their general education peers and teachers, while situating others as problematic and in need of remediation or segregation from general education opportunities (Walton et al., 2016).

In summary, students with autism and intellectual disabilities experience barriers to the benefits of STRs and when they identify as students of color, they experience additional oppressive systems of racism and ableism in classrooms, schools, and communities. Students of color do not experience special education the same as White students with disabilities. The outcomes for students and families are inequitable, unjust, and allow a continued system of segregation and lack of equitable access to education across and within special education. Countering these disparate outcomes, begins with the teachers' beliefs, attitudes, and expectations about students, teaching, and learning. These mindsets influence practitioners' daily interactions, how they develop relationships with students and families, decisions on pedagogical practices, and choice of curriculum and materials.

The Importance of Teachers' Mindsets

As mentioned previously, research has shown that the most significant factor in a student's academic success is an effective teacher (Goodlad, 1990; Marzano et al., 2001). However, being an effective teacher is much more than simply being knowledgeable in the specific content area. It also involves utilizing numerous instructional strategies to teach the content while engaging and interacting with students. When teachers interact with students, what is often taken for granted are the biases and beliefs of the teacher. These biases can impact how often and to what degree teachers interact with students. Deborah Ball (2020) calls these daily interactions discretionary spaces. Discretionary spaces are the day-to-day decisions that teachers make about the interactions they have with students that can positively or negatively impact them based upon the type of interaction.

According to Hammond (2015), being aware of the types of interactions with students, similarities and differences across cultural groups, and understanding how it impacts our cognitive ability is extremely important. Understanding these interactions and this cognitive ability help teachers deepen their understanding that culture and language impact the way we perceive information. Yvette Jackson (2011) calls this our cultural frames of reference. An individual's frame of reference can harness inaccurate beliefs and stereotypes about different groups of individuals, which in turn, could cause a teacher to view students differently simply based on the assumptions or thoughts attributed to particular groups. See the case study below for an example of how this plays out in a classroom from the perspective of the teacher and student.

Case Study 1: Teacher and Student Perspectives

Teacher Perspective

My name is Ms. Smith and I am a White female who teaches fifth grade. I had an African American student with autism named Kyle in my classroom. One day, my class came into the classroom from recess. I stood in front of my class and asked everyone to sit down on their floor spots for group reading time. While students sat down, Kyle paced around the classroom. Since he wasn't listening, I again said to him, "please sit down at the carpet. I am going to start reading a book to the class." Instead of following my instruction and our normal daily routine, Kyle sat down at his desk, groaned at me, and put his hands over his ears to block out my instruction. I calmly directed Kyle again, "No. Don't you know that it's reading time? I said to sit on the carpet. You have until the count of three to sit down on the carpet with the rest of the class." I set a time limit to keep the day and the rest of the class moving. Kyle then told me that I am too loud, that he gets bored when I read, and that he doesn't want to sit on the carpet because it's uncomfortable. I immediately became defensive and started thinking through Kyle's critiques. I had to project my voice so that the whole class could hear me. The curriculum that I am provided might not be fun for all students all the time, but this is what I'm given to work with. All the other students could sit on the carpet for 40 minutes without a problem. Why can't he? The students in class were laughing at me and Kyle and I needed to regain control of the classroom. I again told Kyle, "please follow the rules and join the group." Kyle got angry and hit the table and shouted at me. His defiance was continuing and has escalated to violence. I approached him and told him to move to the carpet with the rest of the students or take

Case Study 1: Teacher and Student Perspectives, (continued)

a timeout. Kyle laid his head on his desk, screamed, and cried. He had lost all control and I had run out of ideas. The rest of the students were quiet and watching us. While Kyle's head was on his desk, I asked him to look at me when I'm talking to him. He refused to show respect and would not make eye contact. We were wasting a lot of time on one student, so I sent Kyle to the principal's office, which was a relief because I didn't know what else to do.

Student Perspective

My name is Kyle and I am a fifth-grade Black student who has autism. One day, my class and I were walking into the classroom from recess. I felt really overwhelmed because there were so many things going on at recess and transitioning from one thing to another is really hard for me. My White teacher, Ms. Smith, stood in front of my class and asked everyone to sit down on their floor spots for group reading time. While students sat down, I paced around the classroom. I paced around because I didn't know what to do. I didn't want to sit on the floor. It's very uncomfortable for me and could trigger one of a few things for me, proximity to other students, the texture of the carpet, and the volume of my teacher's voice. My teacher also always tells us what to do verbally which is hard for me to keep track of because of my autism. Then Ms. Smith again said to me, "please sit down at the carpet. I am going to start reading a book to the class." I sat down at my desk because I wanted to go to my own space. It seemed safe to me. I groaned out of frustration and put my hands over my ears because everything was getting too loud. Ms. Smith said, "No. Don't you know that it's reading time? I said to sit on the carpet. You have until the count of three to sit down on the carpet with the rest of the class." I didn't feel like I had any choices. She wasn't listening to me. I felt a lot of pressure to figure out what to do and it takes my brain a little longer to process everything that she's telling me. I told Ms. Smith that she is too loud, and that I get bored when she reads, and that I didn't want to sit on the carpet because it's uncomfortable. I said this because Ms. Smith's reading lessons are 40 minutes, which is longer than I could sit still. I would rather be learning while moving my body. At home, my family spends a lot of time dancing and moving and doing hands-on learning. My classmates had started laughing at me and I felt embarrassed by the attention. Ms. Smith told me, "please follow the rules and join the group." She still wasn't hearing me. I got angry and hit the table and shouted at her. Ms. Smith walked very close to me and told me to move to the carpet with the rest of the students or take a timeout. I was uncomfortable with how close she was. I laid my head on my desk, screamed, and cried because I didn't know how else to express myself. The rest of the students were quiet and watched us. While my head was on my desk, Ms. Smith asked me to look at her when she was talking. It was hard for me to look directly at people because it causes discomfort and sometimes when I am looking, I have a hard time using my other senses. I continued to look away and kicked a chair. I was sent to the principal's office which was a relief because it's quiet and calm there.

In the case study, Kyle did not follow exact directions; however, he did find an instructional area that met his needs and was ready to listen and participate.

- Did the teacher consider the possible social, communication, or sensory stressors of the student?
- Could the situation have changed if the teacher looked critically at her own interaction and communication style and viewed the student as making a good choice to meet his own sensory and instructional needs?

To avoid projecting negative biases or stereotypical thoughts onto students, Hammond (2015) urges every teacher to widen their frame of reference when identifying potential triggers and utilize proactive strategies for emotional self-management. In the example above, the teacher's response to challenging and unpredictable behavior ended up being more about the teacher's embarrassment and frustration of losing control of the classroom than about the student's behavior. If the teacher widened her frame of reference and interpreted the behavior positively, the outcome may have been different, and the student may still be in class.

The widening of a frame of reference is particularly important if teachers want to better connect with students from different backgrounds and consciously challenge their own biases. According to Ladson-Billings (2020), for teachers to implement culturally relevant or sustaining practices, they must be fluent not only in their own culture but in at least one additional culture. Bi/transcultural teachers are able to deepen their connections to students by understanding how culture influences learning. For instance, teachers exerted efforts to reduce barriers to learning and made instructional and curriculum accommodations for students with disabilities when they believed that it was the environment, rather than student impairment, that was the disabling condition (Danker, Strnadova, & Cumming, 2019). It is the awareness of how cultural competence, rigor, and critical consciousness (Ladson-Billings, 1995) intersect that helps teachers develop a more holistic and inclusive learning environment. Chapter 8 discusses this further. Once teachers understand these three essential components that directly impact their mindset, they can then implement relational, instructional, and technological frameworks, such as establish maintain, and restore (EMR), universal design for learning (UDL) and technological pedagogical content knowledge (TPACK), to increase access and academic success of students with disabilities.

Developing Authentic, Culturally Sustaining Relationships

Relationships are more than social and friendly interactions. The daily interactions between the teacher and student establish the teacher as trustworthy, kind, caring, and credible. Effective relationships require teachers to systematically understand and use knowledge of students' interests, assets, and curiosity to develop authentic and sustainable relationships. Ongoing relationships strategies include ways to affirm children's value, contribution, and create belonging to the classroom community (Lambert, Stillman, Hicks, Kamble, Baumeister, & Fincham, 2013) and most importantly convey belief that students are capable and will grow and learn (Hammond, 2015).

The EMR framework builds culturally sustaining relationship strategies and supports students' engagement (Duong et al., 2018). This framework is designed to improve teachers' skills in cultivating, maintaining, and restoring relationships with students and provides a cost-effective, feasible, and focused approach for improving STRs (Cook et al., 2018). Each component is described in Table 6.2.

Table 6.2 Establish, Maintain, and Restore (ESR) Components	
Establish	Focuses on creating emotional connections and building trust and includes spending time individually with each student, integrating students' lived experiences in the curriculum and instruction, positively greeting the student each day, delivering wise feedback (Yeager et al., 2014) and acknowledging the student through second-hand compliments (e.g., telling the principal or family member).
Maintain	Requires ongoing positive interactions and includes teachers maintaining interaction by using high ratios of positive interactions to negative or reprimand interactions and aiming for 5-1 ratio of positive to negative interaction. This can also include non-contingent attention, such as continuing to use greetings at the door and brief relationship check-ins to continue to affirm students' culture, deepen the understanding of the student, their experiences, and interests. These strategies show that teachers care, which continues to create ongoing interactions demonstrating respect, trust, and value. Hammond (2015) refers to these as affirmations, where educators acknowledge students using words and actions that say, I see you and I care about you, and showing appreciation for all aspects of their personhood. Hammond recommends Trust Generators as one way to maintain relationships.
Restore	Uses restorative communication to repair any harm to the relationship following a negative interaction and includes the teacher taking ownership, using empathy statements, letting go of the incident and starting fresh, conveying care, and engaging in mutual problem-solving to gather perspective, and making a plan to avoid negative interactions in the future. Restorative conversations are brief and delivered privately by the teacher. This final component is another way teachers gain student perspective, validate student experience, convey mutual respect, authenticity, and humanity, and restore the balance of power (Liang et al., 2020).

Through establishing and maintaining rapport and affirmation, teachers and students learn about each other and their strengths and challenge areas. Then teachers can use this information to decide when to push, when to encourage, and when to support. Throughout EMR and especially with restore, teachers need to examine how their own biases and assumptions influence their interactions with students. One way to do this is through reflective supervision/consultation or critical reflective practice to help challenge bias, blind spots, and cultural beliefs. This type of deep reflective practice may require others, such as a supervisor, colleague, or even an educational team to unpack some of the ways the teacher is feeling about the situation. Table 6.3 can help you get started.

Table 6.3 Reflective Practice to Restore Relationships
What happened today? (with a child, with a peer, with a supervisor, with a parent) and how did it make me feel (irritated, frustrated, mad, disrespected, invisible, incompetent)?
Where might those feelings come from?
How might it have felt to be (the child, peer, supervisor, family) and What might have been going on for him, her, or them?
What are my beliefs about this student and am I conveying these beliefs in my interactions with the student? If needed, how do I need to change my beliefs and interactions?

For a more comprehensive discussion of the importance of critical reflection as it relates to classroom interactions, see Howard (2003) and Millner, Cunningham, Delale-O'Connor, and Kestenberg (2019).

Using the EMR framework to develop robust relationships with all students provides the structure teachers need to intentionally use systematic strategies for all students throughout the year and across different classroom situations. By reflecting and examining interactions, teachers can uncover potentially harmful unconscious beliefs that may reproduce patterns of racism and ableism in their interactions and classroom community.

Relationships are critical for students' social emotional well-being and academic success. Effective STRs convey to students, "I see you, I hear you, I like you, I believe in you," and then practitioners use this relational knowledge to select curriculum, provide and scaffold effective instruction and learning activities that are relevant to students' lives and experiences. Universal Design for Learning provides a framework to scaffold instruction to make learning accessible, relevant and rigorous.

Universal Design for Learning (UDL)

UDL is a framework that seeks to make learning accessible for all students (CAST, 2018). For example, just as a ramp helps those who have physical challenges accessing a building, UDL gives students access to learning (Waitoller & Thorius, 2016). The principles of UDL were created following calls for better inclusion practices within the education system. More specifically, "while students with disabilities had gained physical access to the general education classroom, concerns were being raised about how these students would gain access to the general education curriculum" (Edyburn, pg. 34, 2010). The 1997 reauthorization of the Individuals with Disabilities Education Act (IDEA) and the Assistive Technology Act of 1998 defined and integrated practices of UDL (Edyburn, 2010). Then in 2004, the reauthorization of IDEA included UDL as a "scientifically valid framework for guiding educational practice" (Edyburn, 2010).

An important aspect of UDL is designing curriculum and instruction proactively rather than retrofitting it to meet a student's needs. This proactive approach not only provides access to students with disabilities but opens teaching and learning to all students. Without considering student diversity at the forefront, Rose refers to the curriculum as "disabling," rather than the students being dis/abled (Alim, Baglieri, Ladson-Billings, Paris, Rose, & Valente, 2017). The overall goal of UDL is to create expert learners who are purposeful and motivated, resourceful and knowledgeable, and strategic and goal directed (CAST, 2018). The three main principles of UDL, engagement, representation, and action and expression, are described briefly in Table 6.4. For more information on UDL, go to Cast.org.

Table 6.4 Universal Design for Learning Components

Multiple Means of Engagement	Focuses on the "why" of learning and includes ways to include student interest, choice, and support to self-regulate through self-assessment, reflection, and motivation.
Multiple Means of Representation	Addresses the "what" of learning and guides teachers to present information in multiple, flexible formats to honor all students' ways of understanding and make connections across content. This may include alternatives to auditory and visual information, through multiple media and options for language and symbols. The main outcome of this principle is to support comprehension of the content.
Multiple Means of Action and Expression	Addresses the "how" of learning and provides various ways for students to demonstrate knowledge, use technology, express and communicate understanding and competence.

Universal Design for Learning: Contemporary Context

If combined with high-quality instructional strategies, UDL is an effective framework for students with disabilities, especially when technology is integrated (Coyne, Pisha, Dalton, Zeph, & Smith, 2012). Technology can make a dramatic difference for students with disabilities and the use of applications and multimedia need to consider accessibility for individuals with disabilities (Smith & Harvey, 2014). When utilizing UDL and technology with students, it is vital that practitioners consider the students and how linguistic and cultural diversity affects students in the classroom. UDL provides access to the same learning environments and curriculum as those without disabilities. However, if the environment and curriculum are not culturally relevant/sustaining and continue to create opportunities for some students and more barriers for others, then the results may continue to perpetuate low academic performance for students from diverse cultures or racial backgrounds.

Next Steps for Universal Design for Learning

There are many opportunities for UDL, including ways to incorporate UDL in a more culturally sustaining way and application to distance learning. Every aspect of teaching, including UDL, can be improved when practitioners acknowledge and incorporate race, cultural, and linguistic assets and differences in their teaching. Earlier, we discussed how practitioners can learn about their students by developing effective STRs. Through STRs practitioners learn who their students are as individuals, their strengths, interests, and lived experiences and then can incorporate that knowledge as they plan to apply the three principles of UDL. This allows practitioners to use an asset approach and capitalize on the benefits of their students' diversity, rather than viewing students through a deficit lens (Villegas & Lucas, 2002; Yosso, 2005). The use of remote learning has exploded, and online educational resources are constantly changing (Lederman, 2020). Consequently, practitioners are spending more planning time transforming content typically done in-person to an online format (Smith & Lowrey, 2017). Technology opens up the availability of information, providing more opportunities for differentiated assessment and instantaneous feedback. The UDL framework applies to distance learning and can continue to make education accessible to students with disabilities.

Recent research is looking into the effectiveness of combining strategies that support inclusion like UDL with frameworks that integrate TPACK. Practitioners will be able to implement tools to create accessibility and have a guide to how technology and teaching can work together to make students with disabilities academically successful. Hopefully, more strategies will emerge on how to incorporate UDL principles and TPACK to promote the use of technology in teaching and learning (Al-Azawei, Parslow & Lundqvist, 2017).

What is Technological Pedagogical Content Knowledge (TPACK) and How is it Utilized?

In 1986, Lee Shulman identified practices there were specifically used to teach content and called them "pedagogical content knowledge." Koelher and Mishra (2005) then extended Shulman's work to recognize the impact of technology on content and pedagogy by coining the term "technological pedagogical content knowledge." This defined framework consists of identifying three types of knowledge (i.e. content, pedagogical, and technological) and seven knowledge components. These components include technological knowledge (TK), pedagogical knowledge (PK), content knowledge (CK), technological content knowledge (TCK), technological pedagogical knowledge (TPK), pedagogical content knowledge (PCK), and technological pedagogical content knowledge (TPCK).

Breakdown of the Seven Components of TPACK

Content knowledge (CK) highlights the educator's understanding of the specific subject matter and the information that must be taught and learned. It emphasizes the importance of practitioners needing to be subject matter experts prior to teaching the content, whereas technological content knowledge (TCK) adds an additional component of how technology assists in presenting and understanding the content. Pedagogical knowledge (PK) focuses on the educator's knowledge of the methods and practices utilized to convey the information that is being taught. Therefore, pedagogical knowledge (PK) entails integrating learning with how lessons are planned, the classroom management skills that are enacted, and how the content is assessed. When technological pedagogical knowledge (TPK) is applied, it highlights how technological devices and platforms help to support and even enhance the pedagogical decisions and strategies utilized by practitioners. Technological knowledge (TK) encompasses identifying the devices as well as the platforms needed to support the specific content that must be learned. Ultimately, this leads to technological pedagogical content knowledge (TPACK), which uses technology to enhance the teaching and learning of content areas.

Influence of TPACK in Special Education

Recognizing the influence of technology on the way content is taught, TPACK emerged for scholars from all different disciplines to explore. Prior to the theorizing of TPACK, special education viewed assistive technology as the primary use of embedding tools and equipment to support students' learning (Edyburn, 2013). However, due to TPACK, special education is now able to analyze and apply learnings from assistive technology, instructional technology, and the TPACK framework (Edyburn, 2013). Continued research of TPACK allows practitioners in special education to think about and implement the use of technology with their students to support learning specific content areas. Additionally, considering the changing modalities of teaching and whether students are able to learn in-person, remotely, or some combination of the two, TPACK has the potential to provide the disruptive change needed to continue to push the field of special education to explore the juncture between knowing the content, utilizing a variety of strategies to teach the content, and selecting the appropriate technology for the specific content that is being addressed. The case study below provides examples of ways the frameworks described in the chapter can be integrated in a school community to support students and families with disabilities and change mindsets of teachers to develop productive STRs and academic success for students with disabilities and their families.

Case Study 2: Changing Belief Systems About How Teachers Establish, Maintain, and Restore Relationships With Students

What do high expectations for students, a sense of belonging, connection to the classroom community, and culturally sustaining instruction look like together in a school? This case study highlights the experiences of teachers at an elementary school in the upper Midwest.

Specific strategies to nurture authentic relationships with students means being intentional about inclusionary practices and co-teaching. At this school, systems were created by school leaders to embed teacher-student learning partnerships and community building activities. In turn, students with disabilities could feel more connected with their teachers and participate equitably. Teachers consistently implemented CRT strategies, such as integrating "Trust Generators," into their daily routine. Practices such as a morning meeting, positive affirmations, and a collaborative approach to setting daily classroom goals helped build personal regard and "familiarity" between students and teachers. Also, teachers showed "selective vulnerability" by sharing personal challenges they encountered and teaching self-regulation strategies such as "yoga calm" to teach kids to cope with their own challenges (Hammond, 2015). Trust generators, such as familiarity and selective vulnerability, help build strong connections between students and teachers at the school. Students with disabilities had a safe space to share examples of their culture, births or illnesses that were going on in their families, and other life transitions.

It is important to examine how bias influences STRs and responses to managing behavior. During the past seven years, the school put time and effort into changing belief systems about how teachers establish, maintain, and restore relationships with students, hoping that it would have a positive effect on the academic performance, personal satisfaction, and sense of belonging of the students with disabilities. Also, the school put resources and professional development into models such as UDL, TPACK, and culturally responsive teaching; however, the glue that held these systems together, according to the

Case Study 2: Changing Belief Systems About How Teachers Establish, Maintain, and Restore Relationships With Students, (continued)

principal of the school, was "maintaining relationships between teachers and students, especially during the most challenging times" (M. Kalinowski, personal communication, July 29, 2020).

The school's system to manage behavior evolved over time. The school's principal stated, "We saw the same predictable patterns that were present when we had seclusion rooms. Once a student had a significant outburst, they would be sent out of the room and their behavior problem would be outsourced to someone else. There was no repair or connection with the child's teacher after they were sent out of class. Now that we focus on supporting the student–teacher relationship, we're seeing better results." (M. Kalinowski, personal communication, July 29, 2020).

Culturally Sustaining Practices Integrated Across the School Community

Specific strategies to nurture authentic relationships with students means having conversations about race, decentering Whiteness, and learning to adopt a multicultural or transcultural mindset through culturally responsive teaching (CRT). The educators and leaders worked hard to foster strong avenues for communication and trust between general education teachers, special education teachers, support staff, and other related-service professionals and community, keeping conversations about racial equity and access at the forefront. Based on school-wide observation data of every classroom, there were high levels of practices and interactions that signify high expectations, teacher credibility, socio-political and cultural consciousness, and activities that affirm identity. Examples included frequent questioning from teachers, collaborative student activities, multiple pathways to access and present information, scaffolds and differentiation such as anchor charts and visuals, and diverse literature and racial perspectives. Furthermore, when the school examined data and noticed that the use of the behavior room led to a disproportionate number of students of color being sent there and disrupting the STRs, they discontinued it. According to Hammond (2015), relationships are the "on-ramp" to learning in culturally responsive teaching. UDL and TPACK are the beams that support strong relationships.

Flexible Paths to Learning

Before holding students with disabilities to high expectations, we must ensure that there are flexible paths for learning within instructional goals, methods, materials, and assessments (Meyer, Rose, & Gordon, 2014). Educators and school leaders implemented school-wide evidence-based frameworks such as UDL and TPACK to make sure learning was accessible for all students. Students have shown to be successful when they participate in school-wide frameworks

Case Study 2: Changing Belief Systems About How Teachers Establish, Maintain, and Restore Relationships With Students, (continued)

that are "accessible for all students, up-front and not after-the-fact, using both technology and pedagogical strategies" (Kavita, Smith, & Lowrey, pg. 38, 2017). For example, teachers and teacher coaches lead workshops on UDL and other engaging tools and strategies that could be applied to lesson plans and reading, writing, and math curriculum in a culturally sustaining way by building the curriculum based on the racial and cultural experiences of students of color.

Technology Integration to Support Student Success and Access

Due to the COVID-19 pandemic in 2020, thousands of schools in the United States had no choice but to rely on remote learning for schooling (Kamenetz, 2020). Since all learning was remote, it was important to use technology to create spaces to learn but also maintain communication and relationships with families to make sure they were supported. The district of the school in this case study provided free wi-fi access to all families who didn't have the internet at their home, established food pickup spots, and hundreds of educators and other school staff gathered and distributed resources to help families who lacked necessities.

During remote learning, a wide variety of applications were used dynamically for students with disabilities to maintain consistent social-emotional support and maintain relationships with students and families. Teachers addressed servicing students with disabilities virtually by creating adaptive online assignments, virtual conferencing with students, academic interventions and self-regulation instruction, and adapting and modifying general education assignments. Accommodations for students included using mobile device tools that support writing, reading, math, and organizing academic work.

This school demonstrated the mindset that students and families of color are a resource that teachers and educator leaders should tap into rather than an element to be assimilated. As a result outcomes for students improved and more students were included in the general education classroom and school community. Teachers became more skilled at using technology as a tool for differentiation and collaborating with colleagues across domains to create lesson plans that reflect student voice and choice. Suspensions and restrictive procedures used on students decreased since seclusion rooms were discontinued. According to one teacher, "We're truly seeing an environment that's representative of our larger community and beneficial for all students, including those with disabilities. This should be the standard for every school."

Summary

In this chapter, we described the research on STRs and how students with disabilities and of color experience barriers and potentially miss out on the positive effects of STRs. There is not an easy fix and the causes of tenuous STRs are deep and complex. The first step in establishing positive STRs is related to mindsets. Instead of seeing students as broken and using interventions to fix students, practitioners need to consider how bias, racism, and ableism influence daily interactions with students. Then we need to change these mindsets so that children are positioned as sense-makers, capable of doing meaningful work and as humans worthy of love and affirmation (Teachingworks.org). Given the mindset of seeing students as capable and worthy, practitioners are more likely to leverage the frameworks of UDL and TPACK in culturally sustaining ways to lead to academic success for students with ASD and ID.

Guiding Questions

1. What is the importance of building authentic relationships with students with developmental disabilities including autism and intellectual disability through culturally sustaining pedagogy?
2. What are the contributing factors promoting and interfering with building effective relationships with students with developmental disabilities including autism and intellectual disability?
3. What are some relationship strategies and academic frameworks to ensure social emotional learning (SEL) and academic success for diverse students with developmental disabilities including autism and intellectual disabilities?

References

Al-Azawei, A., Parslow, P., & Lundqvist, K. (2017). The effect of universal design for learning (UDL) application on E-learning acceptance: A structural equation model. *International Review of Research in Open and Distance Learning, 18*(6), 54–87.

Alim, H.S., & Paris, D. (2017). What is culturally sustaining pedagogy and why does it matter. In D Paris & H.S. Alim (Eds), *Culturally sustaining pedagogies: Teaching and learning for justice in a changing world* (pp. 1-21). Teachers College Press, New York.

Ashburner, J., Ziviani, J., & Rodger, S. (2010). Surviving in the mainstream: Capacity of children with autism spectrum disorders to perform academically and regulate their emotions and behavior at school. *Research in Autism Spectrum Disorders, 4*(1), 18–27.doi:10.1016/j.rasd.2009.07.002

Alim, H.S., Baglieri, S., Ladson-Billings, G., Paris, G., Rose, D.H., & Valente, J.M. (2017). Responding to "Cross-pollinating culturally sustaining pedagogy and universal design for learning: Toward an inclusive pedagogy that accounts for Dis/Ability." *Harvard Educational Review, 87*, 4-25.

Annamma, S. A., Connor, D., & Ferri, B. (2013). Dis/ability critical race studies (DisCrit): Theorizing at the intersections of race and dis/ability. *Race Ethnicity and Education, 16*(1), 1–31. https://doi.org/10.1080/13613324.2012.730511

Annamma, S.A., & Morrison, D.(2018). DisCrit classroom ecology: Using praxis to dismantle dysfunctional education ecologies. *Teaching and Teacher Education, 73*, 70-80.

Baker, J. A. (2006). Contributions of teacher-child relationships to positive school adjustment during elementary school. *Journal of School Psychology, 44*(3), 211–229. https://doi.org/10.1016/j.jsp.2006.02.002

Ball, D. (2020, July 16). Teaching is powerful [Twitter moment]. Retrieve from https://twitter.com/teachingworks/status/1283808366939308033?s=21

Bierman, K. L. (2011). The promise and potential of studying the "invisible hand" of teacher influence on peer relations and student outcomes: A commentary. *Journal of Applied Developmental Psychology, 32*(5), 297–303.doi:10.1016/j.appdev.2011.04.004

Blacher, J., Baker, B. L., & Eisenhower, A. S. (2009). Student–teacher relationship stability across early school years for children with intellectual disability or typical development. *American Journal on Intellectual and Developmental Disabilities, 114*, 322–339.

Blacher, J., Howell, E., Lauderdale-Littin, S., Reed, F. D., & Laugeson, E. A. (2014). Autism spectrum disorder and the student–teacher relationship. A comparison study with peers with intellectual disability and typical development. *Research in Autism Spectrum Disorders, 8*(3), 324–333.

Blanchett, W. J. (2010). Telling it like it is: The role of race, class, and culture in the perpetuation of learning disability as a privileged category for the White middle class. *Disability Studies Quarterly, 30*. doi:10.18061/dsq.v30i2.1233

Broderick, A., & Leonoardo, Z. (2016). What a good boy: The deployment and distribution of "goodness" as ideological property in schools. In D. J. Connor, B. A. Ferri, & S. A. Annamma (Eds.), *DisCritddisability studies and critical race theory in education* (pp. 55e67). New York: Teachers College Press.

Caplan, B., Feldman, M., Eisenhower, A., & Blacher, J. (2016). Student-teacher relationships for young children with autism spectrum disorder: Risk and Protective Factors. *Journal of Autism Developmental Disorders, 46*, 3653-3666.

CAST (2018). Universal Design for Learning Guidelines version 2.2. Retrieved from http://udlguidelines.cast.org

Cederlund, M., Hagberg, B., Billstedt, E., Gillberg, I. C., & Gillberg, C. (2008). Asperger syndrome and autism: A comparative longitudinal follow-up study more than 5 years after original diagnosis. *Journal of Autism and Developmental Disorders, 38*, 72–85.

Cohen, G. L., Garcia, J., Apfel, N., & Master, A. (2006). Reducing the racial achievement gap: A social-psychological intervention. *Science, 313*(5791), 1307–1310. doi:10.1126/science.1128317

Cook, C. R., Coco, S., Zhang, Y., Duong, M. T., Renshaw, T. L., & Frank, S. (2018). Cultivating positive teacher-student relationships: Preliminary evaluation of the Establish-Maintain-Restore (EMR) method. *School Psychology Review, 47*(3), 226–243. https://doi.org/10.17105/SPR-2017-0025.V47-3

Cook, C.R., Coco, S., Zhang, Y., Fiat, A.E., Duong, M.T., Renshaw, T.L., Long, A. C., Frank, S.| (2018). Cultivating positive teacher–student relationships: Preliminary evaluation of the Establish–Maintain–Restore (EMR) Method, *School Psychology Review, 47*:3, 226-243.

Cornelius-White, J. (2007). Learner-centered teacher-student relationships are effective: A meta-analysis. *Review of Educational Research, 77*(1), 113–143. https://doi.org/10.3102/003465430298563

Coyne, P., Pisha, B., Dalton, B., Zeph, L., & Smith, N. (2012). Literacy by design: A universal design for learning approach for students with significant intellectual disabilities. *Remedial and Special Education, 33*(3), 162–172. https://doi.org/10.1177/0741932510381651

Danker, J., Strnadová, I., & Cumming, T. M. (2019). They don't have a good life if we keep thinking that they're doing it on purpose!": Teachers' perspectives on the well-being of students with Autism. *Journal of Autism and Developmental Disorders, 49*(7), 2923–2934. https://doi.org/10.1007/s10803-019-04025-w

Dekker, M. C., Koot, H. M., van der Ende, J., & Verhulst, F. C. (2002). Emotional and behavioral problems in children and adolescents with and without intellectual disability. *Journal of Child Psychology and Psychiatry, 43*, 1087–1098.

Domina, T., Penner, A., & Penner, E. (2017). Categorical inequality: Schools as sorting machines. *Annual Review of Sociology, 43*, 311–330. doi:10.1146/annurev-soc-060116-053354

Duong, M. T., Pullmann, M. D., Buntain-Ricklefs, J., Lee, K., Benjamin, K. S., Nguyen, L., & Cook, C. R. (2018). Brief teacher training improves student behavior and student-teacher relationships in middle school. *School Psychology Quarterly, 34*(2), 212–221. https://doi.org/10.1037/spq0000296

Edyburn, D. L.(2010). Would you recognize universal design for learning if you saw it? Ten propositions for new directions for the second decade of UDL. *Learning disability quarterly 33*, 33–41.

Edyburn, D.L. (2013). Critical issues in advancing the special education technology evidence base. *Exceptional Children, 80*(1), 7-24.

Eisenhower, A., Blacher, J., & Bush, H. (2015). Longitudinal associations between externalizing problems and student–teacher relationship quality for young children with ASD. *Research in Autism Spectrum Disorders, 9*, 163–173.

Eisenhower, A. S., Baker, B. L., & Blacher, J. (2007). Early student–teacher relationships of children with and without intellectual disability: Contributions of behavioral, social, and self-regulatory competence. *Journal of School Psychology, 45*, 363–383.

Eyal, G. (2013). For a sociology of expertise: The social origins of the autism epidemic. *American Journal of Sociology, 118*, 863–907. doi:10.1086/668448

Fadus, M.C., Ginsburg, K.R., Sobowale, K., Halliday-Boykins-Halliday, C., Bryant, B., Gray, K.M., & Squeglia, L.M. (2020). Unconscious bias and the diagnosis of disruptive behavior disorders and ADHD in African American and Hispanic Youth. *Academic Psychiatry, 44*, 95-102.

Fierros, E. G., & Conroy, J. W. (2002). Double jeopardy: An exploration of restrictiveness and race in special education. In D. J. Losen & G. Orfield (Eds.), *Racial inequity in special education* (pp. 39-70). Cambridge, MA: Harvard Education Press.

Fish, R.E. (2019). Standing out and sorting in: Exploring the role of racial composition in racial disparities in special education. *American Educational Research Journal, 56*, 2573-2608.

Gaffney, C. (2019). When schools cause trauma. Teaching Tolerance, 62. https://www.tolerance.org/magazine/summer-2019/when-schools-cause-trauma

Gay, G. (2010). *Culturally responsive teaching* 2nd Ed. Teachers College Press.

Gillborn, D., Rollock, N., Vincent, C., & Ball, S. J. (2012). 'You got a pass, so what more do you want?': Race, class and gender intersections in the educational experiences of the Black middle class. *Race, Ethnicity and Education, 15*(1), 121-139.

Ginott, H.G., (1972). *Teacher and child: A book for parents and teachers*. Macmillan Company, New York.

Goodland, J.I. (1990). *Teachers for our nation's schools*. Jossey-Bass.

Hammond, Z. (2015). *Culturally responsive teaching and the brain: Promoting authentic engagement and rigor among culturally and linguistically diverse students.* Corwin Press, Thousand Oaks, CA.

Hamre, B. K., & Pianta, R. C. (2001). Early teacher-child relationships and the trajectory of children's school outcomes through eighth grade. *Child Development, 72*(2), 625–638. https://doi.org/10.1111/1467-8624.00301

Harry, B., & Anderson, M. (1994). The disproportionate placement of African American males in special education programs: A critique of the process. *Journal of Negro Education, 63*, 602–619. doi:10.2307/2967298

Hibbard, R., & Desch, L. (2007). Maltreatment of children with disabilities. *Pediatrics, 119*(5), 1018–1025.

Howard, T.C. (2003). Culturally relevant pedagogy: Ingredients for critical teacher reflection. *Theory Into Practice, 42*, 195-202.

Hughes, J. N., & Kwok, O. (2006). Classroom engagement mediates the effect of teacher-student support on elementary students' peer acceptance: A prospective analysis. *Journal of School Psychology, 43,* 465–480. doi:10.1016/j.jsp.2005.10.001

Jackson,Y. (2011). *The pedagogy of confidence: Inspiring high intellectual performance in urban schools*. Teachers College Press.

Jennings, P. A., & Greenberg, M. T. (2009). The prosocial classroom: Teacher social and emotional competence in relation to student and classroom outcomes. *Review of Educational Research, 79*, 491–525. http://dx.doi.org/10.3102/0034654308325693

Kamenetz, A. (2020, July 9). When It Comes to Reopening Schools, 'The Devil's in The Details,' Educators say. National Public Radio. Retrieved July 7, 2020 from https://www.npr.org/2020/07/09/888878030/when-it-comes-to-reopening-schools-the-devil-s-in-the-details-educators-say?utm_campaign=storyshare&utm_source=twitter.com&utm_medium=social

Kavita, R. Smith, S,J., Lowrey, K.A., (2017). UDL and Intellectual Disability: What do we know and where do we go?" *Intellectual and Developmental Disabilities,* 55, 37–47.

Kerns, C., Newschaffer, C., & Berkowitz, S. (2015). Traumatic childhood events and autism spectrum disorder. *Journal of Autism and Developmental Disorders,* 45(11), 3475–3486.

Kincade L., Cook,C., & Goerdt, A. (2020). Meta-analysis and common practice elements of universal approaches to improving student-teacher relationships. *Review of Educational Research* XX, (X), pp. 1–39, DOI:https://doi.org/10.3102/0034654320946836

Koehler, M. J., & Mishra, P. (2005). What happens when teachers design educational technology? The development of Technological Pedagogical Content Knowledge. *Journal of Educational Computing Research*, 32(2), 131-152.

Koerner, K. (2012). *Doing dalectical behavior therapy*. New York, NY: The Guildford Press.

Ladson-Billings, G. (1995). But that's just good teaching! The case for culturally relevant pedagogy. *Theory Into Practice, 34,* 159-165.

Ladson-Billings, G. (2017). The (R) Evolution will not be standardized: Teacher education, hip hop pedagogy, and culturally relevant pedagogy 2.0. In D. Paris & H.S. Alim (eds) *Culturally sustaining pedagogies*. Teachers College Press.

Ladson-Billings, G. (2020, June 23-25). *Culturally Relevant Pedagogy in a Post COVID-19 World* [Conference presentation]. National Urban Alliance Summer Institute, Minneapolis, MN, United States.

Lambert, N. M., Stillman, T. F., Hicks, J. A., Kamble, S., Baumeister, R. F., & Fincham, F. D. (2013). To belong is to matter: Sense of belonging enhances meaning in life. *Personality and Social Psychology Bulletin, 39*(11), 1418–1427. https://doi.org/10.1177/0146167213499186

Lederman, D. (2020, March 18). Will shift to remote teaching be boon or bane for online learning? *Inside Higher Ed,* https://www.insidehighered.com/digital-learning/article/2020/03/18/most-teaching-going-remote-will-help-or-hurt-online-learning

Liang, C. T.H., Rocchino, G.H., Gutekunst, M.H., Paulvin, C., Li, K.M. Elam-Snowden (2020). Perspectives of respect, teacher-student relationships and school climate among boys of color: A multi-focus group study. *Psychology of Men and Masculinities. 21*, 345-356.

Liu, K.-Y. K., King, M. M., & Bearman, P. S. P. (2010). Social influence and the autism epidemic. *American Journal of Sociology, 115*, 1387–1434. doi:10.1086/651448

Longobardi, C., Prino, L. E., Pasta, T., Gastaldi, F. G. M., & Quaglia, R. (2012). Measuring the quality of teacher–child interaction in autistic disorder. *European Journal of Investigation in Health, Psychology and Education, 2*(3), 103–114.

Marzano, R. J., Pickering, D. J., & Pollock, J. E. (2001). *Classroom instruction that works: Research-based strategies for increasing student achievement*. Alexandria, VA: Association for Supervision and Curriculum Development.

Master, B., Loeb, S., & Wyckoff, J. (2014). *Learning that lasts: Unpacking variation in teachers' effects on students' long-term knowledge* (Working Paper 104). New York, NY.

McIntyre, L. L., Blacher, J., & Baker, B. L. (2006). The transition to school: Adaptation in young children with and without intellectual disability. *Journal of Intellectual Disability Research, 50*, 349–361.

Migambi, A., Neal, R.A. (August, 2018). Excluded: The role of race and exclusionary practices in Minnesota's special education. Minnesota Education Equity Partnership (MNEEP).

Millner, H.R., Cunningham, H.B., Delale-O'Connor, L., Kestenberg, E.G. (2019). *These kids are out of control: Why we must reimagine classroom management for equity*. Corwin.

Murray,C. & Pianta, R.,C. (2007). The importance of teacher-student relationships for adolescents with high incidence disabilities. *Theory into Practice*, 46, 105-112.

Ong-Dean, C. (2009). *Distinguishing disability: Parents, privilege, and special education*. Chicago, IL: University of Chicago Press.

Opportunity Gap - Talking Points. (n.d.). Retrieved September 29, 2020, from http://schottfoundation.org/issues/opportunity-gap/talking-points

Pianta, R. C. (1999). Enhancing relationships between children and teachers. *American Psychological Association*. https://doi.org/10.1037/10314-000

Pianta, R. C. (2001). Student–teacher relationship scale: professional manual. Odessa, FL: Psychological Assessment Resources, Inc.

Pianta, R. C., Hamre, B. K., & Allen, J. P. (2012). Teacher-student relationships and engagement: Conceptualizing, measuring, and improving the capacity of classroom interactions. In S. L. Christenson, A. L. Reschly, & C. Wylie (Eds.), *Handbook of research on student engagement* (pp. 365–386). Springer Science. https://doi.org/10.1007/978-1-4614-2018-7_17

Pianta, R. C., Steinberg, M. S., & Rollins, K. B. (1995). The first two years of school: Teacher–child relationships and deflections in children's classroom adjustment. Development and Psychopathology, 7, 297–312.

Quin, D. (2016). Longitudinal and contextual associations between teacher-student relationships and student engagement: A systematic review. *Review of Educational Research*, 87(2), 345–387. https://doi.org/10.3102/0034654316669434

Robertson, K., Chamberlain, B., & Kasari, C. (2003). General education teachers' relationships with included students with autism. *Journal of Autism and Developmental Disorders, 33*(2), 123–130.

Saft, E. W., & Pianta, R. C. (2001). Teachers' perceptions of their relationships with students: Effects of child age, gender, and ethnicity of teachers and children. *School Psychology Quarterly*, 16, 125–141. doi:10.1521/scpq.16.2.125.18698

Scott, T.M.(2017). *Teaching behavior: Managing classrooms through effective instruction*. Corwin.

Serpell, Z. N., & Mashburn, A. J. (2012). Family-school connectedness and children's early social development. *Social Development, 21*, 21–46.

Shulman, L. S. (1986). Those who understand: Knowledge growth in teaching. *Educational Researcher*, *15*(2), 4-14.

Skiba, R., Artiles, A., Kozleski, D., Losen, D., Harry E. (2016). Risks and consequences of oversimplifying educational inequities: A response to Morgan et al. (2015). *Educational Researcher, 45*, 221-225.

Smith, S., & Harvey, E. (2014). K-12 online lesson alignment to the principles of Universal Design for Learning: the Khan Academy. *Open Learning: The Journal of Open, Distance and e-Learning, 29*(3), 222–242.

Smith, S., & Lowrey, K. (2017). Applying the Universal Design for Learning Framework for Individuals with Intellectual Disability: The Future Must Be Now. Intellectual and Developmental Disabilities, 55(1), 48–51.

Spilt, J. Koomen, H.M.Y., & Thijs, J.T., (2011). Teacher wellbeing: The importance of teacher-student relationships. *Educational Psychology Review, 23*, 457-477.

Substance Abuse and Mental Health Services Administration. (2014). Concept of trauma and guidance for a trauma-informed approach. Retrieved September 2020, from http://store.samhsa.gov/product/ SAMHSA-s-Concept-of-Trauma-and-Guidance-for-a-TraumaInformed-Approach/SMA14-4884

Teaching works.org (2020). Building respectful relationships retrieved from: https://library.teachingworks.org/curriculum-resources/teaching-practices/building-respectful-relationships/

Villegas, A. M., & Lucas, T. (2002). Preparing culturally responsive teachers: Reshaping the curriculum. *Journal of Teacher Education, 53*(1), 20-32.

Waitoller, F. R., & Thorius, K. A. K. (2016). Cross-pollinating culturally sustaining pedagogy and universal design for learning: Toward an inclusive pedagogy that accounts for dis/ability. *Harvard Educational Review, 86*(3), 366–389. doi: 10.17763/1943-5045-86.3.366

Walton, J., Priest, N., Kowal, E., White, F., Fox, B., & Paradies, Y. (2016). Whiteness and national identity: Teacher discourses in Australian primary schools. *Race, Ethnicity and Education, 21*(1), 132-147.

Wit, David J. De et al. "Perceptions of Declining Classmate and Teacher Support Following the Transition to High School: Potential Correlates of Increasing Student Mental Health Difficulties." *Psychology in the Schools* 48.6 (2011): 556–572.

Yeager, D. S., Purdie-Vaughns, V., Garcia, J., Apfel, N., Brzustoski, P., Master, A., . . . Cohen, G. L. (2014). Breaking the cycle of mistrust: Wise interventions to provide critical feedback across the racial divide. *Journal of Experimental Psychology: General, 143*(2), 804–824. doi:10.1037/a0033906

Yosso, T. J. (2005). Whose culture has capital? A critical race theory discussion of community cultural wealth. *Race Ethnicity and Education, 8*, 69-91.

Chapter 7

Empowering families by utilizing culturally sustaining strategies in the education of children with multi-layered identities

Jamie N. Pearson, Megan-Brette Hamilton, L. Lynn Stansberry Brusnahan, and Deeqaifrah Hussein

---

Objectives

- Explain legislation in regard to family involvement in special education.
- Describe the intersectional experiences and identify the needs of families participating in the special education process.
- Describe culturally sustaining strategies to effectively empower families to facilitate parent-professional collaboration, and promote self-determination in families.

This chapter provides culturally sustaining strategies to address the identified needs of families who have children with developmental disabilities, such as autism and intellectual disability (ID). Many families of children with disabilities share commonalities with several communities and thus have multiple layered social identities (e.g., an African American male student with autism). This chapter describes the legislation that mandates family involvement in special education and highlights the intersectional experiences of families participating in the special education process. The purpose of this chapter is to provide culturally sustaining practices that are rooted in empowerment and address multidimensionality to strengthen student outcomes. This chapter focuses on supporting empowerment among all families, including those who identify with historically marginalized racial and ethnic groups in the United States. This chapter uses the term "diverse" broadly to describe inclusive groups of individuals across racial and ethnic backgrounds. Additionally, we use the term "caregiver" to refer to fathers, mothers, grandparents, aunts, uncles, siblings, foster parents, legal guardians, and others who serve in the primary care role for a child with a disability.

Table 7.1 Key Terminology	
Caregiver	The person who provides primary care for a child.
Community	A nest of relationships that share commonalities which may include a sense of place, interests, perspectives, and social ties. Individuals can be a part of multiple communities that may or may not be interwoven.
Cultural Humility	The ability to understand the family's cultural perspectives and what they are experiencing in our school settings and make sure families' culture is present in the school community.
Empowerment	A social process of defining what is important, gathering the resources needed, and taking action to achieve desired goals.
Family	A variety of structures that include members who regard themselves as a unit. These relationships may include biological status, marriage or partnership status, living arrangement status, or one's own understanding of family.
Partnership	"A relationship in which families (not just parents) and professionals agree to build on each others' expertise and resources, as appropriate, for the purpose of making and implementing decisions that will directly benefit students and indirectly benefit other family members and professionals" (Turnbull et al., 2011, p. 137).
Power imbalance	Results when difficulties that seem to "belong" to parents are combined with the attitudes and behavior of professionals to produce discourse in which power is loaded on the side of professionals (Harry, 1992).

Legislation and Families

Legislation protects children with disabilities by providing important rights to parents. For families to advocate effectively for their children, they must be aware of these educational rights. One foundational principle of the Individual with Disabilities Education Act (IDEA) is the right of parents to participate in educational decisions regarding their child. The following are key rights of parents in the special education process:

- Parents are members of any evaluation or identification team that determines whether the child is a "child with a disability" and meets eligibility criteria for special education and related services (§300.306(a)(1)).

Chapter 7

- Parents have the right to participate in meetings related to the educational placement decisions and the provision of a free appropriate public education to the child (FAPE) (34 CFR §300.501(b); §§300.501(c) and 300.327).
- Parents are members of the individualized education program (IEP) team that develops, reviews, and revises the program and plan for the child (§300.321(a)(1)).
- If neither parent can attend the IEP meeting, the school is required to use other methods to ensure their participation, including individual or conference calls (§300.322(c)).

One way for families to gain information on their rights is from a Parent Training and Information Center. These centers, located in every state and funded by IDEA, help families of children (birth to age 22) who receive special education services with free support and information on how to make the most of their child's education. Next, we highlight the needs of families who have children participating in special education.

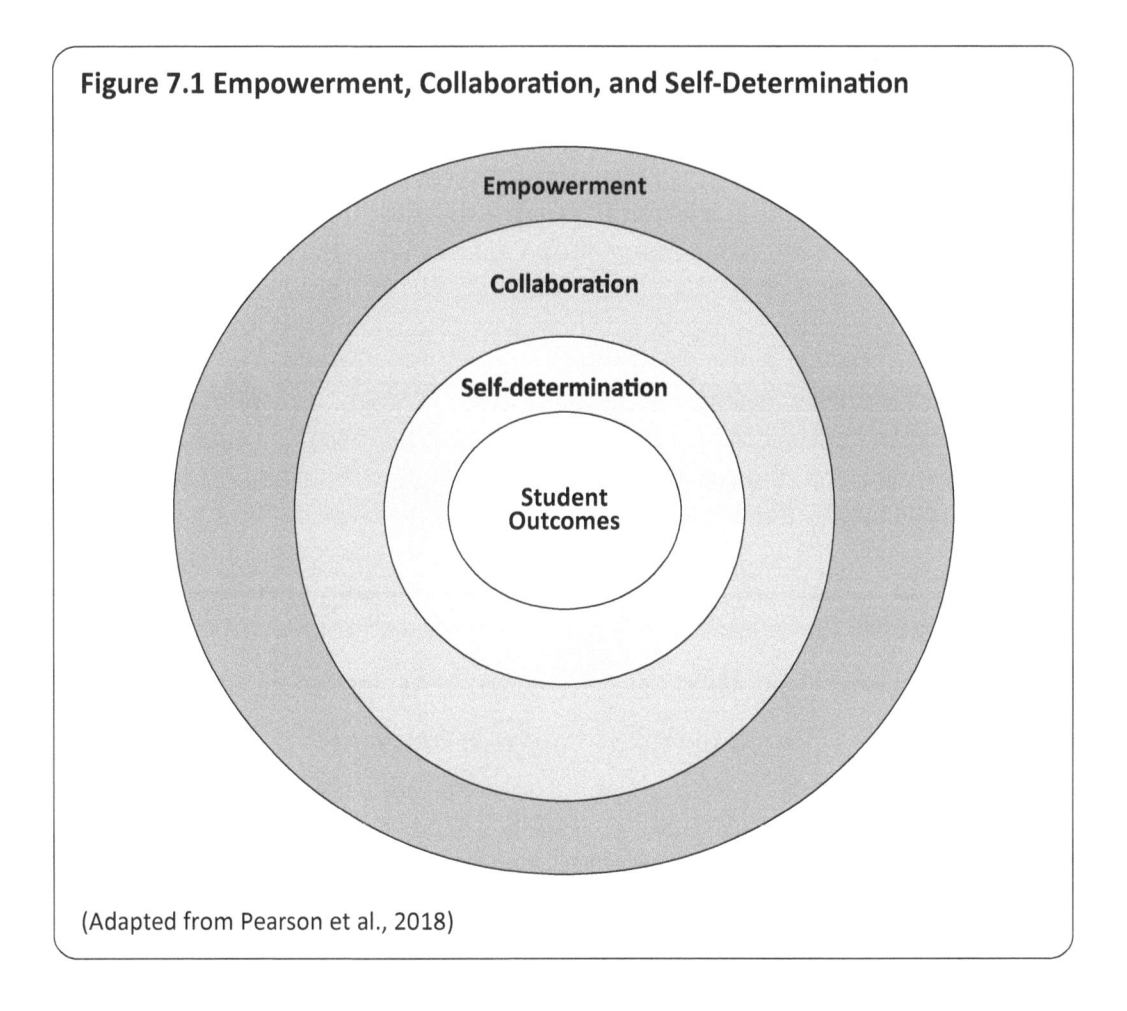

Figure 7.1 Empowerment, Collaboration, and Self-Determination

(Adapted from Pearson et al., 2018)

Understanding the Needs of Caregivers With Children in Special Education

The following literature review examines research about families who have children participating in special education. In these families, the role of the caregiver includes information seeker, problem solver, committee member, public educator, political activist, and spokesperson for the specific needs of the child (Minnes et al., 2003). This review identifies needs and lays the foundation for culturally sustaining strategies that are rooted in empowering families to participate in their needed roles. We explore empowerment through the lens of caregivers participating in special education and we examine some of the identified challenges to having a sense of control over the process. Empowerment is the power (e.g., personal, interpersonal, or political) to take action and work with others to influence and improve situations (Parsons et al. 1998; Whitley et al., 2011). Power is an essential feature of empowerment. There is ample research highlighting caregivers' need for empowerment (Chadiha, et al., 2004; Cox & Parsons, 1996; Dunst et al., 1988; Freire, 1983; Gutierrez, 1994; Kieffer, 1984; Parsons, 1991; Rappaport, 1987).

Early research around caregiver empowerment suggests that empowerment is a central goal in families' efforts to access and improve services for children with disabilities (Koren, et al., 1992). Strengthening empowerment among caregivers is particularly important because of the social injustice that makes families from marginalized communities more susceptible to vulnerability (Whitley et al., 2011). When caregivers feel powerless, they may feel challenged to participate fully in the complex educational process and struggle to advocate successfully to effect change and ensure adequate support for an appropriate education for their child with a disability (Ewles et al., 2014; Pearson et al., 2018). Perceptions of not being empowered can lead to feelings of self-blame and hopelessness, further inhibiting caregivers from taking action to address their child's needs (Kieffer, 1984). Family cultural differences, discrimination, lack of knowledge, lack of access to services, stigma, and poor communication are some of the many "power blocks" that heighten perceptions of powerlessness and are potential barriers to getting the services that children need to reach their full potential (AADM, 2020; Parsons et al., 1998; Pearson, 2015). Power imbalances can occur when difficulties perceived to "belong" to parents are combined with the attitudes and behavior of professionals to produce discourse in which power is loaded on the side of professionals (Harry, 1992).

Racial Inequities in Special Education

U.S. federal laws prohibit racial discrimination in our education system; however, it does not prevent implicit racial biases. Families experiencing discrimination (e.g., Spanish-speaking, African Americans) may experience less empowerment and be at a disadvantage when dealing with schools than those who do not experience discrimination (Delgado-Gaitan, 1990; Harry, 1992a). Historically, children and their families from minority communities have faced many challenges rooted in systemic inequality in U.S. schools (Darling-Hammond, 2000). Due to racial, cultural, and linguistic differences between school and home settings, some caregivers feel disconnected from schools, often resulting in estrangement, alienation, and discrimination when interacting with practitioners and attempting to access services (Adelman, 1994; Bempechat, 1992; Comer & Haynes, 1991; Lovelace et al. 2018). These experiences can lead to caregivers feeling suspicious and distrustful of the educational institution (Brandon et al., 2010). Discrimination and racism are a pervasive and constant element in the schooling experiences for some communities (Castagno & Brayboy, 2008; Deyhle, 1994).

Caregiver Knowledge

Caregivers who have limited experience or knowledge related to typical child development or disability may experience less empowerment. This lack of empowerment can impact caregivers' confidence in advocating for services for children with disabilities. African American parents, for example, rate parent education and training as important and suggest that there is a need for opportunities to access information about disabilities such as autism (Gourdine et al., 2011; Pearson, 2020). While a caregiver may have a child with a disability, they may not understand or be ready to accept the disability (Ho & Keiley, 2003). Denial can be a barrier to children getting the intervention they need (Pearson et al., 2020). Caregivers may not understand the connection between their child's delays or behaviors as they relate to the disability as they may not have observed other children or examined typical child development (Susman, 2007). When caregivers do not understand autism and a professional mentions autism, the caregiver might envision a severe and profound image of disability, given their perceptions of the disability. While some caregivers may not recognize disability characteristics, others may not have the language to describe the characteristics (Pearson & Meadan, 2018). In a study in the Somali community, caregivers reported having a limited understanding of autism and reported a lack of education and awareness about autism (Aragsan, 2016). Some families may not understand the cause of the disability or have a different view of "typical development."

There is high variability in how families select and access services after their child is identified with a disability (Goin-Kochel et al., 2007; Miller et al., 2012). For example, some caregivers may view the child's disability as a medical issue that requires only medical attention and not understand the value of educational interventions. Hispanic immigrant families of children with autism were found to think that autism was a temporary condition that would be cured through divine intervention (Ijalba, 2016). Hmong parents report difficulties understanding the U.S. educational system and a limited understanding of special education (Wathum-Ocama & Rose, 2002) and what is expected of them in their child's education (Lee,

2005). A lack of knowledge can impact caregivers' participation in the educational process, which can contribute to low student achievement (Epstein, 1996). Given the challenges related to equity in access to services, knowledge is a critical need for families so they can gain advocacy skills (Meadan et al. 2010; Mueller and Carranza 2011; Pearson et al., 2020).

Family Support

Family empowerment can be impacted when families lack support (Meadan et al. 2010; Mueller and Carranza 2011; Pearson et al., 2020). For example, African American families of children with autism report difficulties in obtaining support and have identified challenges with finding professionals they trust, who are responsive and empathetic, and who care about their family's needs (Pearson & Meadan 2018). In some instances, families are aware of their needs stemming from power inequities, but may not have the confidence or resources enough to create social support systems (Whitley et al., 2011). When examining support groups, researchers found stark differences in participation; only 2% of Latino and 5% of African American families participated in support groups, compared to 87% of White families (Mandell & Salzer, 2007). Findings indicate that while minority families raising children with autism find the services helpful, in many instances they are unaware that the supports exist in their communities (Pearson et al., 2020). In addition, research indicates that Black families, in particular, prefer more informal resources such as churches, in lieu of more formal supports such as mental health services and vocational rehabilitation (Andrews et al., 2011; Gourdine et al., 2011; Ward & Besson, 2012). Therefore, the way families define and engage in support systems can vary by culture, access, and needs. The reflective exercises from Chapter 1 can help practitioners assess how they are currently supporting (or not supporting) these systems.

Service Access and Utilization

Empowerment can be impacted by caregivers experiencing a need for services and resources (Whitley et al., 2011). Caregivers of children with disabilities can experience poverty, work in low-paying jobs, and receive public assistance without adequate resources to meet all their needs (Poindexter & Linsk, 1999; Simpson & Lawrence-Webb, 2009). Families of children with autism from low socioeconomic statuses (SES) report needing more information about services with parents' knowledge impeding their ability to meet their child's needs (Pickard & Ingersoll, 2016). Pearson et al. (2020) found that 50% of African American parents participating in a program did not know about available autism services in their communities and another 30% who were aware of available services did not use them, suggesting barriers related to knowledge of and access to services. While advocating is a critical step to accessing services for children with autism, many underrepresented families face culturally insensitive service provision (Pearson & Meadan, 2018). In a study, parents of African American children reported providers' lack of concern and negative response delayed access to early intervention services (Pearson et al., 2018).

Two barriers to accessing services are: a) inaccurate and untimely diagnoses and b) disparities in diagnosis (Pearson, 2015; Pearson & Meadan, 2018). Some health care providers do not utilize culturally appropriate screenings and find it difficult to recognize symptoms and signs in African American and Latino children (Zuckerman et al., 2013). Regardless of SES, both African American and Latino children with autism receive evaluations later than White children, with this delay limiting opportunities to receive needed services that could improve quality of life outcomes (AADM, 2020; Centers for Disease Control and Prevention, 2016; Furfaro, 2017). Given the diagnostic disparities among cultural minorities and the importance of early diagnosis and early intervention in addressing the needs (Boyd et al., 2010), disparities can contribute to inequities in access to services for children and their families (Hartlep, 2009; Hosking, 2008; Pearson et al., 2018).

Stigma and Disability

Empowerment can be impacted by caregivers experiencing extreme stigma and social isolation in regard to disability (Harry, 2002; Hewitt et al., 2013). Beliefs can serve as a barrier to empowerment and families advocating for their child's needs (Snell-Johns et al., 2004). For example, social stigma can be a barrier for caregivers getting early identification screening for their children, and thus the assessment process can be delayed in cultural communities (Hewitt, 2013). African American families of children with autism state a stigma of disability exists in their communities (Burkett et al. 2015), which can lead to some families not providing consent to an educational assessment for their child. African American families identify a need for services and supports that can reduce stigma around disability in communities and empower families to advocate for their child's needs (Pearson et al., 2020). In some cultures, there is a great deal of anxiety associated with the special education process as the parents' community mindset and beliefs may not align with the process of identification (Hewitt, 2013). Lack of knowledge of autism, social stigma, and structural barriers can contribute to parental stress and delayed diagnosis (Pisula, 2011). For example, the average age of minority children diagnosis in the Somali community is 7 years old (Wiggins, et al., 2009). The special education process may challenge families to change their opinions, attitudes, and beliefs about the basis of the child's challenges (Gutierrez & Lewis, 1999; Whitley et al., 2011). Parents may blame themselves for their child's disability as has been reported in families of Asian descent (Ghosh & Magaña, 2009).

Family Values

Empowerment can be impacted when practitioners do not demonstrate respect for different family dynamics and parenting styles with the resulting gap created between practitioners and caregivers leading to alienation from the education system (Calabrese, 1989; Harry, 1992b; Scott-Jones, 1987). When professionals are less sensitive to families' customs and values, they are less likely to help them advocate for services as equal partners. In regard to family dynamics, the primary caregiver may be someone other than a mother or father, such as an unsupported grandparent who needs resources and feels a reduced sense of empowerment (Whitley et al., 2011). Practitioners traditionally equate family involvement with parental value of education (Thompson, 2003b; Trotman, 2001). For example, practitioners may assume that low attendance of African American parents at school functions is the result of a lack of concern with their children's education (Lynn, 1997; Mapp, 1997; Thompson, 2003b; Trotman, 2001). Assumptions of parental apathy, disinterest, or indifference may result in practitioners not encouraging caregivers to participate in their child's education (Bloom, 2001). Practitioners' assumptions and cultural perceptions may lead to distrust in the educational system. Research indicates that African American parents want to be involved in their children's education (Adelman, 1994) and that practitioners proactively communicating and encouraging participation increases the likelihood of caregivers' interaction and sense of ownership about the school (Epstein, 1996; Johnson, 1990). Hmong families' unfamiliarity about special education may be a result of the differences in expectations and cultural beliefs of two very different cultures (Wathum-Ocama & Rose, 2002). Some communities view education through different lenses and might see special education as substandard. Professionals need multicultural education to learn about various cultural groups and cultural diversity (Ford. 1992). This includes learning about the learning styles, communication patterns, value systems, and parental perception of disabilities. More information about acknowledging other cultures is in Chapter 3. It is important for professionals to avoid special education jargon that confuses families and make it harder for families to voice their concerns. Furthermore, teachers can empower their students by providing opportunities for culturally sustaining pedagogy.

Caregiver-Practitioner Collaboration

Empowerment can be impacted by a variety of factors that influence collaboration with caregivers from minority communities, which can include poor communication between caregivers and professionals (Blue-Banning et al., 2007; Nelson, & Beegle, 2004; McNaughton et al., 2007; Thompson, 2003b; Tucker & Schwartz, 2013). African American mothers suggest partnerships and open communication are important ingredients in special education advocacy (Stanley, 2015). However, caregivers report feeling unsupported in patronizing school environments causing them anxiety and making them hesitant to communicate with professionals (Burke, 2018; Stanley 2015). Weak communication, connections, and relationships exist when the educational system fails to involve families and communities. Lack of communication and cultural differences has been attributed to a lack of trust with the school system (Halle, et al., 1997). School personnel often have the misconception that parents from diverse cultural groups are apathetic, disinterested, or indifferent to their children's education and may not work to encourage these parents to participate in school (Bloom, 2001). But poor communication between caregivers and professionals may contribute to the lack of caregiver's participation (Greenwood & Hickman, 1991).

Caregiver participation research draws attention to the relatively low involvement of African American parents in the education of their children in both general and special education (Pena, 2000; Rao, 2000; Thompson, 2003a; Winters, 1994). African American caregivers indicate they want to be involved in their children's education, but often experience a breakdown in communication between schools and caregivers (Brown, 2007; Brandon et al., 2010). Moreover, studies confirm that caregivers' input on decision-making and goal setting is frequently ignored (McNaughton et al., 2007). Cultural differences in communication styles (Hart & More, 2013; Pearson, 2015) and systemic barriers that impact families can include both linguistic barriers and dialect differences (Burke, 2018; Cohen, 2013). Schools often struggle to create reliable, two-way communication systems to provide parents consistent, timely, and culturally responsive communication (Lo, 2008; Tucker & Schwartz, 2013; Azad et al., 2016). Power imbalances can cause schools to have difficulty engaging families and diverse communities when the communications styles of the school for engagement don't match the style of the caregivers.

During IEP conferences, research has found that parents experience a wide array of emotions, such as anger, blame, confusion, denial, depression, guilt, isolation, sadness, shock, stress, or disappointment, which can hinder the communication between parents and school personnel (Witherspoon, 2015). Poor professional communication with African American caregivers is one of the factors that contribute to a lack of services for children with disabilities. Cultural perceptions of disability can hinder the collaboration process. Cultural beliefs, practices, and respect are important aspects of caregiving and are embedded in the daily lives of many African American families (Burkett et al., 2016; Ndung'u & Kinyua, 2009).

Self-Determination

Given the active role that parents have in special education processes such as transition services (Wandry & Pleet, 2003), self-determination in students with disabilities is often facilitated by family empowerment and effective family-practitioners collaboration. Self-determination, or an individual's motivation and exertion of control over life circumstances, (Cohen, 2009) includes attitudes, abilities, and skills that allow a person to define personal goals and initiate actions in reaching those goals (Ward, 1998). Self-determination is engaging in intentional self-caused individual actions with aspirations and perseverance even in the face of obstacles (Wehmeyer et al., 2010). The fundamental elements of self-determination behaviors consist of initiation, goal setting, choice-making, decision-making, problem-solving, independent thinking, assertiveness, goal attainment, self-observation, evaluation, reinforcement, internal locus of control, positive attributions of self-efficacy and outcome expectancy, self-awareness, self-knowledge, self-advocacy, self-regulation, and persistence. If the central goal is self-determination for children with disabilities, then practitioners need to help families understand and facilitate self-determination development (Cohen, 2009). Evidence supports active parent involvement in special education processes, including transition services, goals, and objectives, which strongly correlates with the achievement of postsecondary transition success (Destefano et al., 1999; Sinclair et al., 2005; Wandry & Pleet, 2003).

Culturally Sustaining Practices and Implementation Strategies

When practitioners have a clear understanding of the intersectional experiences and identified needs of families participating in the special education process, they are better equipped to address those needs. This section highlights strategies designed to support the needs of caregivers who have youth with developmental disabilities, including autism and intellectual disability (ID). Guided by a framework for supporting the experiences of families (Pearson et al., 2018), we first describe fundamentals for empowering families and then highlight strategies for facilitating caregiver-professional collaboration and promoting self-determination within the context of family empowerment.

Family empowerment strategies are not "one size fits all." First, we need to develop strategies by considering a variety of cultural factors related to families' perspectives of disability. Then we need to implement these strategies by considering the families' cultural background and practices. Chapter 1 discusses the process of infusing C.A.P., which includes: C-cultural self-study, A-acquisition of cultural knowledge, and P-putting the acquired knowledge to practice (Lindo & Lim, 2020). When working with families from various cultural backgrounds, there is a need to understand a few critical factors about cultural backgrounds in general and cultures specifically, including that of the family. It is also important to note that cultural differences aren't just about race and ethnicity. Cultural differences can be in the form of family structure, linguistic background, geographic location, SES, immigration status, and religious background, among others. Next, we describe: a) four fundamentals of culturally-sustaining practices that practitioners should have, and b) specific implementation strategies for empowering families.

Fundamentals of Culturally Sustaining Practices

- Understand how a family describes their child's characteristics.
- Understand how a family makes meaning of the disability (Avdi et al., 2000).
- Understand how a family copes with the disability (Gray, 2003).
- Understand how and where a family decides to seek intervention or not seek intervention for the disability (Hilton et al., 2010).

How Families Describe Child Characteristics

Culture may influence the way a family describes their child's characteristics. While some may view a three-year-old who doesn't talk as "speech delayed," a parent of Asian descent may view a child with a similar profile as "quiet." This is important to understand because practitioners and families need to be on the same page when determining the needs of the child. This is also a critical component when developing strategies because special practitioners need to know how to engage in culturally sustaining conversations with the families. If a parent describes their child as "quiet," a practitioner may ask a caregiver if they would like their child to speak more to family and friends. Recognizing how a family member describes their child's characteristics will help address any concerns the family has, while also showing respect for their cultural perspective.

How Families Make Meaning of Disability

Culture may also influence the way a family makes sense of disability. The following questions can help practitioners better understand how families interpret disability.

- Do the family members, in particular the mother, blame themselves for their child's disability as has been reported often in families of Asian descent (Ghosh & Magaña, 2009)?
- Do the caregivers view the child's disability as a medical issue that requires only medical attention? What value or stigma does the family attach to the disability (Harry, 2002)?
- Is there shame in the family as a result of the child's disability?
- What is the family's view of "typical development?"
- How does the family make meaning of the cause of the disability?

Understanding how a family makes meaning of the disability will help identify the role in which they view practitioners. That is, is the practitioner there to help "fix" or there to counsel and assist? When developing strategies, it is important to provide accurate information to the families, including how a special practitioner can assist in a child's development, while also respecting their cultural beliefs.

How Families Cope With Disabilities

How a family copes with a child's disability can oftentimes be influenced by a variety of cultural factors. For example, many African American families rely on themselves as a strong family unit (including extended) or on religion and spirituality to cope with challenges in their lives. In a study, African American parents who had a child with a chronic illness used their belief in God, their belief that they were getting the best medical care, and their portrayal of strength as coping mechanisms (Allen & Marshall, 2010). Alternatively, some Asian American families tend to move past distressing thoughts quickly and turn to avoidance rather than expressing their emotions outwardly. Other families of Asian descent may want to please other family members and make decisions based on family needs. Much of the research on coping styles in families points to a greater resilience found in ethnically diverse families (e.g., Mexican American and African American families) when compared to European American families (Harry, 2002). When working with families, it is important to not only understand how they cope with distressing factors in their lives, but perhaps what role they may desire and/or expect practitioners to play in order to establish a positive connection. Because every family is different, it is critical to collect information about a family while developing strategies, and prior to implementation.

How Families Decide How and Where to Treat (or Not Treat) a Disability

Oftentimes, when developing strategies to support families, practitioners develop strategies based on their own framework-from their own cultural lens. Views of "right" and "wrong" or "typical" and "atypical," for example, are influenced by cultural background. What happens, however, when the practitioner's own cultural background differs from the cultural background of the family they are supporting? Because the majority of teachers and special practitioners are White females from middle-income backgrounds (Morrell, 2010), the cultures with which they are most familiar can be juxtaposed against the cultures of the students and families with whom they work. This is an important concept to understand because the strategies that practitioners may be most comfortable and familiar with are those that reflect their own cultural lens.

Some families may reach out to medical professionals while other caregivers may seek out practitioners for intervention and support. When practitioners are working with families, it is important for them to agree on the best ways to support their child. Findings indicate that racial and ethnic minorities in the United States are less likely to seek out health services, compared to White families (Andrews et al., 2011; Gourdine et al., 2011; Ward & Besson, 2012). This may be due to factors such as interpretation of the disability, trust/mistrust of the system, or alternative methods for seeking support (Harry, 2008; Pearson & Meadan, 2018). American Indians and Alaska Natives, for example, often rely on traditional healers, and African Americans often rely on ministers as counselors or sources for referral (Avent et al., 2015). Special education practitioners must acknowledge that their role is to respect the choices that families make, while also supporting them with best practices, to the extent that it aligns with the family's preferences. Table 7.2 highlights some empowerment practices and specific strategies for practitioners working with culturally diverse families.

Table 7.2 Culturally Sustaining Empowerment Strategies

Culturally sustaining empowerment practices	Examples of specific strategies for practitioners
Create an authentic dialogue between families, professionals, and schools.	Determine the best and most consistent mode of communication early on (e.g., phone calls, email, text messages, notebook exchange) and communicate with families in the manner that meets their needs.
Develop an understanding of who comprises the family unit.	Ask the family to tell you who the child interacts with each day. This is important because family units may include members who live outside the household.
Ensure that families know their educational rights and how to equitably advocate for their children.	Present families with easy-to-read literature (e.g., less jargon) that discusses IDEA and the IEP process. Talk them through the literature. Define new and unknown terminology. Provide information on a local Parent Training and Information Center.
Help parents understand their due process rights.	Provide families with resources that highlight their rights. Suggest that families prepare and bring their written concerns and questions to meetings. Suggest that they bring paper and a pen to take notes at the IEP meetings.
Understand that families may need some time to accept their child's special needs before being able to dive into the intricacies of their expected involvement.	Listen to how the family discusses their child's needs. Use the same words they use and ask questions about what changes, if any, they would like to see. Highlight the benefits of special education services and the importance of early intervention.
Offer ways to help make family members facilitators.	Teach/coach family members about what they can do in the home in a variety of ways. As needed, demonstrate/model, provide videos, and/or provide literature on practices and strategies that can be used in the home environment.

Table 7.2 Culturally Sustaining Empowerment Strategies (continued)

Culturally sustaining empowerment practices	Examples of specific strategies for practitioners
Provide developmental milestones that are relevant to that family's cultural and linguistic background.	Ask families about their cultural and linguistic background. For example, find information that aligns with the speech milestones concerning that specific background. If no information exists, talk to your family about what patterns they noticed in their community in regard to children and development. Provide typical developmental milestones checklists such as those produced by the Centers for Disease Control and Prevention.
Offer tangible and culturally relevant resources.	Provide families with literature that has photos that resemble their family identity and is written in their language, not just simply translated from English.
Implement strategies that are flexible and family centered.	Ask the family about the daily routines that they already have in place. Do not assume that they implement the same routines you do or that it looks the same. For example, is dinner eaten around a table? As a family? Or does it look different? Create your strategies accordingly.
Work on areas that the family identifies as an area of needed support.	Ask the family what else they need to feel fully supported. Ask if it is access to a computer, transportation, understanding what they should be doing at home, in need of specific materials to use at home, etc.

Implementation Strategies

Once practitioners have a foundational understanding of the role of culture in shaping families' views, perceptions, and decisions, they will be better prepared to implement culturally sustaining practices to support family empowerment. Although it is impossible to develop a one-size-fits-all list of strategies, this section highlights two example implementation strategies to support families of children with disabilities: a) parent-professional collaboration and b) self-determination promotion.

Parent-Practitioner Collaboration

Researchers have noted the positive impact that knowledge and awareness of disabilities can have on families of children with developmental disabilities, including autism and intellectual disabilities (Burke et al., 2019). Given the nature and impact of disabilities on the needs of students in both home and school environments, caregiver-professional collaboration in educational planning and service delivery is critical (Azad & Mandell, 2015). Families from low-income and racial/ethnic minority backgrounds have a history of mistrust with education systems that have resulted in a mismatch between service needs and service utilization (Harry, 2008). For example, due to a history of marginalization and discrimination in educational settings, many African American and Hispanic families have noted their dissatisfaction with special education services (Harry, 2008).

Despite the aforementioned barriers, there are several strategies that school-based professionals can employ to build positive relationships with families. In their work on building family-professional partnerships with culturally and linguistically diverse families of young children, Pearson and colleagues (2019) identified several strategies to engage in positive relationship-building with families. Building on the foundational empowerment strategies, we highlight implementation strategies to support parent-professional collaboration in Table 7.3.

Table 7.3 Culturally Sustaining Collaboration Strategies
Get to know the students and their families.
Practice responsive, multimodal communication.
Communicate with parents in ways that are accessible and convenient for them.
Provide written and oral information in the family's language and/or dialect as necessary.
Use an interpreter when necessary to explain difficult concepts; be sure the interpreter speaks the same language and dialect of the family.
Seek ways to build trust with family members by being dependable, authentic, consistent, and respectful.
Collaborate with cultural liaisons and train them in the special education process.
Support family-centered goals by talking to parents about their families' experiences, priorities, needs, and goals. Strategies should not focus on "fixing" problems not seen as a problem.
Co-construct strategies for children with disabilities.
Be willing to ask questions that you do not know the answers to.
Be willing to listen to what the family members have to say.

Self-Determination Promotion

Little research to date has explored the impact of students' cultural identities on their self-determination behaviors and practices (Trainor, 2005). Given the increasingly diverse compositions of U.S. classrooms, promoting self-determination among historically marginalized students is critical (Trainor, 2005). In some cases, caregivers' visions for their child (parent-advocacy) and the child's vision for themselves (self-determination) may not align. This may be particularly true in families of color (Trainor, 2005). Therefore, in addition to supporting family empowerment, and parent-teacher collaboration, practitioners must also facilitate the development and acquisition of self-determination skills in students with disabilities. See Chapter 8 for more details. Table 7.4 highlights specific strategies for facilitating self-determination through a culturally sustaining lens (Trainor, 2005).

Table 7.4 Culturally Sustaining Self-Determination Strategies
Individualize transition plans for each student.
Include students in Individualized Transition Planning (ITP) meetings, while honoring the families' values.
Align curricular plans with student goals.
Maintain multidisciplinary Individualized Transition Planning teams.
Support student and family development and involvement in self-determination activities.

Bringing it all Together

For many years, families raising children with developmental disabilities such as autism and intellectual disabilities have documented challenges and needs related to special education services. Recommendations from caregivers and practitioners have consistently highlighted the need to increase agency and service-access for families of children with disabilities through culturally sustaining service delivery, including empowerment practices, and collaborative partnerships (Harry, 2008; Pearson & Meadan, 2018). The challenges and needs that families face are often exacerbated among historically marginalized racial and ethnic groups in the United States. Therefore, to strengthen outcomes for children with intersecting identities, special education practitioners and related service providers must engage families using culturally sustaining methods that are designed to support families' agency and empowerment.

Case Study: Yasmine

When teachers mentioned that Yasmine's son might need an initial evaluation to see if he would meet the criteria for special education services, this mother was crushed. She saw behavioral differences in her son and knew he needed support but did not know exactly what support. She thought that eventually her young son would grow out of the behavioral differences and that this would be a temporary childhood phase her son was going through. When the practitioners mentioned autism, Yasmine struggled with accepting this educational label as children on the spectrum were becoming disproportionately represented in her Somali community.

Through authentic dialogue and listening to Yasmine's concerns, the team learned it was not accessing special education services that were hard for her to accept, but the social stigma associated with autism. In the Somali community, children with autism are perceived to be on the severe end of the spectrum, mostly non-verbal, and are rarely seen in community settings. She thought of the children with autism she saw that were shunned from the community. The only thing she could think of was the non-verbal children that did not make eye contact or acknowledge others. She thought, "my son speaks and makes eye contact, the teacher must be mistaken." With a verbal child, Yasmine was finding it hard to accept the label. Yasmine was doing everything in her power to protect her son's educational trajectory, but she lacked knowledge. Yasmine wanted what was best for her son and if she knew the benefits of early identification and early intervention, she would be the first in line to get it.

Frustrated and feeling defeated, Yasmine was ready to switch schools and enroll her son in another school or district. The practitioners, sensing Yasmine's frustration, provided developmental milestones that were relevant to her family's cultural and linguistic background. The team realized that the interpreter was having difficulty translating the special education terminology and made sure to take the time to explain difficult concepts in easy to understand language. By communicating, the team educated Yasmine about the label by providing accessible resources that presented the full spectrum of characteristics associated with autism. Yasmine spoke to her son's teacher and asked the practitioners to look at other labels so that her son could receive the support. At the time, Yasmine's son was young and could receive services and benefits under the broader label of developmental delay. The practitioners explained that while this label would get Yasmine's son special education services, autism-specific interventions available in the community might not be available. Yasmine lacked empowerment and was unsure about how to advocate for resources. Yasmine wanted to protect her son from the autism label but she also wanted him to have the support he needed in the classroom. Her limited knowledge was a barrier to early autism-specific interventions such as the social skills training her son needed to thrive with his peers.

Case Study: Yasmine (continued)

Yasmine wasn't the only parent in the Somali community who wanted to refuse the autism label. Teachers were used to Somali families' apprehension toward autism. Teachers were using the developmental delay label to get early special education services for students that met the criteria to avoid the challenging conversations that come with having to explain to a caregiver that their child might qualify for disability services under autism. This was not the case with Yasmine's son's practitioners. Yasmine's educational team understood that families may need some time to accept their child's special needs before being able to dive into the intricacies of their expected involvement. The team also understood that a label like developmental delay could impact families' access to autism-specific resources and supports from organizations (e.g., Somali Parents Autism Network, Autism Society, and Autism Speaks). Yasmine's practitioners ensured that she knew her educational rights and due process by providing her information on workshops provided by the state's Parent Training and Information Center (PACER) where she could learn how to advocate for her child. Yasmine was struggling with her son at home and the practitioners provided her with visual schedules to help organize routines and other strategies that were flexible and family-centered based on areas that Yasmine identified as areas of needed support.

As a result of this educational team's communication with Yasmine about autism and providing her resources, they equipped her with advocacy skills. Yasmine was later able to accept the label of autism for her son and gained the empowerment skills she needed to advocate for services to meet his needs both in academic and community settings. Yasmine continued to build strong partnerships with her son's team and became an active member of his school by attending parent-teacher conferences and volunteering for school-based activities.

Summary

This chapter described the intersectional experiences and identified needs of families participating in the special education process. We provided culturally sustaining strategies to effectively empower families to facilitate parent-professional collaboration and promote self-determination in families. School-based professionals should support families' understanding of their special education rights so caregivers feel more knowledgeable and are better prepared to advocate for their child's needs. In addition, professionals should strive to understand the diverse complexities of families who are partners in special education. Finally, school-based professionals must employ practices that amplify the voices of marginalized children with disabilities and their families. That is, schools must demonstrate a sense of cultural humility by ensuring that they understand families' perspectives and experiences, and then use those perspectives and experiences to foster a culture where families feel empowered and prepared to engage in special education partnerships. Despite the challenges that both school-based professionals and caregivers face in establishing effective special education partnerships, empowering caregivers by utilizing culturally sustaining strategies is critical for ensuring both positive family engagement and strengthened student outcomes.

Guiding Questions

1. What are the intersectional experiences and needs of families participating in the special education process?

2. What are some culturally sustaining strategies to effectively empower families to facilitate parent-professional collaboration, and promote self-determination in families?

References

Adelman, H. S. (1994). Intervening to enhance home involvement in schooling. *Intervention in School & Clinic, 29*, 276–288.

American Psychiatric Association. (2013). *Diagnostic and statistical manual of mental disorders* (5th ed.) Washington, DC: Author.

Andrews, S., Stefurak, J., & Mehta, S. (2011). Between a rock and a hard place? Locus of control, religious problem-solving and psychological help-seeking. *Mental Health, Religion & Culture*, 855–876. https://doi.org/10.1080/13674676.2010.533369

Atwater, S. C. (2008). Waking up to difference: teachers, color-blindness, and the effects on students of color. *Journal of Instructional Psychology, 35,* 246–53.

Autism and Developmental Disabilities Monitoring (ADDM) Network (2020). Community report on autism: A Snapshot of Autism Spectrum Disorder among 8-year-old Children in Multiple Communities across the United States in 2016. Centers for Disease Control and Prevention (CDC) United States Department of Health and Human Services.

Avent, J. R., Cashwell, C. S., & Brown-Jeffy, S. (2015). African American pastors on mental health, coping, and help seeking. *Counseling and Values, 60*(1), 32–47. doi.org/d7d9

Azad, G. F., Kim, M., Marcus, Sheridan, S. M., & Mandell, D. S. (2016). Parent-Teacher Communication about Children with Autism Spectrum Disorder: An Examination of Collaborative Problem-solving. *Psychology in the Schools, 53*(10).

Avdi, E., Griffin, C., & Brough, S. (2000). Parents' constructions of the 'problem' during assessment and diagnosis of their child for an autistic spectrum disorder. *Journal of Health Psychology, 5*(2), 241-254.

Bloom, L. R. (2001). "I'm poor, I'm single, I'm mom, and I deserve respect": Advocating in schools and with mothers in poverty. *Educational Studies*, 32(3), 300-316.

Boyd, B. A., Odom, S. L., Humphreys, B. P., & Sam, A. M. (2010). Infants and toddlers with autism spectrum disorder: Early identification and early intervention. *Journal of Early Intervention, 32,* 75–98.

Brandon, R. R., Higgins, K., Pierce, T., Tandy, R., & Sileo, N. (2010). An Exploration of the Alienation Experienced by African American Parents From Their Children's Educational Environment. *Remedial and Special Education*, 31(3), 208–222.

Burke, M. M., Lee, C. E., & Rios, K. (2019). A pilot evaluation of an advocacy programme on knowledge, empowerment, family–school partnership and parent well-being. *Journal of Intellectual Disability Research*, 63(8), 969-980.

Calabrese, R. L. (1989). Public school and minority students. *Journal of Educational Thoughts*, 23, 187–196.

Castagno, A. E., & Brayboy, B. M. J. (2008). Culturally responsive schooling for indigenous youth: A review of the literature. *Review of Educational Research*, 78(4), 941-993.

Centers for Disease Control and Prevention. (2016). Prevalence of autism spectrum disorders among children aged 8 years—Autism and developmental disabilities monitoring network, 11 Sites, United States, 2012. *Morbidity and Mortality Weekly Report. 65,* 1–23.

Center for Parent Information and Resources https://www.parentcenterhub.org/qa2/#ref5

Chadiha, L. A., Adams, P., Biegel, D., Auslander, W., & Gutierrez, L. (2004). Empowering African American women informal caregivers: A literature synthesis and practice strategies. *Social Work*, 49(1), 97–108.

Cheatham, G. A., & Ostrosky, M. M. (2011). Whose expertise?: An analysis of advice giving in early childhood parent-teacher conferences. *Journal of Research in Childhood Education*, 25, 24–44.

Cohen, S. R. 2013. Advocacy for the "Abandonados": Harnessing cultural beliefs for Latino families and their children with intellectual disabilities. Journal of Policy and Practice in Intellectual Disabilities, *10*, 71–78.

Comer, J. P., & Haynes, N. M. (1991). Parent involvement in schools: An ecological approach. Elementary School Journal, 91, 271–277.

Coots, J. J. (1998). Family resources and parent participation in schooling activities for their children with developmental delays. *Journal of Special Education*, 31, 498–520.

Cox, E., & Parsons, R. (1996). Empowerment-oriented social work practice: Impact on late life relationships of women. Journal of Women & Aging, 8, 3–4.

Darling-Hammond, L. (2000). New standards and old inequalities: school reform and the education of African American students. *Journal of Negro Education*, 69, 263–87.

Davis, C., Brown, B., Bantz, J. M., & Manno, C. (2002). African American parent's involvement in their children's special education programs. *Multiple Voices*, 5(1), 13–27.

Delgado-Gaitan, C. (1990). *Literacy for empowerment*. New York: Falmer Press.

Deyhle, D. (1995). Navajo youth and Anglo racism: Cultural integrity and resistance. Harvard Educational Review, 65(3), 403-444.

Dunst, C. J., Trivette, C. M., & Deal, A. G. (1988). Enabling and empowering families: Principles and guidelines for practice. Cambridge, MA: Brookline Books.

Epstein, J. L. (1996). Advances in family, community, and school partnerships. New Schools, New Communities, 12(3), 5–13.

Folger, J., Poole, M. S., & Stutman, R. K. (2000). Working through conflict: Strategies for relationships, groups, and organizations (4th ed.). New York, NY: Longman.

Freire, P. (1983). Pedagogy of the oppressed. New York, NY: Seabury Press.

Furfaro, H. (2017, November 20). Race, class contribute to disparities in autism diagnoses. *Spectrum*. Retrieved from https://spectrumnews.org/news/race-class-contribute-disparities-autism-diagnoses/

Goin-Kochel, R. P., Myers, B. J., & Mackintosh, V. H. (2007). Parental reports on the use of treatments and therapies for children with autism spectrum disorders. *Research in Autism Spectrum Disorders, 1*, 195–207.

Gourdine, R,, Baffour, T., & Teasley, M. (2011). Autism and the African American community. Social Work Public Health., 26, 454–70.

Gray, D. E. (2003). Gender and coping: The parents of children with high functioning autism. *Social Science & Medicine, 56*(3), 631-642.

Greenwood, G. E., & Hickman, C. W. (1991). Research and practice in parent involvement: Implication for teacher education. Elementary School Journal, 91, 279–288.

Gutierrez, L. M. (1994). Beyond coping: An empowerment perspective on stressful life events. Journal of Sociology and Social Welfare, 21(3), 201–220.

Halle, T., Kurtz-Costes, B., & Mahoney, J (1997). Family influences on school achievement in low-income, African-American children. *Journal of Educational Psychology*, 89, 527-537.

Harry, B. (1992a). *Cultural diversity, families, and the special education system: Communication and empowerment*. New York: Teachers College Press.

Harry, B. (1992b). Restructuring the participation of African Americans in special education. *Exceptional Children, 59,* 123–131.

Harry, B. (2002). Trends and issues in serving culturally diverse families of children with disabilities. *The Journal of Special Education, 36*(3), 132-140.

Harry, B. (2008). Collaboration with culturally and linguistically diverse families: Ideal versus reality. *Exceptional children, 74*(3), 372-388.

Hartlep ND. Critical race theory: an examination of its past, present, and future implications. ERIC. 2009; https://files.eric.ed.gov/fulltext/ED506735.pdf

Ho, K. M., & Keiley, M. K. (2003). Dealing with Denial: A Systems Approach for Family Professionals Working with Parents of Individuals with Multiple Disabilities. *The Family Journal.* 11 (3), p.239-247

Hosking DL. Critical disability theory: a paper presented at the 4th biennial disability studies conference at Lancaster University, UK. 2008. http://www.lancaster.ac.uk/fass/events/disabilityconference_archive/2008/papers/hosking2008.pdf 2008. Accessed 18 Oct 2018.

Kieffer, C. H. (1984). Citizen empowerment: A developmental perspective. Prevention in Human Services, 3, 9–36.

Lee, S. (2007). The truth and myth of the model minority: The case of Hmong Americans. Narrowing the Achievement Gap, 171-184.

Mautone, J. A., Marcelle, E., Tresco, K. E., & Power, T. J. (2015). Assessing the quality of parent-teacher relationships for students with ADHD. *Psychology in the Schools*, 52, 196–207.

Miller, V. A., Schreck, K. A., Mulick, J. A., & Butter, E. (2012). Factors related to parents' choices of treatment for their children with autism spectrum disorders. *Research in Autism Spectrum Disorders, 6,* 87–95.

Minnes, P, Nachshen, J., & Woodford, L. (2003). The Role of Families. In I. Brown and M. Percy (Eds.) Developmental Disabilities in Ontario (2nd Ed.). Toronto: Ontario Association on Developmental Disabilities, 663-676.

Morrell, J. (2010). Teacher preparation and diversity: When American pre-service teachers aren't White and middle class. *International Journal of Multicultural Education*, *12*(1).

Morris, J. E. (1999). A pillar of strength: An African American school's communal bonds with families and community since Brown. *Urban Education*, 33, 584–605.

Mueller, T. G. & Carranza, F. (2011). An Examination of Special Education Due Process Hearings. *Journal of Disability Policy Studies,* 22(3) 131–139.

Parsons, R. (1991). Empowerment: Purpose and practice principle in social work. *Social Work with Groups*, 14(2), 7–21.

Pearson, J.N., Hamilton, M-B., & Meadan, H. (2018). "We Saw our Son Blossom": A Guide for Fostering Culturally Responsive Partnerships to Support African American Autistic Children and their Families. *Perspectives of the ASHA Special Interest Groups, 3,* 84-97.

Pearson, J. N., Hamilton, M-B., Meadan, H. (2018). *"We Saw Our Son Blossom" A Guide for Fostering Culturally Responsive Partnerships to Support African American Autistic Children and Their Families.*

Pearson J. (2015). Disparities in diagnoses and access to services for African American children with autism spectrum disorder. *DADD Online Journal*. 2015; 2:52–65.

Pearson J, & Meadan H. (2018). African American mothers' perceptions of diagnoses and services for children with autism. Education and Training in Autism and Developmental Disabilities.53,17–32.

Pearson, J. N., Trafcante, A. L., Denny, L. M., Malone, K., & Cod, E. (2020). Meeting FACES: Preliminary Findings from a Community Workshop for Minority Parents of Children with Autism in Central North Carolina. *Journal of Autism and Developmental Disorders*. 50 (*1*), 1-11. https://doi.org/10.1007/s10803-019-04295-4

Pena, D. C. (2000). Parent involvement: Influencing factors and implications. Journal of Educational Research, 94, 42–54.

Rao, S. S. (2000). Perspectives of an African American mother on parent–professional relationship in special education. Mental Retardation, 38(6), 1–14.

Rappaport, J. (1987). Terms of empowerment/exemplars of prevention: Toward a theory for community psychology. American Journal of Community Psychology, 15(2), 121–149.

Scott-Jones, D. (1987). Mothers-as-teachers in the families of high and low-achieving low-income Black first graders. Journal of Negro Education, 56, 21–34.

Smalley, S. Y., & Reyes-Blanes, M. E. (2001). Reaching out to African American parents in an urban community: A community university partnership. Urban Education, 36, 518–533.

Susman, L. (2007). Effects of Increased Parental Knowledge of Development of Children with Disabilities (Doctoral dissertation). Available from ProQuest.

Thompson, G. L. (2003). No parent left behind: Strengthening ties between educators and African American parents/guardians. Urban Review, 35(1), 7–23.

Ward, E. C., & Besson, D. D. (2012). African American men's beliefs about mental illness, perceptions of stigma, and help-seeking barriers. *The Counseling Psychologist*, *41*(3), 359–391. https://doi.org/10.1177/0011000012447824

Wathum-Ocama, J. C., & Rose, S. (2002). Hmong immigrants' views on the education of their deaf and hard of hearing children. American Annals of The Deaf, 147(3), 44-53.

Whitley, D. M., Kelley, S. J., & Sipe, T. A. (2001). Grandmothers raising grandchildren: Are they at increased risk of health problems? Health & Social Work, 26, 105–114.

Wright, J. (2016). Disparities in diagnoses might harm minority groups. https://spectrumnews.org/news/disparities-in-autism-diagnosis-may-harm-minority-groups

Zuckerman KE, Mattox K, Donelan K, Batbayar O, Baghaee A, Bethell C. Pediatrician identification of Latino children at risk for autism spectrum disorder. Pediatrics. 2013;132:445–53.

Chapter 8

Teaching diverse students with disabilities sociopolitical consciousness and self-advocacy

Peggy J. Schaefer Whitby, Elizabeth A. Harkins Monaco, Djanna Hill, and Kelly McNeal

---

Objectives

- Understand the sociopolitical constructs that impact people from oppressed populations' ability to advocate for themselves and others.

- Articulate how the intersection of multiple sociopolitical constructs further impact people with disabilities' ability to advocate for themselves and others.

- Identify their own bias that may impact how they teach diverse students from traditionally oppressed populations to self-advocate.

- Identify ways to teach self-advocacy while addressing the sociopolitical constructs using a cultural competency approach.

Chapter 8 provides information on the intersection of sociopolitical constructs as it affects one's ability to self-advocate. The intersection of multiple sociopolitical constructs affects youth with developmental disabilities (DD), including those with autism and intellectual disability (ID). The intersection of sociopolitical constructs and disability as a marginalized population has a significant impact on their ability to be heard and treated equitably by mainstream institutions such as schools. The skills needed to advocate for oneself within sociopolitical constructs can be taught to practitioners as well as students. However, many practitioners do not understand the impact of these constructs or how their own biases may affect how they practice and teach self-advocacy to a diverse population. The purpose of this chapter is to provide an overview of the sociopolitical constructs that impact a person's ability to self-advocate, impact a practitioner's ability to practice and teach self-advocacy skills, and to provide recommendations for increasing practitioners' abilities to teach self-advocacy skills to people with disabilities from marginalized populations.

Table 8.1 Key Terminology	
Cultural Competence	The ability to build understanding, communicate and interact with people across cultures in a way that demonstrates respect and openness to different cultural perspectives and strengthens cultural security.
Cultural Relevance	A pedagogical strategy that "uses the cultural knowledge, prior experiences, frames of reference, and performance styles of ethnically diverse students to make learning more relevant and effective." (Gay, 2010).
Marginalization	To relegate to an unimportant or powerless position within a society or group (Merriam Webster).
Sociopolitical Constructs	A combination of social and political ideas that have been created and accepted by a society (Merriam Webster).

The self-advocacy movement for people with disabilities stems from the civil rights movements of the 1950s and 1960s (Test et. al, 2005). Self-advocates challenged the idea that people with disabilities needed protection and were dependent on others to make decisions for them. Disability self-advocates fought for the right to have autonomy in making decisions about their own lives to the greatest extent possible. Self-advocacy skills are crucial for the successful transition to adulthood and those with demonstrated self-advocacy skills have better post-school outcomes (Wehmeyer & Palmer, 2003). Test et al. (2005) developed a framework for teaching self-advocacy to people with disabilities; it includes the constructs of knowledge of self and rights, communication, and leadership. The framework directly aligns with research literature on people with disabilities and provides special education practitioners the areas to be addressed for successful self-advocacy instruction. If self-advocacy skills lead to better post-secondary outcomes (Wehmeyer & Palmer, 2003) and practitioners have a framework for teaching self-advocacy (Test et al., 2005), then why aren't more students with disabilities using the learned skills to effectively self-advocate in post-school settings (Cawthorn & Cole, 2010)? There appears to be a significant disconnect. Lindsay, Cagliostro, and Carafa (2018) suggest that stigma and discrimination are two such barriers that impact disability disclosure and use of accommodations in postsecondary settings.

For practitioners to successfully teach self-advocacy, they must first understand the history of oppression of marginalized populations and the existing systemic issues in our schools today, along with their own position and biases within the institutional practice (see Chapter 2 for more on understanding your own biases).

Practitioners can then create environments that honor differences and allow for diverse populations to safely express their needs and wants. The intersectionality of race/ethnicity, gender, socioeconomics, poverty, and disability makes it more difficult to find safe places in which a person from diverse intersections can successfully self-advocate.

The Sociopolitical Lens and Intersectionality

As introduced in Chapter 1, viewing special education through a sociopolitical lens asks practitioners to consider social and political factors. This chapter pays particular attention to the intersection of the social constructs of the identities of people with autism and ID, and how they intersect with other identities such as race and poverty, and how these social constructs intertwine with the political context of disability, education, and society.

The identification of disabilities is entangled with historical, institutional, racist practices underpinned by deficit thinking. As forced integration of schools in the United States happened in the 1950s, there was a growing trend of an overrepresentation of non-White students separated from the White mainstream and put into special education (Reid & Knight, 2006). While the Supreme Court ruling in *Brown v. Board of Education* (1954) ended the legal segregation of schooling, de facto segregation of schools continued through federal, state, and local-level policies and legislation. Segregation continues today and builds on generations of mistrust many non-White parents and communities feel toward American institutions such as schools. This mistrust is often elevated when conversations take place regarding exclusionist practices such as "classifying" students for special education or providing special education services in non-inclusive classrooms.

More recently, it has been suggested that schools in the South may be under-identifying students of color in special education (Morgan et al., 2020). This shift represents yet another means to impose de-facto segregation of students because children with disabilities served under IDEA may not be suspended more than 10 days and must be served in the least restrictive environment (IDEA, 2004). Therefore, when non-White children's disabilities are not recognized and they are not classified, they are not protected under IDEA and can be easily expelled and sent to alternative learning environments, segregating them from their White peers. National data indicates that Black/African American children are being expelled and suspended at a much higher rate than their peers (National Center for Educational Statistics, 2019). Expulsion, when analyzed across the social construct of race, is another type of racial segregation.

Cultural differences have often been viewed through a deficit lens by White mainstream schools. This means that students who may not come to school prepared for the expectations of this school were often seen as deficient and had a higher risk of being labeled with a disability (Harry & Klingner, 2006). Remember the biopsychosocial model from Chapter 1? The medical model of disability views disability differences as deficits that need to be corrected. An inclusive view requires practitioners to reject the medical model of disability in favor of a social model that views disability as diversity and the education of students with disabilities as an issue of civil rights and social justice (Lalvani, 2012, p. 16). Lalvani's study revealed that teachers hold multiple interpretations of inclusive education, and that teachers who demonstrate little support for inclusive education have a deficit perspective of students with disabilities based on the medical model and beliefs about students with disabilities related to IQ and ability (p. 14). In contrast, teachers who supported inclusion viewed it through the lens of democracy and social justice. Use the reflective exercises from Chapter 1 to assess how you support inclusion.

"The sociopolitical context of society includes laws, regulations, policies, practices, traditions, and ideologies" (Nieto & Bode, 2018, p.3). Therefore, when we speak of strategies for guiding self-reflection and for teaching self-advocacy when working with diverse populations, we must first acknowledge that education is political and therefore advocacy is not a neutral act. As you start to come to terms with your role in this process, remember to use the reflective questions from Chapter 1. Focus on understanding that education and advocacy are related to the social, political, legal, and economic structures which construct and regulate the institutional framework in society. It becomes dysfunctional when stakeholders, such as practitioners, try to teach advocacy and do not name the realities of the societal structures that created the actual sociopolitical constructs surrounding an issue. This naming of the issues aids stakeholders to work toward setting realistic goals for change.

Advocacy

To teach advocacy in special education, one must first reflect on one's own practices and be aware of what Ware (2010) calls "critical special education," which means

a) that which refers to special education's overreliance on the medical model of disability,

b) the impulse to "fix" the unfit child,

c) the rush to equate human difference with limited capacity and individual pathology, and

d) the paradigmatic change that was urgently needed to coax the field away from its exclusively behaviorist and reductionist worldview (p. 254).

Oyler (2010) describes an elementary inclusion preparation program for practitioners in which practitioners focus on child study, self-reflection, principles of universal design, and critical multicultural multi-level instruction. Practitioners also spend a semester taking a course called *"Collaborative Communication in*

Cultural Contexts" (p. 210). The purpose of the course is to work as an effective team member and prepare practitioners to "take on (sic) the difficult work of collaborating across differences. A key aspect of the curriculum of the course relates to developing strong partnerships with families. This involves looking carefully at discourse and authority patterns" (p. 210). To better collaborate with families and students, practitioners need to better understand and respect their funds of knowledge (Moll, 1990; Gonzelez, Moll, & Amanti, 2005). Institutional practices are frequently mismatched to student and family funds of knowledge, and this can promote deficit thinking and practices in practitioners and further maintain institutional racism.

Zion and Petty (2014) focus on youth and adult partnerships as a means for creating student success and social justice. Tantamount to success is students having "voice" (p. 42). Significant attention is paid to the meaning of "dialogue" between adults and students, and particularly listening to students whose voices have been historically silenced. It is not possible to engage with students or to teach them to advocate for themselves if we, as special education practitioners, have not truly "heard" them. Social justice advocates want to create safe spaces in which they can engage students, share power, and build trust. To do this practitioners must ask themselves

- Do you believe that all students have the right to engage in dialogue and prepare to fully participate in society?
- Do you believe that there are those who are too young, belligerent, are criminal offenders, have particular kinds of disabilities, espouse particular beliefs, are from particular racial/ethnic and other backgrounds, have different learning patterns or particular ways of communicating, or lack particular skills sets and have forfeited their right to fully participate in society?

These are important questions to ask. The key issue here is that we ask these and other questions, especially about what we are creating amongst ourselves if we do not fully engage all of society's members and support each other in our ability to participate in the co-creation of and benefit from our social systems (p. 43). How we "see" students has significant impacts on successful schooling experiences.

To create the type of self-advocacy or activism that Zion and Petty (2014) discuss, they note that students must be engaged in dialogue about the issues and there must be skill building for both the students and the adults involved. The skills to be addressed are comprehensive and include social, cultural, interpersonal, academic, moral, civic, organizational, analytical, and cultural competency. The skills learned in this framework are similar to those taught to the teacher candidates in Oyler's (2010) Critical Special Education Core (p. 209). Learning is not solely the responsibility of the students; it is the responsibility of the practitioner/adult/advocate as well.

Teacher Bias and Student Outcome

Everyone has biases, or preferences, for or against something or someone (Harry et al., 1999). Implicit or hidden biases are stereotypes held by all individuals (Staats et al., 2015), but most people are unaware that they exist. We suggest two main reasons for this oversight:

1) implicit biases are often not consistent with individuals' conscious ethical systems and,

2) individuals tend to only acknowledge their conscious ethical systems (Chugh et al., 2005; Banaji & Greenwald, 2013; Bertrand, et al., 2005; Sever et al., 2015).

The fact is, acknowledging one's implicit biases is uncomfortable for people and this essentially makes them blind to the very structures in society (Murray Law, 2011) that promote systemic discrimination, unequal outcomes, and the marginalization of certain populations (Banaji, Bazerman, & Chugh, 2003; Chugh, Bazerman, & Banaji, 2005; Tenbrunsel & Messick, 2004).

Most special education practitioners are members of dominant social groups in terms of race, language, and ability (White, English speaking, and typically developing), and have not experienced systemic prejudice or oppression, something their students most likely experience regularly. Many believe they are open-minded (Murray Law, 2011), but they are likely unaware that their teaching practices are shaped according to their implicit biases. This makes it that much harder to address or combat such biases (McIntosh, 1989; Messick & Bazerman, 1996; NASP, 2016; Sever, Gino, & Bazerman, 2015). An example is when a White practitioner misjudges the actions of a student of color who has a disability and responds with discipline. These kinds of responses exacerbate the risks for multiple minoritized students (Crenshaw, 1991), despite the practitioners' intentions.

Let's examine biases that exist in special education programs. "Having never been the victim of racism and prejudice, [special education practitioners] can dismiss the importance of cultural differences" (Spring, 2000, p. 87). This prevents practitioners from recognizing when people with multiple minoritized identities experience oppression; understanding the actions, feelings, and needs of those who have been "othered" (Spring, 2000); and admitting their roles in creating or supporting unjust systems (NASP, 2016; Niles & Harkins Monaco, 2019). The reality is that these kinds of biases tend to be ignored in schools, which creates toxic conditions that impact learning and have long-term, negative effects on students and their families. This is devastating for students with disabilities, who are at increased risk due to their multiple minoritized identities. "Practitioners' levels of multicultural competence can no longer rest on what feels most comfortable or how one personally identifies .... Practitioners must all be committed to doing the hard work to look at these biases, especially around disability" (Niles & Harkins Monaco, 2019, p. 115). Teaching self-advocacy skills can only be effective if students are provided opportunities to engage in meaningful discourse regarding the sociopolitical constructs that impact them every day, and if practitioners address the implicit bias that may impact students' willingness to engage in this discourse and self-advocate. In this chapter, we will use Ladson-Billings' (2009) model to show how to infuse culturally responsive advocacy in the classroom.

Culturally Relevant Strategies to Teach Self-Advocacy

Ladson-Billings (2009) suggests that culturally relevant pedagogy best promotes student learning. This means practitioners must simultaneously promote academic success while helping students develop positive ethnic and cultural identities; and recognize, understand, and analyze existing, social inequalities. In other words, students whose identities and experiences are "othered" in multiple ways need to see themselves, their experiences, and their values in their education to best benefit from their education (Villegas, et al., 2013; Waitoller & Thorius, 2016). This starts with the practitioner themself.

Consider disability, for example. If you learn to "interrogate how [your] perceptions of disability were socialized and how that socialization intentionally or unintentionally affects students and [develop] the ability to be creative when recognizing multiple layers of identity" (Niles & Harkins Monaco, 2019, p. 115), practitioners will better be able to empower their students with DD, including those with autism and ID, academically, socially, emotionally, and politically. Not only that, but students without disabilities will also benefit. In fact, all social groups – dominant or minoritized – benefit from this kind of approach (Ladson-Billings, 2009).

Strategies for Teaching Self-Advocacy in Cultural Competence

Ladson-Billings' (2009) pedagogical framework has three core tenets. The first tenet is cultural competence. As described in Chapter 6, this refers to when one is aware and substantiated in their own culture while becoming fluent in another culture. Essentially, this means practitioners need to develop an understanding of their own cultural identities and how their identities have shaped their perspectives. Then they should actively learn and prioritize their students' cultures and perspectives. Practitioners should first deconstruct their own social identities, and therefore their own biases, prior to considering others' social complexities (Howard-Hamilton, Cuyjet, & Cooper, 2011). When one can fully affirm that their personal social identities and experiences are different from others around them, they will better be able to build strong relationships with students across the students' social identities. Essentially, practitioners must be able to acknowledge how they benefit from systemic social privilege. This is challenging, but incredibly important.

The next step is for practitioners to learn the students' cultural (background) knowledge while providing students opportunities to connect their personal experiences to new information (National Academies of Sciences, Engineering, & Medicine, 2018; Hammond, 2015). Create initiatives to infuse this into the climate and culture of the classroom (Osher & Berg, 2018; the Aspen Institute, 2018). Ask yourself questions like

- How can I help students make connections to this content?
- How might their experiences relate?
- How can I engage students and help students "see" themselves in this content?

Once these questions are asked, give students the time and space to answer these questions and develop their own voices (Zion & Petty, 2014). While students' voices are developing, practitioners' listening skills should become refined and they should make sure students feel heard. Provide students opportunities to connect similarities and differences across these conversations. Be sure to include the students' backgrounds and experiences directly into the content (Tatum, 2009; Tatum, 2006; Wood & Jucius, 2013; Dysarz, 2018; Chiefs for Change, 2019). Ultimately the goal should be that the languages, cultures, and identities of students and their communities are reflected and valued in every facet of the education provided to them.

Finally, examine the public face of whichever content area you teach. Show students who the most relevant scientists, mathematicians, authors, or leaders are. Discuss the [lack of] representation of multiple minoritized populations in this field and emphasize why representation is important. Show how the experiences of multiple minoritized individuals have been erased or excluded into the foundations of the discipline. Explore how multiple minoritized identities *are* represented. Are there ways this discipline has contributed to systems of privilege or oppression? Shape your instructional materials, assignments, and readings to reflect these minoritized voices (Harkins Monaco, 2020).

Strategies for Teaching Self-Advocacy in Sociopolitical Consciousness

The second central tenant is sociopolitical consciousness, or the ability to use one's education to identify and solve current social, cultural, civic, environmental, and political problems. Ladson-Billings (2009) calls this the "so what" factor and challenges practitioners to go beyond the curriculum to teach students that with a strong education, they are equipped to address social injustices. In other words, instructional practices should build students' knowledge and understandings of injustices in their communities. Help guide students' thinking about injustices they see in their communities or in their peers' communities. Ladson-Billings (2008) emphasized the importance of "humanely equitable" (Wilson, 1972) social relationships beyond the classroom. Offer examples as needed. Finally, help students identify how to work towards changing these inequalities. Advocacy is one way to actively address social change.

Strategies for Teaching Self-Advocacy in Social-Emotional Learning

Social-emotional learning (SEL), or the development of self-awareness, self-management, and relationships, is incredibly important in schools (Osher & Berg, 2018; the Aspen Institute, 2018). These skills are multifaceted and complex and so we recommend focusing on the following: 1) self-awareness of self; 2) self-management of behavior; 3) social management and relationships; and 4) self-awareness of the greater community (Adams, 2013). The importance of these skills cannot be overstated; individuals who develop a positive sense of identity, for example, are more invested in connecting with people of different backgrounds (Rivas-Drake, et al., 2014), and a strong racial/ethnic identity is linked to higher self-esteem, better attitudes about learning, healthier lifestyles, and the skills to navigate prejudiced systems (Phinney, et al., 1997).

What does this mean for students with disabilities? Youth with DD, including those with autism and ID, require learning modalities that are coordinated and consistent across settings. This applies to social-emotional learning too! Provide explicit instruction and individualized supports in each area, across environments. Table 8.2 shows recommendations for shaping four SEL tenants with students.

Table 8.2 Shaping SEL Tenants With Students
1. Self-awareness (I am): Recognize who I am, what I need, and how I feel relative to the world around me.
2. Self-management (I can): Manage my behavior in prosocial ways.
3. Social management (I will): Interact with others in meaningful and productive ways.
4. Self-Awareness (I care): Demonstrate an awareness of the role and value of others in the greater community (Adams, 2013, p. 110-111).

When teaching, the four SEL tenants with students, take the opportunity to identify intersections of diversity and discuss the difficulty these intersections can impose. This provides students with a strong base with which they can develop self-advocacy skills.

Case Study: Randy

Randy is a senior in high school. Like most of us, he has multiple identities that drive his personality and impact how he engages with his community. Randy is a gay Hispanic male with autism, living in the rural South. He succeeds academically and aspires to become the first person in this family to go to college. Randy is an accomplished musician and has practiced playing the piano, guitar, and violin since he was 5 years old. He experiences the world from different identities, many of which have historically been oppressed. As a male, Randy is expected to lead his family and experiences pressure to conform to male stereotypes. The community assumes he lives in poverty and many people assume he will stay in the community working at his family's restaurant. Living in the South, he has few opportunities to interact with the LGBTQ community. In fact, homosexuality is considered a sin by most in his Southern Baptist community. His family fears for his safety should anyone outside of the immediate family discover his sexual identity. However, he does have a few allies at his school. His special education teacher, along with his music instructor, support his college goals but are concerned that Randy will not discuss his need for accommodations at the college level. Without accommodations to address issues related to his autism, Randy may not reach his full potential. In high school, Randy received extra time on assignments and tests, he is able to take tests in a quiet area, and he is provided notes on all lectures. Randy has had self-advocacy instruction but does not use the skills outside of his special education classroom. They have talked to him several times about this and Randy says he will use the skills but doesn't use them. They are frustrated and wonder why. They discuss the issue at an IEP team meeting and decide as a group to dig a little deeper to determine how to help Randy. First, they allow Randy to choose which teacher he would like to work with to help dissect issues of intersectionality that Randy may be experiencing. He chooses his special education teacher. Randy has a good understanding of himself and how he feels his diversity may impact others. Randy needs to learn how to self-advocate in situations that may be uncomfortable as well as advocate for change on behalf of the multiple identities he represents. Figure 8.1 outlines Randy's identities and concerns.

Next, Randy's special education teacher helps him analyze his concerns and how not self-advocating in other environments can adversely impact his goals. The teacher helps him navigate these concerns, many of which are valid, and develop solutions should problems arise. Randy chooses chemistry class as the most difficult course in which he is not receiving accommodations. The chemistry teacher is ex-military and is also the school's football coach. He is strict but fair and expects hard work. The chemistry teacher's identities are intimidating to Randy, who does not see himself at all in this teacher and who fears his attempts to self-advocate could be taken harshly, affecting his social standing with others in his small community, such as the football team. The special education teacher agrees to talk to

Case Study: Randy (continued)

Figure 8.1

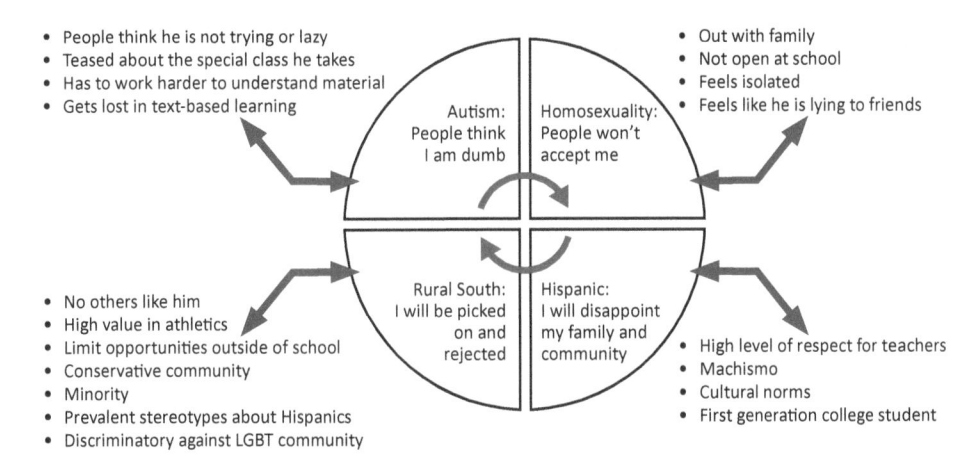

- People think he is not trying or lazy
- Teased about the special class he takes
- Has to work harder to understand material
- Gets lost in text-based learning

Autism: People think I am dumb

Homosexuality: People won't accept me

- Out with family
- Not open at school
- Feels isolated
- Feels like he is lying to friends

Rural South: I will be picked on and rejected

Hispanic: I will disappoint my family and community

- No others like him
- High value in athletics
- Limit opportunities outside of school
- Conservative community
- Minority
- Prevalent stereotypes about Hispanics
- Discriminatory against LGBT community

- High level of respect for teachers
- Machismo
- Cultural norms
- First generation college student

the chemistry teacher to set up a safe environment for Randy to self-advocate for his special education accommodations. This allows the special education teacher to provide support and education to the chemistry teacher while supporting Randy in practicing these skills. The chemistry teacher begins to self-assess ways in which his identities (male, athletic, traditional) may be displayed in the classroom in terms of both teaching examples and language he uses in the classroom. After his reflection, he understands that his comments such "Man up and get the job done" or "You aren't going to get special treatment when you leave high school so get used to the real world" can be intimidating for Randy. In this classroom Randy feels like he must act like the man his teacher thinks boys should be and that if you ask for "special help" you are weak. The teacher looks for terminology that he can use to motivate students without placing judgment. As he is reviewing the curriculum, he notices that there are few women or minorities represented in the courses, so he decides to do some research and add a few new examples to the lessons. But the chemistry teacher does not stop there. He not only adds content about the contributions of Hispanics and other minorities in chemistry, he also tries to get to know Randy and learn what may interest and engage him in chemistry content, so that Randy can "see" himself in the curriculum. The teacher begins to include non-traditional assessments and strategies such as project-based learning. The teacher realizes Randy's love and accomplishment in music and finds ways to include it in chemistry class. It is important that Randy and the chemistry teacher be successful in this interaction so that they will use the skills learned in other situations.

Next, the IEP team discusses the idea that if Randy feels this way, other students may be limiting their engagement due to their intersections of diversity. They

Case Study: Randy (continued)

approach their principal and ask for professional development on the topic. They wish to embed diversity across the curriculum, address situations that occur in the classroom as teachable moments, and provide practitioners with activities and strategies to promote interaction and collaboration across multiple identities. To begin this process, they develop a diversity committee thatwill begin exploring cultural competency and intersectional pedagogy at the school. First, they evaluate and consider their own cultural identities and bias. Next, they discuss identities that are different than their own and how these differences may impact student engagement. Then they agree to intentionally evaluate the curricula they are using and point out underrepresentation of diverse leaders. After, they decide to shape the four tenets of social emotional learning across courses and to seek curricula to help guide their teaching.

Finally, the special education teacher works with the transition team on identifying colleges that are inclusive that may support Randy's academic and personnel needs, identifying a person at the disability resource center on campus who can assist with accommodations and help Randy be his best self-advocate. Randy, his family, and his IEP team work together to identify online support networks that can help Randy feel connected and comfortable with his identities. By doing this, the special education teacher is helping Randy develop sociopolitical consciousness.

While the team cannot be assured that Randy will use his self-advocacy skills at college, they know that they have set up supports and systems for Randy and his family that increase the likelihood he will use the skills and his family can help him intervene should problems arise. Furthermore, they used this experience to build their intersectional pedagogy to support all students in the future.

Summary

The inequities in special education services and outcomes have been well documented in this chapter. These inequities have a long-term impact on how people with disabilities engage with their environment and how they are included in the community. Tools have been established to teach self-advocacy skills to students with disabilities. However, unless practitioners understand the impact of multiple oppressed or marginalized populations and the role these intersections play in the classroom, practitioners will be unable to understand why students from intersectional backgrounds are not using the self-advocacy skills they teach. Practitioners must adopt an intersectional pedagogy that becomes a norm in the classroom, seize the teachable moments in the classroom to address discriminatory practices, point out discriminatory literature in curricula, and introduce learners to leaders across all content from diverse backgrounds. Once the classroom and curricula represent our students and address the issues of oppression, the environment can be a safe place for students to practice their self-advocacy skills.

Guiding Questions

1. What are the sociopolitical constructs that impact people from oppressed populations' ability to advocate for themselves and other?
2. How does the intersection of multiple sociopolitical constructs further impact people with disabilities' ability to advocate for themselves and others?
3. What are your own biases that may impact how you teach diverse students from traditionally oppressed populations to self-advocate?
4. How can you teach self-advocacy while addressing the sociopolitical constructs using a cultural competency approach?

References

Adams, D. (2013). The application of social-emotional learning principles to a special education environment. *KEDI Journal of Educational Policy,* 103-118. https://www.researchgate.net/profile/David_Adams6/publication/257138287_The_application_of_social-emotional_learning_principles_to_a_special_education_environment/links/0c9605246f61e20e2a000000.pdf

Aspen Institute Education & Society Program (2018). *Pursuing social and emotional development through a racial equity lens: A call to action.* Aspen Institute

Banaji, M.R., Bazerman, M.H., & Chugh, D. (2003). How (un)ethical are you? *Harvard Business Review. 81*, 56-65.

Banaji, M.R. & Greenwald, A.G. (2013). *Blindspot: Hidden biases of good people.* Delacorte Press.

Bertrand, M., Chugh, D., & Mullainathan, S. (2005). Implicit discrimination. *American Economic Review, 95*(2), 94-98. Brown v. Board of Education, 347 U.S. 483 (1954).

Cawthon, S. W., & Cole, E. V. (2010). Postsecondary students who have a learning disability: Student perspectives on accommodations access and obstacles. *Journal of Postsecondary Education and Disability, 23*(2), 112-128.

Choudhury, S. (2015). *Deep diversity: Overcoming us vs. them.* Between the Lines.

Chugh D., Bazerman M.H., & Banaji, M.R (2005). Bounded ethically as a psychological barrier to recognizing conflicts of interest. In Moore, D., Cain, D., Loewenstein, G., Bazerman, M. (Eds.), *Conflict of interest: Challenges and solutions in business, law, medicine, and public policy.* Cambridge, UK: Cambridge University Press.

Crenshaw, K. (1991). Mapping the margins: Intersectionality, identity politics, and violence against women of color. *Stanford Law Review, 43*(6), 1241–1299.

Dysarz, K. (2018). *Checking in: Are math assignments measuring up?* The Education Trust.

González, N., Moll, L., & Amanti, C. (Eds). (2005). *Funds of knowledge: Theorizing practices in households, communities and classrooms.* Erlbaum.

Hammond, Z. (2015). *Culturally responsive teaching and the brain: Promoting authentic engagement and rigor among culturally and linguistically diverse students.* Corwin Press.

Harkins Monaco, E. A. (2020). Intersectionality in the college classroom. *Excellence in College Teaching, 31*(3).

Harry, B., Kalyanpur, M., & Day, M. (1999). *Building cultural reciprocity with families.* Paul H. Brookes.

Harry, B., & Klingner, J. K. (2006). *Why are so many minority students in special education? Understanding race and disability in schools.* Teachers College. Honoring origins and helping students succeed: The Case for cultural relevance in *high-quality instructional materials* (February, 2019). Chiefs for Change.

Howard-Hamilton, M. F., Cuyjet, M., & Cooper, D. (2011). *Multiculturalism on campus.* Stylus Publishing.

Ladson-Billings, G. (2009). *The dreamkeepers: Successful teachers of African American children.* 2nd ed. Jossey-Bass.

Lalvani, P. (2012). Privilege, compromise, or social justice: Teachers' conceptualizations of inclusive education, *Disability & Society, 28*(1), 14-27. doi:10.1080/09687599.2012.692028

McIntosh, P. (1989). White privilege: Unpacking the invisible knapsack. *Peace and Freedom Magazine*, (10-12).

Messick, D.M., Bazerman, M.H. (1996). Ethical leadership and the psychology of decision making. *Sloan Management Review, 37*, 9-22.

Moll, L. C. (Ed.). (1990). *Vygotsky and education: Instructional implications and applications of socio-historical psychology.* Cambridge University Press.

Murray Law, B. (2011). Retraining the biased brain: Is it possible to break people of unconscious prejudice? *American Psychological Association, 42*(9), 42.

National Academies of Sciences, Engineering, and Medicine (2018). *How people learn II: Learners, contexts, and cultures.* National Academies Press.

National Association of School Psychologists. (2016). Understanding intersectionality. [handout]. Bethesda, MD: Author.

National Center for Educational Statistics (2019). Percentage of students receiving selected disciplinary actions in public elementary and secondary schools, by type of disciplinary action, disability status, sex, and race/ethnicity, 2000-2016). *Digest of Education Statistics*, (2017)

Nieto, S., Bode, P. (2018). *Affirming diversity: The sociopolitical context of multicultural education (7th edition).* Pearson

Niles, G. and Harkins Monaco, E.A. (2019). Privilege, social identity and autism: Preparing preservice practitioners for intersectional pedagogy. *DADD Online Journal (DOJ), 6*(1), 112-123.

Osher, D. and Berg, J. (January 2018). *School climate and social and emotional learning: The integration of two approaches.* Issue brief, Pennsylvania State University.

Oyler, C. (2011). Teacher preparation for inclusive and critical (special) education. *Teacher Education and Special Education, 34*(3) 201-218

Phinney, J. S., Cantu, C. L., and Kurtz, D. A. (1997). Ethnic and American identity as predictors of self-esteem among African American, Latino, and White adolescents. *Journal of Youth and Adolescence 26*(2), 165-185.

Reid, D., & Knight, M. (2006). Disability justifies exclusion of minority students: A critical history grounded in disability studies. *Educational Researcher, 35* (6), 18-23. http://www.jstor.org/stable/3876749

Rivas-Drake, D., Syed, M., Umaña-Taylor, A., Markstrom, C., French, S., Schwartz, S. J., Lee, R., and Ethnic and Racial Identity in the 21st Century Study Group (2014). Feeling good, happy, and proud: A meta-analysis of positive ethnic–racial affect and adjustment. *Child Development*, 85(1), 77–102.

Sever, O., Gino, F., and Bazerman, M.H. (2015). Ethical blind spots: Explaining unintentional unethical behavior. *Current Opinion in Psychology*, 6, 77-81.

Spring, Joel (2000). The intersection of cultures: Multicultural education in the United States and the global economy. McGraw Hill Higher Education.

Staats, C., Capatosto, K., Wright, R. A., & Contractor, D. (2015). State of the science: Implicit bias review 2015. https://kirwaninstitute.osu.edu/wp-content/uploads/2015/05/2015-kirwan-implicit-bias.pdf

Tatum, A. W. (2009). *Reading for their life:(Re)Building the textual lineages of African American adolescent males*. Heinemann.

Tatum, A. W. (2006). Engaging African American males in reading. *Educational Leadership, 63*(5), 44. Tenbrunsel, A. E. and Messick, D.M. (2004). Ethical fading: The role of self-deception in unethical behavior. *Social Justice Research*, 17, 223-236.

Villegas, L., Villegas, T., and Villegas, A.M. (2013). Preparing linguistically responsive teachers: Laying the foundation in preservice teacher education. *Theory Into Practice, 52*(2), 98–109.

Waitoller, F. R., and Thorius, K.A.K. (2016). Cross-pollinating culturally sustaining pedagogy and universal design for learning: Toward an inclusive pedagogy that accounts for dis/ability. *Harvard Educational Review, 86*(3), 366– 389.

Ware, L. (2010). Disability studies in education. In S. Tozer, A. Henry, B. Gallegos, M. B. Greiner, & P.G. Price (eds.), *The Handbook of Research in the Social Foundations of Education* (pp. 244 – 260). Routledge.

Wilson, T. L. (1972). Notes toward a process of Afro-American education. *Harvard Educational Review, 42*, 374-389.

Wood, S. and Jucius, R. (2013). Combating "I hate this stupid book": Black males and critical literacy. *The Reading Teacher 66*(9), 661–669.

Zion, S., & Petty, S. (2014). Student voices in urban school and district improvement: Creating youth – adult partnerships for student success and social justice. In E. B. Kozleski & K. King Thorius (Eds.), *Ability, Equity, & Culture*. Teachers College

Chapter 9

Preparing practitioners and coaching cultural competence and disability awareness

Marcus C. Fuller, Kelly M. Carrero, and William Hunter

Objectives

- Understand how the Cultural Proficiency Continuum can help identify healthy and unhealthy behaviors when conducting coaching.
- Learn how to provide clear expectations between coach and coachee.
- Identify practices and strategies to use during coaching sessions on culture and diversity and disability awareness.

Chapter 9 discusses how developing culturally proficient or sensitive practitioners requires clear guidance and coaching (Robins, Lindsey, Lindsey, & Raymond, 2002). However, coaches often face challenges finding (a) strategies that can move their coachees to the next space along the *Cultural Proficiency Continuum* model (CPC; Lindsey, Robins, & Terrell, 2009), and (b) ways to assess and provide feedback to their coaches about the CPC. The cultural proficiency of the coaches themselves plays a contributing factor in creating and maintaining culturally proficient educators. This chapter will guide the coach through (a) understanding how the CPC can help identify *healthy* and *unhealthy* behaviors, (b) providing clear expectations between coach and coachee, and (c) identifying practices and strategies to promote cultural, diversity, and disability awareness while constructing successful coaching experiences.

Table 9.1 Key Terminology	
Coaching	A professional development (PD) activity that is ongoing, intimate, and teacher-oriented to gain a new skill, strategies, or understanding (Cornett & Knight, 2009; Denton & Hasbrouck, 2009; Kraft, Blazar, & Hogan, 2018; and Joyce & Showers, 1981).
Coachee	The individual who is receiving coaching (Fluckiger, et al., 2017).
Performance Feedback	Personal interaction with the oral, written, and/or gestural communication regarding the progress towards the desired outcome. (Brock & Carter, 2017; Brock, et al., 2017; Cavanaugh, 2013, Kraft, Blazar, & Hogan, 2017; and Solomon, Klein, & Politylo, 2012).
Cultural Proficiency	Educating all students to high levels through knowing, valuing, and using as assets their cultural backgrounds, languages, and learning styles within the context of our teaching.
Cultural Informant	A person who is highly self-aware of his/her own cultural values, norms, and appropriate behaviors and who understands the nuances well enough to express this knowledge to others who are less familiar with the culture.
Critical consciousness	Allows for an individual to question the authenticity of what's taught in the educational system and pose powerful questions about culture and socio-economics problems within a democracy that attempts to serve a diverse population of people (Ladson-Billings, 2018).

The literature on coaching provides an array of definitions depending on (a) the relationship between the coach and the coachee, (b) the skill(s) needed to be coached, and (c) many other factors such as intensity, duration, and immediacy of providing performance feedback. Kraft, Blazar, and Hogan (2018) completed a meta-analysis outlining key hallmarks of a good coaching model. They suggest that coaching should be an intense process that uses frequent sessions for an extended period. Coaching should also be a personal experience featuring one-on-one or small group observations centered around the coachee(s). The coaching experience should promote the betterment of a specific skill, intervention, mindset, and/or strategy. Finally, coaching is context-specific; meaning the observation and coaching should take place where the coachee is supposed to implement the target skill, intervention, mindset, or strategy. Coaching within the natural environment where the skill is to be implemented, such as the classroom environment, helps the coachee infuse the targeted skill in their everyday practice.

Moreover, coaches may be able to immediately troubleshoot issues that threaten to impede the coachee from reaching high levels of implementation fidelity when observing them in the natural setting.

The intimacy and duration of the coaching process can cause the experience to drift away from the desired goal. Moreover, coachees may become complacent or distraught when results are not immediate. A good way to ensure this does not happen is to construct the coaching process within a framework, or specific guidelines, to keep the experience centered on the goal. When working with coachees to understand and process their own biases about working with students and colleagues who are from backgrounds different than their own, the CPC (Lindsey et al., 2009) serves as an effective framework. CPC highlights six points along a continuum that helps school personnel identify their own behaviors as *healthy* or *unhealthy*. Using the CPC in coaching permits a pragmatic approach to rethinking how diversity is represented in the school community. *Figure 9.1* illustrates the six points of the CPC and offers a brief description of each point. The first three points on the continuum--*Cultural Destructiveness*, *Cultural Incapacity*, and *Cultural Blindness*—are categorized generously as tolerating diversity and are considered unhealthy behaviors. People who exercise these *unhealthy* behaviors uphold the mindset that the "*other*" is the problem and may say statements such as, "This student is always acting up and keeps me from being an effective teacher." The second three points on the continuum—*Cultural Precompetence*, *Cultural Competence*, and *Cultural Proficiency*—are categorized as transformative actions for equity and are considered *healthy* behaviors. Using *healthy* behaviors allows individuals to transform their mindset from "The "*other*" is the problem" to "How am I and/or my biases contributing to this problem?" Practitioners practicing *healthy* behaviors may make a statement such as, "Are my current academic practices effectively engaging my student, promoting my student's strengths, and promoting my student as a valuable member of the classroom community?" Moving along the CPC (i.e., from *Cultural Destructiveness* to *Cultural Proficiency*) requires a shift in coach-coachee conversations and thinking; specifically, moving from blaming others to acknowledging changes the coachee can make to support their students (CampbellJones, CampbellJones & Lindsey, 2010).

One way to move along the continuum is to incorporate the following concepts into the coaches' and coachees' understanding, as well as using these concepts as the foundation of educational practices.

Figure 9.1 Cultural Proficiency Continuum

Compliance based tolerance for diversity			Transformation for equity		
Cultural Destructiveness	Cultural Incapacity	Cultural Blindness	Cultural Precompetence	Cultural Competence	Cultural Proficiency
Practices that seek to eradicate cultures remnants other than that of the dominant culture	Practices that demean and seek to show cultures other than the dominant culture as wrong, savage, or violent	Practices in which the dominant culture refuses to acknowledge the cultures of other	Practices that create awareness of what one knows or does not know about working in truly diverse settings	Practices that are additive to cultures that are different than the dominant culture	Practices that seek to continuously learn about other cultures in a positive manner and are inclusive and celebratory of all groups in the school community

(Derived from Lindsey, Robins, & Terrell, 2009)

First, coaches and coachees must assess their own cultural knowledge, this includes understanding your own culture (See Chapter 2), as well as understanding cultures you come into contact with (See Chapter 3). To do this, practitioners must be aware of their own cultural identity and how their culture affects others (Shepherd & Linn, 2015). By assessing cultural knowledge, one becomes aware of (a) their understanding of that specific culture, (b) their reactions to different cultural practices, and (c) methods for navigating cross-cultural experiences with people from different cultures. Secondly, practitioners must become comfortable with being uncomfortable (Sue, 2016). Managing conflicts and viewing these conflicts as a normal and natural part of cross-cultural experiences is essential to creating an inclusive and welcoming classroom climate. Creating a classroom climate where uncomfortable conversations about one another's culture are welcomed and valued when done in positive, constructive ways, can facilitate negotiating cultural dissonance between all classroom members (e.g., students, teachers, staff, volunteers) and provide opportunities to practice real-world problem-solving techniques in a safe space. Chapter 1 offers you resources in how to start assessing your classroom climate. Furthermore, collectively problem-solving culturally based conflicts introduces the possibility that disagreements may be due to a cultural difference instead of a personality flaw (e.g., "She never looks at me when I am talking to her").

Another concept that helps one move along the CPC is valuing diversity. Valuing diversity involves being inclusive of viewpoints and experiences of others that differ from your own. Furthermore, to value diversity is to (a) welcome a diverse group of individuals into the classroom environment, (b) acknowledge those traits that differ from the educator, and (c) use these experiences to create teachable moments with the students. After the coachee begins to value diversity, the coach can support the coachee in adapting to diversity. More specifically, the coachee can seek education about other cultures and identify ways to use the experiences derived from other cultures in educational settings (Rogoff et al., 2007). This can be accomplished by using cultural informants to increase your own understanding and inviting them as featured speakers during in-class discussions.

The final concept to help one move along the CPC is to institutionalize cultural knowledge. The institutionalization of cultural knowledge presents the opportunity to display and celebrate the growth that the coachee experienced, both in the coachee's own life and in common classroom practices, as they move along the continuum. This notion of institutionalization of cultural knowledge can, and likely should, be expanded beyond the classroom to affect culturally proficient changes in educational policies and district-wide practices to represent the values of all community members.

It is important to note that becoming culturally proficient is not a holistic achievement. Rather, people seeking to become culturally proficient should be self-aware of where they currently fall on the CPC each time they come in contact with a person who is from a culture or background they are unfamiliar with or find themselves making assumptions about. For example, if a teacher worked through the continuum to be culturally proficient with a particular Mexican-American culture because she had a student in the classroom who was Mexican-American and then next year she has a student on her roster who has recently immigrated from India, the practitioner should not assume that s/he is already culturally proficient in that culture as well. Instead, the teacher should go through the same steps described above to assess where she falls on the continuum for that particular culture and begin moving along the CPC. Becoming culturally proficient is not a destination, but a practice. Consistent work along the continuum and constant reflective evaluation of the practitioner's current points along the continuum is needed for each culture with whom they come in contact. Promoting the knowledge and experiences one gain about other cultures and sharing one's insights with fellow practitioners and administrators is critical to the disruption of systemic and institutionalized racism that is prevalent in schools, and many other systems in our country. Only then can one create educational practices that are truly culturally proficient (see Chapter 6 for more information on culturally sustaining pedagogies).

Identifying Clear Roles and Expectations

To coach a professional in how to be culturally responsive, the coach must assume the role of assisting the professional--or coachee--to engage in the coachee's own journey of self-awareness and other-awareness. As the coachee moves into the transformative points (*Cultural Precompentence, Cultural Competence,* and *Cultural Proficiency*) of the CPC, the coach is then free to teach the coachee how to engage in the *Cultural Reciprocity Model* (Kalyanpur & Harry, 1997). The *Cultural Reciprocity Model* was born out of the understanding that in order to ethically and genuinely collaborate and program for a person, one must be prepared to engage in a dialogue with their collaborative partner(s) to negotiate cultural differences in values and traditions that may exist between two persons in order to arrive at the most culturally relevant course of action (Kalyanpur & Harry, 1997, 1999). Moreover, employing a "posture of cultural reciprocity" (Kalyanpur & Harry, 1997) helps mitigate cultural assumptions of the dominant culture that can often drive "culturally responsive practices" by approaching the activity with the full awareness that your values and beliefs are culturally grounded and may not be shared by your collaborative partner. Most of the literature about cultural reciprocity in special education applies to professionals collaborating with families (e.g., Harry et al. 1999; Kalyanpur & Harry, 1997; Kalyanpur & Harry, 2012; Rao et al., 2020); however, here we apply the model to the coach-coachee relationship (*See Figure 9.2*).

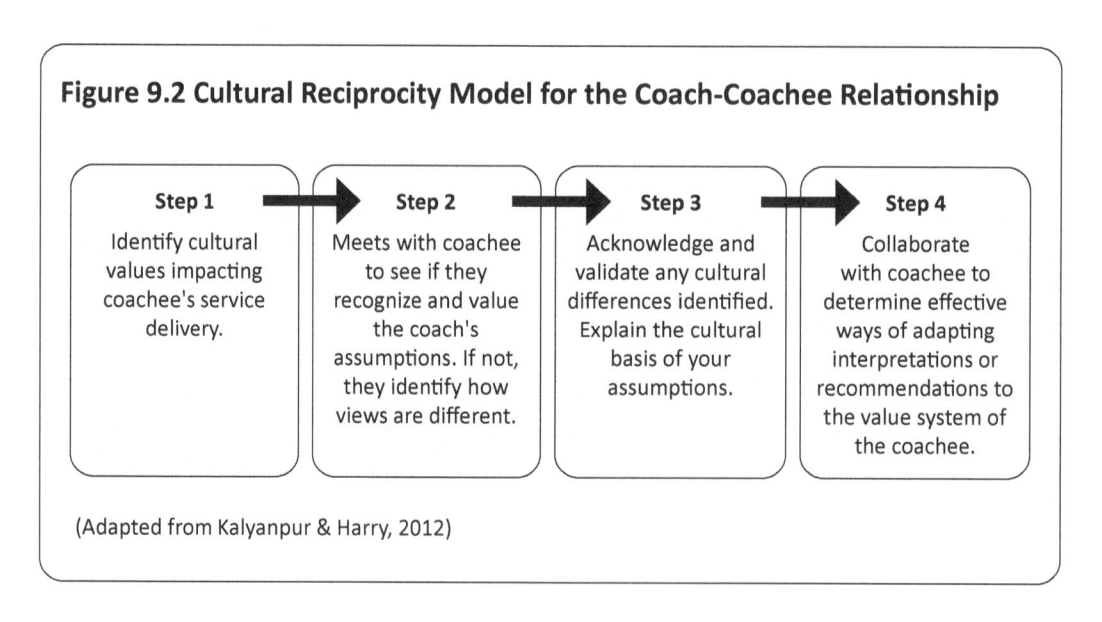

Figure 9.2 Cultural Reciprocity Model for the Coach-Coachee Relationship

Step 1	Step 2	Step 3	Step 4
Identify cultural values impacting coachee's service delivery.	Meets with coachee to see if they recognize and value the coach's assumptions. If not, they identify how views are different.	Acknowledge and validate any cultural differences identified. Explain the cultural basis of your assumptions.	Collaborate with coachee to determine effective ways of adapting interpretations or recommendations to the value system of the coachee.

(Adapted from Kalyanpur & Harry, 2012)

It is beneficial that the coach and coachee practice the guiding steps of the *Cultural Reciprocity Model* by engaging in the model as a part of the feedback loop (Lawley & Linder-Pelz, 2016; and Linder-Pelz & Hall, 2008). While employing the *Cultural Reciprocity Model* with the coachee, the coach should also point out how the coachee could use this same model when partnering with families. This process of teaching the coachee how to transition the skills and framework learned from their experience working with the coach into the role of serving as a "coach" with families or students, is described as meta-coaching (i.e. coaching on how to coach). The way in which the coach will train the coachee on employing the model is through experience and reflective coaching. For example, after the coach and the coachee work through the model together for their own working relationship and understanding, the coach will have the coachee consider what that same kind of transaction or exchange might look like when working with a family or a student. It is important to note, that cultural reciprocity is a posture; it is a way of approaching a collaborative, or transactional, relationship (Kalyanpur & Harry, 1997; 2012). Therefore, the coach should expect to work through the *Cultural Reciprocity Model* each time there is a major programming consultation meeting (i.e. when determining goals and/or outcomes). It is in this space of planning and partnership that proactively negotiating any potential cultural dissonance is vital to the success of the collaboration.

Consulting All Stakeholders

To best ascertain the cultural values, norms, and expectations of the coachee, the coach must consult multiple stakeholders. Within the context of a school, these stakeholders include the special education director or coordinator, the school principal, other teachers in the building (not just the special education teacher), paraprofessionals, and related staff (e.g., school nurse, occupational therapist, speech-language pathologist, transition specialist, etc.). The coach must make sure the coachee is aware of the cultural values and norms of these stakeholders. For school districts and building personnel, there are typically explicit declarations of cultural norms and values; however, it is important to note that often how these declarations are actually achieved may vary from school to school and from teacher to teacher. Consequently, it is best if the coach and coachee seek to first identify and then consult with temporal stakeholders (i.e., those with the most direct interaction and impact with the setting and/or student that is being targeted for the coaching sessions) to establish a clear understanding of varied and collective perspectives. A simple socio-cultural map will serve as a useful tool to organize practical steps to achieve this end when coaching the coachee to glean information for their students (*see Figure 9.3*).

Figure 9.3 Bronfenbrenner Ecological Model

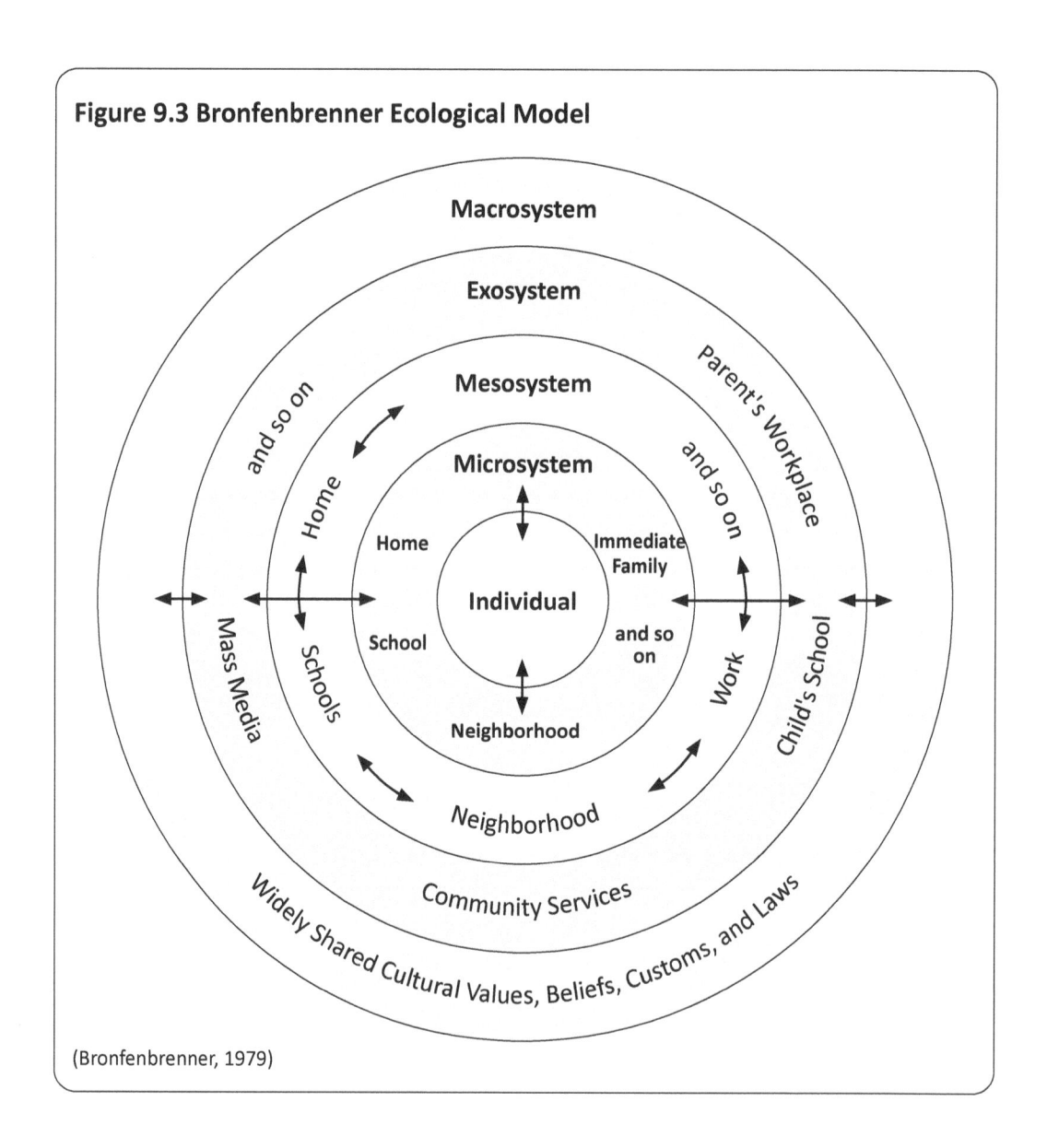

Macrosystem — Widely Shared Cultural Values, Beliefs, Customs, and Laws; Mass Media; and so on

Exosystem — Parent's Workplace; Child's School; Community Services; and so on

Mesosystem — Home; School; Neighborhood; Work; and so on

Microsystem — Home; Immediate Family; Neighborhood; and so on

Individual

(Bronfenbrenner, 1979)

Including Cultural Informants

Once the coachee has entered into the *Cultural Precompetence* point of CPC, they will see the value of actively seeking cultural informants to share their experiences. A cultural informant is defined as a person who is highly self-aware of their own cultural values, norms, and appropriate behaviors and understands the nuances well enough to express this knowledge to others who are less familiar with the culture (Coan & Gottman, 2007; Romney et al., 1986). Cultural informants can provide vital insight to facilitate the adaptive process as the coachee moves along the CPC. Although it is ideal to establish a relationship with people from various backgrounds to assist with understanding different cultures, it is important to note that just because someone is from a diverse background (i.e., a background that is different from the coachee), does not mean they are (a) able to speak on behalf of their entire culture, race, or demographic; and (b) self-aware of their own nuanced cultural experiences. It is recommended that the coachee seek out multiple cultural informants and triangulate the information gathered from each experience, so as to not have a limited viewpoint (e.g., just gaining information from the social media feed of a young celebrity from the culture of interest).

Understanding Cultural Bias When Selecting Practices

When providing support to the coachee, it is vital for coaches to understand what cultural bias is when selecting culturally responsive practices within a professional development plan. It is critical for practitioners (coaches and coachees) to use cultural knowledge to make learning experiences more relevant and effective for students within a K-12 and post-secondary classroom (Gay, 2013). The culture of power is an important concept to establish within educational spaces to guard against the potential for cultural bias within the classroom (Delpit, 2006). A student's success is predicated on the acquisition of the culture of those in power within the institution of school/educational settings. From an educational perspective, the definition of a cultural bias includes the notion that prejudice is highlighted in which a certain viewpoint suggests a distinct preference of one culture over another (Banks, 2006). Cultural bias highlights differences among persons and groups which includes differences in levels of socioeconomic status, language, race, ethnicity, and religion (Shockley & Banks, 2011).

Cultural bias has been found to be a factor impacting educational and health care opportunities for people. For example, special education is designed to support students to ensure that all students receive an inclusive, free appropriate education; however, Black students in special education experience cultural bias through the initial identification process, compromised educational practices, receiving inadequate educational resources, and receiving more restrictive placements than their non-black counterparts (Molett, 2013; Whitford & Carrero, 2019). Black students are overrepresented in "soft" or subjectively-identified disabilities such as intellectual disability (ID), emotional disturbance, and specific learning disabilities (see Sullivan & Bal, 2013; USDOE, 2017)[1] and Black students who are identified with autism are twice as likely to be identified with comorbid ID, compared to their White, non-Hispanic peers (Baio et al., 2018). From the time parents of Black children begin noticing symptoms consistent with autism to the time the child is diagnosed is approximately three years (Constantino et al., 2020). Barriers to expedient diagnoses are incredibly problematic, particularly when research indicates early and intensive intervention provides children with autism and/or ID the most promising outcomes across several areas of functioning (Linstead et al., 2017). Finally, Black students are underrepresented in postsecondary programs for students with moderate to severe exceptionalities (Wagner, Newman, Cameto, & Lavine, 2005). Socioeconomic factors also play a role in education as students with moderate to severe exceptionalities from marginalized backgrounds are less likely to attend post-secondary programs (Newman et al., 2011). These are a few factors for coaches to consider when selecting culturally responsive practices to have coachees implement the classroom/educational setting.

Strategies and Activities

Practitioners, coaches, and other professionals may fully engage in becoming more culturally responsive in their practice, yet most struggle to know how to turn this desire into actionable steps. To inspire and guide invested professionals in moving towards cultural proficiency, this section provides specific strategies and activities for educational professionals.

Moving Along the CPC

Moving along the CPC requires a shift in mindset from tolerating diversity to incorporating transformative actions for equity into everyday activities (CampbellJones, CampbellJones & Lindsey, 2010). It requires a change in understanding from finding the problem in your students that impact their education, to realizing how you, as the teacher, work with people from different cultures to ensure equity and social justice (Robins, Lindsey, Lindsey, & Raymond, 2002). Two important strategies to help make this mind shift are the use of reflection and dialogue. Reflection invites the teacher to have a conversation with themselves about what practices they currently use and where these practices may fall on the CPC. Dialogue invites others in the school, group, or grade level to the conversation about these practices.

In addition, there are various strategies that are easy to implement for zero, or low, cost. As a coach, assign the *Cultural Proficiency: A Manual for School Leaders* (Lindsey, Robins, & Terrell, 2009) for a book club and then have the group journal and discuss their thoughts with guided questions. The manual outlines the CPC, barriers to *healthy* behaviors, and strategies to help understand the CPC. Another strategy is to invite cultural informants to faculty meetings as a way to become informed about the cultures present in the school. When there are limited opportunities to develop relationships with potential cultural informants from a variety of backgrounds and identities, encourage the coachee to do their own research on the background they are seeking to gain more information about. There are several wonderful and visible social media channels, blogs, and YouTube channels that do an excellent job confirming and discussing the common value systems and cultural behaviors most often experienced and practiced by those who identify with the group. Whichever strategy coaches use with their coachees, it is most important to ensure that there is "buy-in" with coachees. It is better to start with a small group that is motivated to move along the CPC than with an entire grade level where some believe "this is just another PD requirement." Engagement helps ensure that the reflections and dialogue will be genuine and represent an effort to move towards *Cultural Proficiency*.

Evaluations Using CPC

Coaches must identify ways to evaluate their coachees' movement along the CPC and give constructive feedback on where they are on the CPC. There are two easy ways to evaluate them. First, the coach can conduct in-classroom observations and identify practices that showcase *Cultural Competence* and *Cultural Proficiency*. These two farthest-right points on the continuum include practices that recognize and incorporate different cultural practices into everyday teaching and foster an ongoing learning environment about cultures in an inclusive and positive manner. Another way is to evaluate the coachees' understanding of the CPC. Have the coachee identify where various statements about students and culture may fall on the continuum and then ask the coachee to rewrite these statements from a *Cultural Proficiency* point-of-view. Statements such as, "If they are in my classroom they will speak English" would fall under *Cultural Destructiveness*, while statements like "We are implementing a culture month across subjects and inviting community leaders to speak" would fall under *Cultural Proficiency*. In disability advocate circles, it can be considered *Cultural Blindness* or, maybe even *Cultural Incapacity* to say, "the student is wheelchair-bound." Culturally competent educators say, "the student uses a wheelchair" recognizing that a wheelchair is a tool that provides the student with the ability to move around more independently. Understanding where various statements fall along the CPC helps coachees identify where their own practices fall on the CPC and within schoolwide and district practices.

Selecting Culturally Responsive Practices

The first step recommended for coaches before selecting culturally responsive practices (CRP) to incorporate in coaching is to determine their own cultural bias, as discussed in other chapters in this book. This also includes examining the power of their culture within a classroom setting (Delpit, 2006). By understanding their own cultural bias, coaches/coachees are less likely to misconstrue the behaviors of students from culturally diverse backgrounds, which can have a positive impact on how they interact with students within educational settings (Dray & Wisneski, 2011). Through the self-examination of culture, the hope is for the coach to develop critical consciousness that then can be transferred to the coachee through the coaching process.

Critical consciousness allows for an individual to question the authenticity of what is taught in the educational system and pose powerful questions about culture and socio-economic problems within a democracy that attempts to serve a diverse population of people (Ladson-Billings, 2018). For example, the coach can consider disproportionality in the (over) identification of black males in special education and (under) identification within gifted education (Ford, Wright, Washington, & Henfield, 2016), Another consideration is the need for (more) diverse post-secondary programs for students with moderate to severe exceptionalities (Wagner et al., 2005). Having these factors in mind can assist with the selection of culturally responsive practices that can be used within a PD.

When selecting culturally responsive practices within PD, it is recommended that coaches focus on student learning (focus on intellectual growth), construct a plan developing students' own movement along the CPC (which includes helping students recognize and appreciate their culture of origin) and develop a student's critical consciousness, which are tenets of culturally sustaining pedagogy (see Chapter 8) (Ladson-Billings, 2018). To do this, the coach must facilitate a PD that includes a forum for a discussion centered around how a coachee can obtain the knowledge of the student's cultures that they will be working with. Within the PD, the coaches should create a safe space (Singleton, 2014) to discuss self-examining one's culture and potential cultural bias eventually developing an understanding of the (K-12/post-secondary) student's culture that they are serving.

Case Study: Mia

Mia, a curriculum coach, has recently been put in charge of helping the fifth grade English teachers implement more CRP in their classrooms. Mia decides to facilitate peer coaching using the CPC model to help increase the teachers' implementation of CRP. First, she meets with the teachers to set expectations and define roles. During this meeting, Mia describes the CPC to the teachers and illustrates how the CPC is used to establish *Cultural Proficiency* and promote the use of CRP. Secondly, Mia provides information on how the coaching process will be conducted. Mia describes how observations will be conducted by herself, as well as how the teachers will conduct sessions with each other, and describes how feedback will be delivered. Next, Mia shows the teachers the observation form, describes what the targets are and how to fill out the form. Finally, Mia has the teachers rehearse using the form and ask any questions they have about the coaching process.

During observation sessions, Mia and the teachers use the observation form to identify different strategies being used in their classrooms and where those strategies fall on the CPC. At the end of the school day, the coach provides feedback to the teacher on what strategies were identified. The coach also brainstorms with the teacher ways to move those strategies across the CPC

Case Study: Mia (continued)

towards *healthy* behaviors. Once a month Mia meets with the whole team to discuss progress, answer questions and concerns, and introduce new strategies or elements that promote *Cultural Proficiency*. Mia informs her teachers how cultural bias plays a big part in the teachers' pedagogy and strategies they use in the classroom, and how critical consciousness can combat cultural biases. Mia also began to identify different cultures represented in the teachers' classroom and provided ways for teachers to become more informed about those cultures, such as seeking out cultural informants.

In addition to the group meetings, Mia has quarterly one-on-one meetings with each teacher. Mia uses these one-on-one meetings to assess and provide feedback on the teacher's understanding of the CPC model and where the practices that the teacher uses fall on the continuum. First, Mia assesses that the teacher has a clear understanding of how to identify practices and determine where they fall on the CPC. After Mia has ensured that the teacher has that understanding, she discusses with the teacher the practices that were identified during observations and where they are on the CPC. Practices that are *unhealthy* are revamped or replaced with practices that promote *healthy* behaviors. Mia practices using the *Cultural Reciprocity Model* with the teacher and talks about how the teacher can use this model with the students and their families. Finally, Mia uses meta-coaching strategies to help transition the skills and techniques she used to help the teachers implement CRP and practice *Cultural Proficiency* in themselves to coaching their students to practice *Cultural Proficiency* as well.

Summary

This chapter began by introducing CPC as a coaching framework to help coaches increase the implementation of CRP in school personnel. This section described each point on the continuum and how to move along the continuum into transformative practices. It is important to reiterate that a coachee or a coach reaching Cultural Proficiency with one person/student does not automatically mean they have reached that point with others from different cultures. Remember, Cultural Proficiency is more of a journey than a destination. Next, the authors described how coaches provide clear roles and expectations between them and coachee. Both coaches and coachees need to be prepared to be reflective throughout this process and understand how to deliver as well as receive feedback. The coach should also examine the practices used in the coaching process and identify where they fall on the CPC. Coaches and coachees need to understand the position of various stakeholders that affect the classroom environment and how cultural biases play a part in selecting CRP. Another role to use in the coaching process is that of a cultural informant who can provide vital insight into cultures that the coachee(s) may be unfamiliar with. Finally, this chapter provided strategies and activities to help coachees move along the CPC, help coaches use the CPC to evaluate coachees, and select CRP before illustrating this process with a case study for a curriculum coach named Mia.

Now that this chapter has described the significance of being culturally aware when planning and implementing coaching, the chapter lends itself to a series of next steps that readers should consider. Implementing practices of Cultural Proficiency takes true buy-in and willingness to undergo this change in thinking. Start with a small group or yourself. These practices can begin at a small scale. Start with a few strategies that promote *healthy* behaviors and identify ways to incorporate them in the classroom; begin in one subject area and then broaden it to other subjects throughout the day. As a coach, be mindful to not create undesired stress from changes that in turn might create a negative coaching experience. Finally, consider your impact. When culture and diversity are at the core of creating a classroom climate, all members of that class can feel safe and welcome and ensure that the learning environment is conducive to the success of all its students.

Chapter 9

Guiding Questions

1. How can practitioners use the CPC to identify *healthy* and *unhealthy* behaviors?
2. Describe the importance of providing expectations for coaching.
3. What are strategies and practices that promote cultural competence that should be implemented when conducting coaching?

References

Banks, K. (2006). A comprehensive framework for evaluating hypotheses about cultural bias in educational testing. *Applied Measurement in Education, 19*(2), 115–132.

Bronfenbrenner, U. (1979). *The ecology of human development.* Harvard University Press; Cambridge, MA

CampbellJones, F., CampbellJones, B., & Lindsey, R. (2010). *The cultural proficiency journey: Moving beyond ethical barriers toward profound school change.* Thousand Oaks, CA: Corwin

Coan, J. A., & Gottman, J. M. (2007). The specific affect coding system (SPAFF). *Handbook of emotion elicitation and assessment*, 267-285.

Cole, M., & Packer, M. (2011). *Culture in development.* Psychology Press.

Cornett, J., & Knight, J. (2009). Research on coaching. *Coaching: Approaches and perspectives,* 192-216.

Cross, T. (1988). Cultural Competence Continuum.

Denton, C. A., & Hasbrouck, J. A. N. (2009). A description of instructional coaching and its relationship to consultation. *Journal of Educational and Psychological Consultation*, 19, 150-175.

Dray, B. J., & Wisneski, D. B. (2011). Mindful reflection as a process for developing culturally responsive practices. *Teaching Exceptional Children*, 44(1), 28-36.

Delpit, L. (2006). Other people's children: Cultural conflict in the classroom. *The New Press.*

Ford, D. Y., Wright, B. L., Washington, A., & Henfield, M. S. (2016, September). Access and Equity Denied: Key Theories for School Psychologists to Consider When Assessing Black and Hispanic Students for Gifted Education. In *School Psychology Forum* (Vol. 10, No. 3).

Gay, G. (2013). Teaching to and through cultural diversity. Curriculum inquiry, 43(1), 48-70.

Joyce, B., & Showers, B. (1981). Transfer of training: The contribution of "coaching". *Journal of Education*, 163(2), 163-172.

Kalyanpur, M., & Harry, B. (1997). A posture of reciprocity: A practical approach to collaboration between professionals and parents of culturally diverse backgrounds. *Journal of Child and Family Studies*, 6(4), 487-509.

Kalyanpur, M., & Harry, B. (1999). *Culture in special education: Building reciprocal family-professional relationships*. PH Brookes Pub..

Kalyanpur, M., & Harry, B. (2012). *Cultural reciprocity in special education: Building family-professional relationships*. Baltimore, MD: Paul H. Brookes Publishing.

Kraft, M. A., Blazar, D., & Hogan, D. (2018). The effect of teacher coaching on instruction and achievement: A meta-analysis of the causal evidence. *Review of Educational Research*, 88, 547-588.

Ladson-Billings, G. (2018). From big homie the OG, to GLB: Hip-hop and the reinvention of a pedagogue. In # HipHopEd: The Compilation on Hip-hop Education (pp. 21-26). Brill Sense.

Ladson-Billings, G. (2014). Culturally relevant pedagogy 2.0: aka the remix. *Harvard Educational Review,* 84(1), 74-84.

Lawley, J., & Linder-Pelz, S. (2016). Evidence of competency: Exploring coach, coachee and expert evaluations of coaching. *Coaching: An International Journal of Theory, Research and Practice*, 9(2), 110-128.

Linder-Pelz, S., & Hall, M. (2008). Meta-coaching: a methodology grounded in psychological theory. *International Journal of Evidence Based Coaching & Mentoring*, 6(1).

Lindsey, R. B., Robins, K. N., & Terrell, R. D. (2009). *Cultural proficiency: A manual for school leaders.* SAGE. Molett, M. (2013). Academic and cultural bias in the classroom: A qualitative examination of the overrepresentation of African American students in special education. *McNair Scholars Research Journal,* 6(1), 8.

Newman, L., Wagner, M., Knokey, A. M., Marder, C., Nagle, K., Shaver, D., & Wei, X. (2011). The post-high school outcomes of young adults with disabilities up to 8 years after high school: A report from the National Longitudinal Transition Study-2 (NLTS2).

Rao, S., Pancsofar, N., & Monaco, S. (2020). Effective practices for collaborating with families and caregivers of children and young adults with disabilities. *Oxford Research Encyclopedia of Education*. DOI: 10.1093/acrefore/9780190264093.013.1017

Robins, K., Lindsey, R., Lindsey, D., & Raymond, T. (2002). *Culturally proficient instruction: A guide for people who teach* (2nd ed.). Corwin

Rogoff, B., Moore, L., Najafi, B., Dexter, A., Correa-Chávez, M., & Solís, J. (2007). Children's

Development of Cultural Repertoires through Participation in Everyday Routines and Practices. In J. E. Grusec & P. D. Hastings (Eds.), *Handbook of socialization: Theory and research* (p. 490–515). The Guilford Press.

Romney, A. K., Weller, S. C., & Batchelder, W. H. (1986). Culture as consensus: A theory of culture and informant accuracy. *American Anthropologist, 88*(2), 313-338

Rose, C. (2018). Toward a Critical Hip-hop Pedagogy for Teacher Education. In # HipHopEd: The Compilation on Hip-hop Education (pp. 27-37). Brill Sense.

Shepherd, T. L., and Linn, D. (2015). Behavior and classroom management in the multicultural classroom: Proactive, active, and reactive strategies. Sage Publications.

Singleton, G. E. (2014). *Courageous conversations about race: A field guide for achieving equity in schools*. Corwin Press.

Shockley, K. G., & Banks, J. (2011). Perceptions of teacher transformation on issues of racial and cultural bias. *Journal of Transformative Education, 9*(4), 222-241.

Sue, D. W. (2016). *Race talk and the conspiracy of silence: Understanding and facilitating difficult dialogues on race*. United Kingdom: Wiley.

Wagner, M., Newman, L., Cameto, R., & Lavine, P. (2005). Changes over time in the early post-school outcomes of youth with disabilities. A report of findings from the National Longitudinal Transition Study (NLTS) and National Longitudinal Transition Study -2 (NLTS-2). Menlo Park, CA: SRI International. http://www.nlts.org/reports/2005_06/nlts2_report_2005_06_complete.pdf

Whitford, D. K., & Carrero, K. M. (2019). Divergent discourse in disproportionality research: A response to Kauffman and Anastasiou (2019). *Journal of Disability Policy Studies, 30*(2), 91-104.